"Secret Judgments of God"

What causes the Indians to die and to diminish in number are secret judgments of God beyond the reach of man. But what this witness has observed during the time he has spent in these parts is that from the province of Mexico have come three or four pestilences on account of which the country has been greatly depopulated.

—Pedro de Liévano,
Dean of the Cathedral of Guatemala
1582

"Secret Judgments of God"

Old World Disease in
Colonial Spanish America

Edited by
Noble David Cook and
W. George Lovell

University of Oklahoma Press : Norman and London

Also by Noble David Cook

Demographic Collapse: Indian Peru, 1520–1620 (New York and
London, 1981)
People of the Colca Valley: A Population Study (Syracuse, 1982)

Also by W. George Lovell

*Conquest and Survival in Colonial Guatemala: A Historical Geography of
the Cuchumatán Highlands* (Kingston and Montreal, 1985)
Conquista y cambio cultural (Guatemala, 1990)

Library of Congress Cataloging-in-Publication Data

Secret judgments of God : Old World disease in colonial Spanish
America / edited by Noble David Cook and W. George Lovell. —
1st ed.
     p.   cm. — (The Civilization of the American Indian series)
Selected and edited papers from the 46th International Congress
of Americanists, held in Amsterdam, Netherlands, in 1988.
Includes bibliographical references and index.
ISBN 0-8061-2372-9
     1. Indians—Diseases—Congresses.   2. Indians—Popula-
tion—Congresses.   3. Indians—History—Congresses.
4. Epidemics—Latin America—History—Congresses.   I. Cook,
Noble David.   II. Lovell, W. George (William George), 1951–   .
III. International Congress of Americanists (46th : 1988 :
Amsterdam, Netherlands)   IV. Series.
E59.D58S43   1991
614.4'28—dc20   91-50301
                                                                          CIP

Illustrations from the Florentine Codex by John V. Cotter.

The paper in this book meets the guidelines for permanence and
durability of the Committee on Production Guidelines for Book Lon-
gevity of the Council on Library Resources, Inc.⊗

*"Secret Judgments of God": Old World Disease in Colonial Spanish
America* is Volume 205 in the Civilization of the American Indian
series.

To the memory of Sherburne F. Cook,
Carl O. Sauer, and Lesley B. Simpson,
whose example continues to inspire

CONTENTS

TABLES

Editors'
Preface

Swelling of the Throat (*Florentine Codex*)

Our knowledge of the impact of Spain in America has recently gone through important changes. These changes have led not only to reformulation of the kinds of questions scholars ask but, more significantly, have also increased public awareness that the arrival of Europeans on American shores unleashed on native peoples sustained and unprecedented destruction. It is not a pleasant story to tell or to hear. Everywhere one looks, disaster abounds.

That the causes of Indian demise were complex, myriad, and interwoven is indisputable, as indisputable as the fact that some native peoples fared much better than others in the face of European settlement and colonization. Consensus is finally emerging where dissent prevailed before. This consensus acknowledges not only that Amerindian numbers dropped precipitously following conquest by imperial Spain but also that native population decline may be attributed in large part to the introduction of Old World diseases against which New World inhabitants were immunologically defenseless.

While the disease factor is now widely recognized as a key variable in explaining patterns and processes of Indian survival, few attempts have been made thus far to devote an entire volume to its study. Our intent in this collection of essays, therefore, is to examine the role disease outbreaks played in shaping the colonial experience of native peoples throughout Spanish America.

The essays gathered here are the result of years if not decades of individual initiatives that took on a decidedly collective dimension when the contributors met in Amsterdam in July 1988 to present papers at the 46th International Congress of Americanists. The quality and range of the presentations, we think, warrant their being brought together in the present form. Most edited collections seem to suffer from a lack of focus born of frustrated efforts to relate disparate parts to an elusive whole. In an attempt to minimize this occurrence, we decided to select from the Amsterdam session only those contributions that deal primarily or exclusively with the impact of Old World disease on native peoples during the colonial period in Spanish America.

Woodrow Borah served to draw discussion to a close in Amsterdam by assessing the "state of the art" in our chosen field. It seems fitting, indeed something of a natural reversal, that what were first conceived as concluding remarks now serve as an opening statement. Borah's original charge called for him to review pertinent research not just on Spanish America but for the entire New World. The hemispheric coverage of his first draft Borah then pruned to meet our revised terms of reference. In a letter to us, he rightly argued: "The difficulty is that disease does not politely conform to political boundaries. For that matter, in the sixteenth century and much of the rest of the colonial period, there were few political boundaries of importance anyway." While the analysis of available literature that forms the introduction to this volume sees Borah delimit his critical faculties at our request, he nonetheless evaluates "titles that fit into the Spanish period in the northern borderlands and those that relate to certain general phenomena that may have been detected north of the Río Grande but are of importance south of it as well." Other chapters also incorporate valid findings from various parts of the world, but the focus remains, in time and in space, colonial Spanish America.

After Borah sets the scene, several contributors present chronologies of the diseases that swept through different regions at different times. Hanns J. Prem pieces together an epidemic sequence for central Mexico in the sixteenth century. Of particular interest in Prem's reconstruction is his appraisal of Indian records that augment better-known, though not always fully utilized, Spanish texts. Prem scrutinizes his sources with caution before venturing an opinion as to what possible diseases match the symptoms and characteristics described. He delineates what may have been epidemic waves of measles and typhus occurring at roughly thirty-year intervals and contends that, following contact, the downward curve of population movement was not continuous, but jagged, and plummeted with each major bout of sickness. Elsewhere in Mesoamerica, W. George Lovell establishes a disease chronology for Guatemala which indicates that as many as eight pandemics struck Maya peoples there between 1519 and 1632, during which time dozens of other more localized outbreaks of sickness also occurred. The argument Prem makes for central Mexico is supported by Lovell's interpretation of the materials extant for Guatemala: because of inadequate, ambiguous, or contradictory evidence, it is often impossible to determine precisely what certain pandemics were, especially when more than one disease was present. Loss of life, however, was pronounced, as were the social and economic repercussions of disease outbreaks.

Linda A. Newson then reconstructs the epidemic history of sixteenth-century Ecuador. She concludes that, in contrast to what some scholars maintain, disease outbreaks had a major impact on the native population. At least five pandemics can be identified between 1524 and 1591, with, as in the case of Guatemala, numerous other outbreaks of sickness occurring at the local level. Newson also finds little evidence to support the unhealthy reputation the coast of Ecuador earned in the minds of contemporary Spaniards. Similarly, she finds nothing of significance in the accounts of the expeditions of Francisco de Orellana or Pedro de Ursúa and Lope de Aguirre to indicate that diseases from Ecuador spread into the Amazon during the first half-century or so of Spanish movement. Farther north, for the Chibcha of the Sabana de Bogotá, Juan and Judith Villamarín chart the incidence and impact of epidemics for almost the entire colonial period, 1536 to 1810. The Villamaríns, in addition, glean information from records relating to the parish of Chía to provide a more specific appreciation of what events might look like at the community as opposed to the regional level of analysis. Theirs is an investigative approach sensitive to the nuances, and connections, of locale.

If Chía serves as a community study whose case particulars both reflect and refine the larger context of which it forms part, so also does another Andean microhistory. Brian M. Evans traces mortality patterns in Aymaya, a community in Alto Perú, from 1580 to 1623, using as his data base court records arising from disputes about Indian tribute obligations. Called upon to furnish the baptismal and burial rolls of Aymaya in the course of legal proceedings, local clergymen submitted detailed accounts that enable Evans to document the crippling impact of smallpox in 1590 and again in 1608 and 1610.

A shift from countryside to town is marked by Suzanne Austin Alchon's study of eighteenth-century Quito. Alchon, like Evans and the Villamaríns, takes care to situate what happened in Quito in historical and geographical context. The population of Ecuador, following sixteenth-century collapse, doubled in size between 1590 and 1670 through immigration and natural increase. This growth was cut short by several disease outbreaks between 1692 and 1695, which prefigured a series of epidemics that struck throughout the eighteenth century. Quito did not escape these visitations and, as a result, declined in population during the 1740s and beyond. The city was particularly hard hit by an epidemic of measles in 1785–88. Also dealing with disease impact in the late colonial period, but in a natural and cultural setting quite unlike eighteenth-century Quito, is Fernando Casanueva's study of smallpox in the frontier zone along the Bío-Bío river in southern Chile in 1791. Significant here is the role of government policy, especially the question of imposing quarantine measures to curtail the spread of disease, and indigenous response to the ravages of smallpox. The weakened condition of native peoples in the wake of the epidemic enabled Spaniards to assert their authority over a region that had long eluded effective imperial control.

Following these essays, which reveal the benefits that accrue when historians, geographers, and anthropologists work together, our concluding essay outlines the evolution of a web of disease that developed in the New World in the wake of European expansion. Wave after wave of Old World disease swept the Americas, following well-established routes of trade and communication. Disease impact varied according to a number of factors, but by the seventeenth century aboriginal numbers had been massively reduced and native ways irrevocably altered. Sickness that had raged in epidemic form in the sixteenth century by the eighteenth had become endemic, occurring more sporadically among an Indian population that in most regions had begun to recover from the epidemiological shock of conquest. Important strands that mesh and connect are readily identifiable, but other features of the web of disease await patient and rewarding research. If this volume accomplishes nothing more than to persuade readers that much of enduring worth and relevance remains to be done before the meaning of 1492 can properly be known, we will be well pleased.

Acknowledgments

Every book, especially a multiauthored volume such as this, carries with it a myriad of dues. Our contributors identify certain people and institutions to whom and to which they feel indebted. We wish here, as coeditors responsible for the final product, to express our gratitude to several individuals whose talents, guidance, initiative or support helped us steer the project from idea to fruition.

A special vote of thanks at the outset belongs to Henry F. Dobyns, for it was through him that the editors first met each other in person, at a conference he organized on Native American Historic Epidemiology, held at the Newberry Library in Chicago in December 1983. Henry's bringing us together marked the beginning not just of an intellectual partnership but also a friendship that has made all the difference to the way we approach scholarly collaboration. We owe Henry much and have benefitted considerably from his painstaking commentary as manuscript reader.

Plans for a volume of essays on native peoples and Old World disease in colonial Spanish America derive from conversations we had while attending a symposium convened by David J. Robinson at Syracuse University in October 1986. We agreed then to solicit papers and coordinate a session on the topic for the 46th International Congress of Americanists, which met in Amsterdam in July 1988. Our session in Amsterdam extended over two days and included presentations from Maria Luiza Marcilio, Robert McCaa, Maria Alice Rosa Ribeiro, and Leon Yacher in addition to the contributions included here. We thank all participants, as well as those who attended to listen and comment, for making the Amsterdam symposium lively and stimulating.

After we decided to proceed from symposium to book, the work of two of our contributors called for feats of translation that, during the process, meant inevitable transformation of original submissions. We and the authors concerned, Hanns J. Prem and Fernando Casanueva, played our parts, but Chapters 1 and 7 in large measure reflect the translation skills, respectively, of Alexandra Parma Cook and Anthony Higgins.

Our subject of necessity addresses issues pertaining to epidemiology and the history of medicine. As historians, geographers, and anthropologists, however, we stray often into technical realms in which none of us is professionally trained. In order to reduce the margin of error inherent in our collective use of medical vocabulary, we sought assistance from George J. Hill, M.D., F.A.C.S., professor of surgery and chief of the Division of Surgical Oncology at the University of Medicine and Dentistry of New Jersey. Professor Hill's scrutiny of the manuscript prior to publication helped us enormously and allowed us to move into print with greater confidence. His input, like that of Daniel W. Gade, was quite exceptional, and we learned much from his critical remarks.

Preparation of the manuscript involved the computing and word-processing expertise of Armando J. Alfonzo, Guisela Asensio Lueg, Vincent Cook, Stephen Elliott, and Heidi Fielder. Mapwork and illustrations were handled by John Cotter of the University of Texas at Austin, who reworked graphic material earlier provided by Ross Hough, George Innes, and the contributors themselves. William L. Sherman provided helpful suggestions, as did John Drayton, editor-in-chief at the University of Oklahoma Press. John actually expressed an interest in seeing the results of the project even before the symposium in Amsterdam was held, a gesture appreciated both by ourselves and our contributors. Frederick E. Hoxie, director of the D'Arcy McNickle Center for the History of American Indian, encouraged us over the years that a book like this was needed and that we were the ones who could oversee its creation.

Our thanks, in closing, go to each of our contributors, for we surely exhausted patience and goodwill many times between first solicitation and final copyediting. Their understanding allowed us the freedom to shape an edited volume without excessive sacrifice of personal style or intended meaning. Striving for unity while leaving room for diversity is certainly not easy. If nothing else, we now recognize the truth of that popular academic saying, that it is indeed more challenging to edit a book than to sit down and write one.

NOBLE DAVID COOK AND W. GEORGE LOVELL

"Secret Judgments of God"

Abbreviations

APP-SI	Archivo del Ayuntamiento de Puebla, Suplemento al Libro (Indice)
AG	Audiencia de Guatemala
AGCA	Archivo General de Centroamérica, Guatemala City
AGI	Archivo General de Indias, Seville
AGN	Archivo General de la Nación, Buenos Aires
AHNC	Archivo Histórico Nacional de Colombia, Bogotá
AJC	Achivo Jijón y Camano
AL	Audiencia de Lima
AMQLC	Archivo Municipal de Quito, Libros de Cabildo
ANHQ	Archivo Nacional Histórico, Quito
AQ	Audiencia de Quito
ASF	Audiencia de Santa Fe
CDHM	*Colección de documentos para la historia de México.* Edited by Joaquín García Icazbalceta. 2 vols. Mexico, 1858–66.
CDI	*Colección de documentos inéditos relativos al descubrimiento, conquista y organización de las antiguas posesiones españolas de América y Oceanía.* Edited by L. Torres de Mendoza. 42 vols. Madrid, 1864–84.
CDIE	*Colección de documentos inéditos para la historia de España.* 112 vols. Madrid, 1842–95.
ENE	*Epistolario de Nueva España, 1505–1818.* Edited by Francisco de Paso y Troncoso. 16 vols. Mexico, 1939–42. Biblioteca histórica de obras inéditas, ser. 2.
PNE	Papeles de Nueva España. Edited by Francisco del Paso y Troncoso. 9 vols. Madrid and Mexico, 1905–48.
RGI	*Relaciones geográficas de Indias: Perú.* Edited by Marcos Jiménez de la Espada. 3 vols. Madrid: Biblioteca de Autores Españoles, 1965.

INTRODUCTION

Woodrow Borah

Coughing (*Florentine Codex*)

Study of the history of epidemics among Indians in colonial Spanish America faces the peculiar difficulties inherent in any topic that covers a continent and a half in a wide interdisciplinary range. Perhaps worst of all, from a scholarly standpoint, is the painful fact that we are living in a period of transition between forms of storing information, moving from card catalogues to the memory banks of computers. Coverage means that the topic must include research and publications on social units of varying size and complexity, from a small village to an entire country. Intent and purpose range from nonprofessional recording for local histories of disastrous illnesses to the careful laboratory research of a team of medical specialists. The interdisciplinary nature of the theme exposes the inadequacies of our bibliographies and indexes, especially those arranged by field of study. The topic, it seems, falls between the interstices of anthropological, historical, and even medical indexes, including the *International Medical Index*. Excellent though they are, card catalogues organized accord-

ing to the specifications of the International Congress of
Brussels or those of the Library of Congress cover only
books acquired up to 1977, in university libraries in the
United States. Since that time, information has been
handled in microfiche and computer catalogues that are
far from complete. Vaunted nationwide guides and indexes currently on computer seldom give coverage that
was available before 1977, although we should be grateful for what is listed and hence incorporate it. One is
left, in the end, with the assessment that the *International Medical Index* and that old standby, the *Handbook
of Latin American Studies,* though far from complete, still
do the best job. Despite months of searching, the following discussion is based on what must be regarded as
no more than a sample and by no means a representa-
tive one, for it reflects serious problems of coverage.

Classification of Epidemic Studies

Reports of epidemics may occur as short notices by travellers or chroniclers. They blend into longer reporting
that would rank as studies. Studies, in turn, embodying
work done to date, may occur as parts of inquiries subordinate to more general themes or as quite sharply
focused examinations of occurrences of disease. They
display an almost infinite variety. Any attempt at cate-
gorization must be crude if not simplistic, with much
crossing of boundaries. The term of reference is treatment of epidemics, whether or not the purpose of the
work as a whole is that or something else.

Five different categories of reports can be identified.
First, perhaps, are casual reports of epidemics by travellers or chroniclers, as in the accounts by Cieza de León
(1984–85, 1:36, 219–20, 309–10) of the disease that devastated the Inca realm in the mid-1520s or the epidemic
of 1546 in the same area. Second might be accounts
and studies of individual epidemics. Such are the reconstruction by MacLeod (1986) of *matlazáhuatl* in the
Guadalajara region in 1737–38 and the depiction by

M. Simmons (1966) of the smallpox epidemic of 1780–81 in New Mexico, to name but two examples. Third, there are histories of a single disease, like the attempt by Micheli (1979) to bring together the story of all the smallpox epidemics in colonial Mexico and the now classic tracing by Carter (1931) of the origins and occurrences of yellow fever. Into this category fits the lively study of Zinsser (1935), which, after long accounts of the ravages of disease in various historical contexts, deals with typhus. It is, to be sure, global in its coverage, as is Carter's book, but does include Spanish America.

A fourth, catchall category is the study of epidemics as they affected a tribe, a group of tribes, or a region. The category, certainly, is a broad one, but the components shade so easily one into another that they are best kept together without further differentiation. Here would fit, inter alia, studies by Malvido (1975) of Cholula, by Denevan (1966:112–20) of the Mojos region of eastern Bolivia, by Sweet (1966) of the upper Amazon in the seventeenth and eighteenth centuries, and by Larraín Barros (1980, 2:33–41, 78, 82–87, 97) of the northern sierra of Ecuador in the sixteenth century.

Fifth would be systematic listings of epidemics for a country or a large region embracing several countries for long periods of time. A notable study of this kind is the one by José Toribio Polo (1913), an attempt at chronological listing of all epidemics in the central Andes, quoting or citing sources. Recent studies of this type, if of more limited scope, include Balcázar (1956), Dobyns (1963), N. D. Cook (1981:60–61), Browne (1984), and, in the present volume, Prem, Lovell, Newson, and the Villamaríns. For Mexico we have the two volumes edited by Florescano and Malvido (1986), a notable effort to collect contemporary accounts and later studies of epidemics and agricultural crises. Florescano and Malvido reproduce much important source material, including the detailed description of the symptoms of the

1576–81 epidemic in Mexico written by the noted natu-
ralist and doctor, Francisco Hernández. Also for Mex
ico, we have the tables compiled by Gibson (1964:448–
51) and Gerhard (1972:22–28). Jackson (1981) seeks a
similar end for the missions of Baja California. For Central America, MacLeod (1973:98–100) has developed
tables even more complete than Gibson's or Gerhard's.
More recently MacLeod's work has been paralleled and
superseded by Newson for Honduras (1986:314) and
Nicaragua (1987:119–22, 247, 327–28).

All of these categories cover the various ways in
which disease outbreaks are reported. Another approach would be to examine past occurrences analyti-
cally, with a view to more critical identification of the
epidemics involved. Most of the studies cited above are
concerned more with providing descriptions than ana-
lytical reasoning. One could reclassify all of the studies
listed so far by the criterion of the amount of analysis
each contained. In addition, other studies aim at analysis, in one form or another, rather than mere reporting.
Foremost among these would be attempts to identify
diseases that were not clearly recognized at the time.
Although Spanish and native reporting identified the
cause or causes of sickness during some outbreaks, in
others available sources do not, or reveal conflicting evidence. Scholars today have had great difficulty in re-
solving the doubts and continue to disagree. One explanation lies in the nature of medical knowledge at the
time: measles and smallpox, for example, were not distinguished by most members of the medical profession
until a period ranging from the late fifteenth to the early
seventeenth century (Ball 1977:237). A notable exception was the great Persian physician Rhazes (ca. 865–
923 or 932), whose *De variolis et morbillis* (A Treatise on
the Smallpox and Measles) properly identifies and describes both. Another explanation, which further com-
plicates our work, is that many outbreaks of sickness

consisted of several diseases, what we might call compound epidemics. Thus, although the Spaniards clearly recognized the disease they introduced during the conquest of Mexico as smallpox, the epidemic that broke out in central Mexico in 1595 was identified by Fray Jerónimo de Mendieta, an eyewitness, as measles, typhus, and mumps, clearly a compound epidemic. What was the murderous epidemic of Katun 4 Ahau in Yucatán? The description of symptoms we have might indicate yellow fever (Guerra 1986; Bustamante 1958:8–10). And what were the disease components of the devastating epidemics of 1545–48 and 1576–81 in Mexico and Central America?

In a fine piece of sleuthing, Guerra (1985) has identified the epidemic that accompanied Columbus's second expedition and laid low the natives of Hispaniola as influenza, type A, transmitted by the hogs loaded in the Canaries to Spanish sailors and from them to the Indians. Guerra argues that influenza spread quickly to the mainland. This evidence supports McBryde (1940), who claimed the epidemic of 1523 among the Cakchiquel Maya was influenza, disputing identification with smallpox that spread south from Mexico.

Regarding the nature of the sickness that struck Mexico and Central America from 1545 to 1548 and again from 1576 to 1581, the problem was well propounded by N. León (1919). Solution has been more difficult: Mendieta (1945, 3:172–79) and Humboldt (1811, 1:352–53, or bk. 2, ch. 4) state that the sickness was typhus. More recently, MacLeod (1973:98–99), Dobyns (1983:18), and Malvido and Viesca (1985) conclude that it was an outbreak of plague in pneumonic form. Prem and Lovell, in this book, offer their own assessments.

Virgin Soil Epidemics

Related to the identification of disease is the concept of virgin soil epidemics. Basically, this involves the idea that a disease introduced among populations which never before had experienced the illness, or which had been free from it for so long that any acquired immunity had disappeared, will be attacked in a massive onslaught, with no age group or sex spared infection. Mortality, in consequence, will be high, perhaps even total. Such diseases appear with extraordinary virulence and at times exhibit symptoms quite unlike the ones we normally associate with them. After a period of acclimatization, which may last three or four generations, say, eighty to one hundred years, a virgin soil epidemic will usually settle down to a somewhat milder form with the symptoms that we are accustomed to. It may even subside into a childhood disease with little or no mortality. In its more elaborate formulations, the concept holds that during their passage through the temperate and arctic zones of northeastern Asia to reach the New World, the ancestors of Native Americans gradually shed tropical and subtropical diseases and avoided such temperate diseases as had not yet evolved in Eurasia. Within the vast land mass of Eurasia, diseases slowly became part of local pools in India, China, and the Mediterranean, and eventually merged into a unified disease pool by the beginnings of the Renaissance. The Eurasian disease pool mixed with the disease pool of tropical Africa at the time of the slave trade. Later improvements in vessels and techniques of navigation made possible swifter voyages, thus increasing the likelihood that air- and vector-borne diseases could survive an Atlantic crossing. Meanwhile, Native American ancestors retained some of the diseases of temperate and arctic Eurasia and perhaps developed a few of their own, ready for exchange with Eurasia and Africa. On the whole, though, American Indians had relatively few diseases and, aside from natural disasters such as floods or droughts causing crop failures, seem to have enjoyed especially good health.

The concept of virgin soil epidemics was expressed in an incipient form by Sticker (1924, 1931, 1932–33), Hrdlicka (1932), S. F. Cook (1937, 1945), Graham-Cumming (1967), Jarcho (1964), and Vogel (1970). Their formulations were elaborated upon by Crosby (1972:35–63; 1976[a]; 1978), McNeill (1976:199–234), and Dobyns (1976[a]; 1983:11–23), all of whom stress the formation of Old World disease pools, their unification and transmission to America, and their subsequent destructive impact in virgin terrain. Supporting but modifying the theory are a number of other writers. Long (1935) points out that while tuberculosis probably existed among Native Americans before the coming of Europeans, crowding and dislocation caused by the latter's presence meant that the disease attained epidemic proportions and became a major killer. Black et al. (1976) report that with measles in virgin soil conditions, nursing care reduced mortality. Their conclusion is that inability to provide care for the sick, as in epidemics in earlier centuries among Indian tribes, must be considered an important contributor to deaths. They agree that, in the end, there is a residual excess mortality in such populations. Further strengthening the idea of a different immunological development between American and Eurasian peoples, Heinbecker and Irvine-Jones (1928) indicate that the Inuit are susceptible to upper respiratory infections on contact with visitors from outside their world, who, although not apparently suffering from the infection, pass it on nonetheless. On the other hand, the Inuit apparently possess a hereditary resistance to diphtheria and scarlet fever. Since the Renaissance, such divergences have been fast disappearing (Borah 1962) through what LeRoy Ladurie (1973) calls "l'unification microbienne du monde." Had not American Indians been infected and killed by the new diseases, their lands emptied of people, then the course and nature of European settlement would have been far different (J. W. Simmons 1932; Crosby 1978; 1986:95–216; Dobyns 1976ᵃ)

Disease Origins and Diffusion

The virgin soil concept of disease action automatically evokes another topic of discussion, namely, the place of origin of diseases, for the concept assumes that diseases originated in one part of the world and spread from there to others. For most diseases, there is little question that they originated in the Old World and were introduced into the New, but for some there is dispute. Malaria is a good example of the latter. Its existence in the New World has been posited on the basis of reports of pre-Columbian foci in Peru. Against this argument, however, Dunn (1965) and Wood (1975) provide substantial support for the theory of Old World origin, while Zulueta and Ayala (1978) reject reports of pre-Columbian foci on the grounds of shoddy research.

Of the disease known as *enfermedad de robles* (onchocerciasis), transmitted by black flies and believed to have been brought to America as a result of the slave trade, Fragoso Uribe (1979) claims to have encountered evidence of its presence during pre-Columbian times both in skeletal remains and in the depictions on the sculptured stones known as the *danzantes*, at Monte Albán in Oaxaca. He agrees that the disease is caused by the same agent as in Africa but believes that it is carried by different black flies. Further evidence of pre-Columbian origin is the existence, in Zapotec, of an ancient, largely obsolete term for the ailment. Onchocerciasis is endemic rather than epidemic. Uribe's theory, pending further investigation, has to be considered more possible than probable.

Another issue is the origin of yellow fever, certainly one of the most destructive diseases known. Bustamante (1958:8–31) makes the case for American origin, citing the reports in Mayan codices of pre-Columbian epidemics with symptoms resembling those of yellow fever. He also ascribes to yellow fever the emptying of the tropical lowlands of the Caribbean coast, although symptom descriptions are too vague for identification until the mid-seventeenth century. On the other hand, Carter (1931) indicates an Old World origin. Yellow fever is transmitted by the *Aedes aegypti* mosquito, which is not native to America.

Perhaps the most charged dispute about origins and diffusion involves syphilis. Proponents of the theory of an American origin have pointed to the return of Columbus from his first voyage, the travel of crew members to the court of Ferdinand and Isabella in Barcelona, and the outbreak there of the first recorded instances of syphilis. Afterwards, some crew members went to Naples, where syphilis broke out in an epidemic that spread across much of Europe. On the other hand, Sticker (1923), citing Avicenna, argues for the presence of syphilis in Europe during previous centuries, pointing also to the existence in Africa of yaws, a close relative. A mutation in 1493 may have produced the forms of syphilis we know today. The issue is complicated by the fact that *pinta* in America, yaws in Africa, and epidemic and venereal syphilis are all caused by spirochetes, which under laboratory inspection are difficult to distinguish (Guerra 1978; Hoeppli 1969). Some of the latest contributors to the debate are Bullen (1972) and Iscan and Miller-Shaivitz (1985), who report discoveries of syphilitic lesions in pre-Columbian skeletal remains found in Florida. Guerra (1978) seeks to reconcile all factions by a Solomonic declaration that pre-Columbian America had all four forms of spirochetic infection, that the Old World had three (yaws in Africa, endemic and venereal syphilis in Europe), but that Columbus on his first voyage did indeed return with infected crewmen to Europe. Obviously, the dispute is far from settled, as recent discussion by Baker and Armelagos (1988) and Dobyns (1989[b]) attest. How proponents of a pre-Columbian European form of syphilis explain their

case—that the treponemas causing all four forms are
the same and that the different diseases or forms of the
disease are the result of the way the spirochete enters
the host—is far from satisfactory. Clearly, further research is needed (Hudson 1965; Fieldsteel 1983; Hovind-Hougen 1983). It may well be that a more highly
refined form of laboratory inspection will disclose that
there are differences in the treponemas causing the four
related diseases.

Future Research Strategies

The observations made above may suggest that much
more work has been done than really has, for gaps
abound. Let me now indicate what in my view is
needed to fill these gaps and move ahead. Comprehen-
sive coverage in bibliographical indexes is an obvious
need. This should be interdisciplinary, even to including items from local journals that do not circulate
widely, and international to the extent of indexing journals and books published in all the countries of North
America, Central America and the Caribbean, South
America, Africa, Europe, and Asia. The field truly is
international. Increasingly, countries like the Soviet
Union, China, Japan, and India will discuss these top-
ics. Perhaps the computer, of which so much is expected, will help us in this tedious but essential task.

In addition to improving access to information, we
need much more exact listings of epidemics by region
and country, including a history of the course of each
epidemic, as detailed descriptions as possible of symptoms and treatments, and analysis of the effects in
terms of morbidity, mortality, and changes in vital statistics and in economic and social structure. Manuscript
sources have been but little explored; even printed
sources have not been fully exploited. Under systematic
examination, items such as parish registers, town records, minutes of *cabildo* (city council) meetings, and
accounts of efforts to meet the emergencies created by

catastrophe should provide us with fairly good chronologies for urban centers. Herrera and Enríquez (1916) and Alchon, in Chapter 6, show what can be done from the records of the *cabildo* of Quito. For the early colonial period, little private correspondence survives, although far more is extant than has been utilized. State and church correspondence survives in great volume but has been little examined for reports of disease and epidemics. Again, the reports of colonial officials were often more concerned with the damage to the royal treasury than with the human tragedy, but they do contain indications of it, as Evans makes clear in Chapter 5 and Casanueva in Chapter 7. Secular and regular clergy writing to their superiors may yield a richer return. In the Jesuit annual reports and letters we have an invaluable source, for the writers were unusually well-trained observers and obligated to inform their superiors of what they knew, saw, or heard. Reports by doctors are sporadic and usually not helpful. There were, to begin with, few doctors in Spanish America, and most, locked in the humoral theory of the time, reported poorly. Francisco Hernández (1959–60) stands out as an exception in his remarkably full statement of the symptoms of the 1576–81 epidemic in New Spain, but even he was constrained by prevailing medical philosophies (Risse 1987:43–45).

One kind of clue to identification and transmission lies in the search for parallel phenomena in Europe and elsewhere. Diseases usually come from somewhere, and in areas linked by interoceanic shipping, the place of origin would usually be one or more ports. Fortunately, the charting of epidemics and development of histories of disease and medicine for regions and cities of Europe is far more advanced than for the Americas. Students of epidemics in colonial Spanish America should make use of this resource, as applicable. Ruth Pike (1972), for example, provides a useful overview of demographic trends, sanitary conditions, and public health (or the lack of it) in sixteenth-century Seville, an overview Spanish scholars have elaborated not just for Seville but also for other Andalusian port cities (Carmona García 1979; Hermosilla Molina 1970).

When one deals with later colonial centuries, private correspondence survives in fuller form, and official and church correspondence becomes even more voluminous. By the late eighteenth century, as more trained doctors resided in the colonies and their training increasingly discarded the theory of humors, descriptions are longer and better. For the nineteenth century, records become quite abundant and their survival more certain. In effect, the rule of recency applies, namely, that the more remote in time the period, the greater the loss of records, and the more recent the period, the better the chance of survival.

Records, of course, tell us almost exclusively about areas of European penetration and settlement. They seldom have anything to say about areas beyond European control and may even avoid areas about which Europeans had good reason to be silent. It is quite likely that, from time to time, unrecorded as well as recorded vessels would make landings on the coast for supplies and other purposes, and, if they encountered Indians, engage in trade and other pursuits. Are we to believe that Europeans had no diseases among them in mild or more serious form and that they did not transmit them to the natives? It seems far more likely that, from the late fifteenth to the seventeenth centuries, European vessels seeded a number of epidemics, which spread along lines of native communication and eventually burned themselves out. Milner (1980:41–49), in discussing European exploration and settlement in the southeastern United States, identifies striking depopulation due to early disease introduction by Ayllon, DeSoto, and other Spanish settlers in Florida, as well as in the Mississippi Valley.

What applies to the southeastern part of present-day Anglo-America must hold for other parts of the New World also. Amazonia was traversed in the sixteenth century by European expeditions and afterwards by European traders and slavers. Did these movements have no epidemiological effects? Similarly, the basin of the Río de la Plata and even Patagonia were explored at intervals, and southwestern Paraguay and the mouth of the Río de la Plata were settled. In later years the area toward the Andes became the scene of much movement of contraband. Yet again it seems reasonable to posit epidemiological effects beyond the reach of European records. The epidemic that devastated the Inca realm in the middle 1520s, killing the reigning Inca and his heir and unleashing the war of succession that opened the realm to Spanish conquest, likely came from Europeans in the Río de la Plata basin, for the disease moved from south to north in the Andes. Even in so remote and unknown an area as California, Spanish exploration and the regular landing of the Manila fleet to replenish wood and water may well have left an epidemiological residue. Robert Heizer, for example, once commented to me that in excavations around Sacramento, he found evidence of mass burials, which he considered might well date to the sixteenth century. In general, in all areas for which we lack detailed reports, there is little recourse but to apply with care rules of general theory in accordance with such evidence as we have on the nature and density of European penetration and the paths of Indian communication.

The spread of epidemic disease along lines of Indian communication and trade brings us to the concept of pandemics. Some pandemics have been recorded, as in the case of worldwide cholera outbreaks in the nineteenth century. But the absence of records does not mean that pandemics did not occur. On the contrary, their presence may reasonably be inferred from the outbreak of a virulent disease, especially one occurring under virgin soil conditions. Pestilence would not stop courteously at the limit of recording but would certainly spread outward into areas for which we have no records for the time. It would continue until it reached a barrier in the form of climatic conditions unsuitable for survival or a density of population too low for successful, continued infection. The smallpox epidemic that started in 1518 in Hispaniola and subsequently spread from there to Cuba and then to Mexico has also been traced to Central America. It almost certainly moved along traditional lines of Indian trade deep into the Mexican north and what is today the Southwest of the United States, even though we have no records to confirm this. Dobyns (1963; 1983:12–13) detects evidence of its reach into West Texas and believes it to be the legendary epidemic that devastated the Inca Empire in the mid-1520s. He postulates a vast pandemic of smallpox, which struck much of North America and South America. The concept of pandemics advanced by Dobyns, if questionable as regards Peru in this instance, is eminently reasonable but does require careful attention to evidence in application (Dobyns 1989a; Henige 1989; Snow and Lanphear 1989). The great epidemics of *matlazáhuatl* of 1545–48 and 1576–81 in Mesoamerica and Central America must have moved beyond the borders of those regions, but how far we cannot know, for evidence is lacking.

Related to the study of disease and epidemics must be contemplation of the immediate and long-term changes in vital characteristics and social and economic structures. For vital characteristics, the most immediate effect would be an increase in morbidity and mortality, but longer-term effects would depend upon the age groups and sexes who were attacked and the extent to which the shattered population moved to reconstitute family units. If cohorts of childbearing age suffered onslaught, the birthrate would drop (McFalls and McFalls 1984). As for social and economic consequences, they may range from relatively few and unimportant to myriad and profound. Dobyns (1983:313–28), whose writings have opened so many paths of inquiry, has proposed a theory of adaptation and transformation in instances of catastrophic depopulation such as would occur in virgin soil or repeated epidemics. Those who survived, he contends, could no longer maintain formerly elaborate structures, for the supporting social surplus and specialization of economic activities would decrease or even vanish according to the degree of loss of population. Social structures and religious and cultural forms would become more simplified and might change quite drastically according to the degree of loss of surplus for their support. Patterns of settlement might change as the group abandoned villages and concentrated the survivors or even moved to new ones. If the loss in population brought the town or tribe below the necessary number to maintain communal life, it might merge with a neighboring group and cease to exist in its own right.

Some of the evidence we need to detect the ravages of epidemics and pandemics have recently come from the field of archaeology, where techniques of excavation and assessment are always being refined and new procedures invented (Mitchem and Hutchinson 1987; Ramenofsky 1987; M. T. Smith 1987). Exploration and yield will come slowly since results depend upon highly localized examinations, which only through time and number can achieve reasonable coverage and arrive at generalizations. Examples of such local explorations are Malvido, Mansilla, and Pompa (1986), who report on the excavation of a cemetery in the Mexican township of Huexotla, which was apparently a mass burial dating to an epidemic two-thirds of the way through the sixteenth century. Storey (1985, 1986) also reports on evidence of age of death and prenatal mortality in pre-Columbian Teotihuacán. At least two impediments exist that affect the application of archaeology to the study of epidemic disease: first, popular and religious objections may prevent excavation of burial sites; and second, the abundance of burial sites may require so much effort that, as has been said for Mexico, the entire adult population would have to train as archaeologists for adequate exploration to be mounted. In addition, disease can be detected only through the survival of tissue and in effects upon bone. Increasing knowledge may widen the possibility of application.

For the immediate future, if one may venture a prediction, a risky business at best, the greatest advances in our knowledge of the history of epidemics in colonial Spanish America, as elsewhere, are likely to result from research into disease in all its forms and nuances. Here are involved the fields of epidemiology and immunology, including questions of communicability, resistance, and adaptation of man and malady; the study of elements of the blood and knowledge of their development; and the evolution of diseases and their relation to animals and man. Cockburn (1977) provides some answers. Continued studies may finally solve the question of which intestinal ailments were present in the New World when the Europeans arrived. They may also shed light on the extent to which Europeans entered into an exchange of diseases, especially the much-debated question of the origin of syphilis and its relation to other forms, whether the causal treponema is the same, differentiated in its effects only by the way it enters the human body, or whether techniques of laboratory inspection have not yet been refined enough to detect four closely related forms. A combination of historical investigation and medical research may be required to illuminate the spread of diseases that require a carrying vector. The various forms of malaria moved as native anopheline mosquitoes transmitted parasites brought from the Old World throughout the New. Could malaria therefore have been one of the diseases that, within a decade, converted densely populated zones into wastelands of contagion through which passengers from Europe moved as quickly as possible? Once infected, the indigenous species of mosquitoes of the order Anophelinae served as substitutes. Similarly, yellow fever apparently is limited to the settling-in of its carrying vector, the *Aedes aegypti* mosquito. How soon could it arrive, and what role did it play in the initial emptying of the humid tropical lowlands? Guerra's (1986) indication of transmission as early as the third voyage of Columbus and epidemic spread at that time hardly seems plausible. Even more complex are the questions of the settling-in of typhus and bubonic plague in its non-pneumonic form, for these two diseases require the services of double carriers. Could native fleas and mice have served as New World vectors, or did the European fleas and rats spread with such rapidity that, by 1545–48, there could have been an epidemic either of bubonic plague or typhus, or both, as the identification of the disease by later scholars indicates? We have, indeed, much to learn, for the unification of the globe by microbes and viruses, even in its narrower application to the Americas, remains a wide-open field of inquiry.

Disease Outbreaks in Central Mexico During the Sixteenth Century

Hanns J. Prem

Burning of a Corpse (*Florentine Codex*)

The native peoples of the Americas were exposed, through contact with Europeans and Africans, to numerous and multifarious adverse effects. Without doubt, the most drastic of these was the transfer to the New World of hitherto unknown diseases, which manifested themselves in the form of devastating epidemics. It was, above all else, epidemic outbreaks that brought about the alarming drop in indigenous numbers (90 percent and more in certain cases) and the virtual depopulation of vast regions (Joralemon 1982). Other factors, including population loss due to violent wars of conquest, food shortages caused by disruption of agricultural routines, the depressed psychological state of the vanquished, or the end of political, economic, and cul-

NOTE: I am grateful to Professor Woodrow Borah of the University of California at Berkeley and Professor Helmut Stickl of the Bavarian State Inoculation Institute in Munich for important references and suggestions made in relation to an earlier version of this chapter. The Deutsche Forschungsgemeinschaft funded the investigation with a stipend under reference number Pr 83/9.

tural autonomy were crucial, but most likely did not, alone or in mutually reinforcing interaction, unleash such accelerated population decline.

In the central Mexican context, general agreement prevails that, following conquest, epidemics were indeed the primary cause of native population decline. Opinion, however, varies widely with respect to the magnitude of Indian depopulation and, consequently, the impact of disease outbreaks. Until now, seeking to resolve this issue has rested on a rather crude demographic assumption: that an exponential curve reflecting the magnitude of population loss reached its maximum extent around the middle of the sixteenth century, leading eventually to stationary population levels, similar to the situation at the time of conquest.

While the process is fundamentally indisputable, it carries the implicit assumption that, after conquest, the intensity of population loss increased steadily. Only around the middle of the sixteenth century, several decades after the conquest, did the intensity of the population decline reach its peak, subsequently to drop again. This schematic view was applied by Cook and Borah (1971; 1974) because it allows a relatively easy procedure of mathematical backprojection, starting with the earliest, most reliable population counts from the middle of the century.

A gradual process of increasing population decline, however, seems implausible, for some of the most important causes of depopulation (warfare, social disruption, the impact of sickness, and exploitation of Indian labor) must have had an immediate and massive effect. The schematic backward calculation of population must therefore be replaced by a more discerning method of analysis, one in which the demographic effects of single epidemic events are taken properly into account. Such an analysis was in fact planned by Cook and Borah (1979: v), but the death of the former intervened.

A prerequisite for any assessment of the effects of ep-

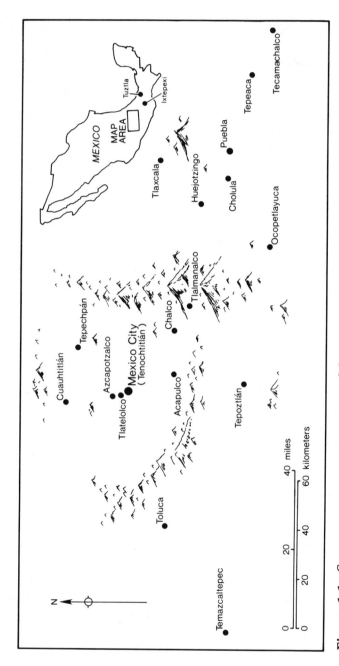

Figure 1.1. Sixteenth-century Central Mexico

idemics is their identification based on contemporary accounts, an undertaking all too often overlooked (Joralemon 1982:113). Although accounts compiled by Europeans as well as Indians who experienced and survived the epidemics frequently contain descriptions of disease symptoms, their use as indicators of the nature of illness is restricted, given the scarce medical knowledge of the time and imprecise or untrustworthy terminology. Furthermore, the authors of these accounts seldom had any medical training, and so the quality of their testimony ranks even farther below contemporary standards of medical expertise. To these difficulties must be added the uncertainty that derives from our being offered more than one diagnosis of a specific disease outbreak. Also, the available sources usually contain only sparse statements regarding mortality and the area affected by disease. Data for regions of Mexico other than the central highlands—the area encompassed by the valley and environs of Mexico City, Toluca, Puebla, and Morelos—are especially scant. Any attempt at epidemic identification, therefore, must for the present be limited to this territory.

Considerable risks are involved, then, when we attempt to identify epidemics solely from accounts in the sources. These risks can be reduced, however, by incorporating analogous medical data from similar epidemic situations (Joralemon 1982:115). Such data can also supplement the information lacking in the sources about levels of mortality. In doing so, however, we must not fail to acknowledge the possibility that the epidemic characteristics of a particular illness, at that time or under specific Mexican conditions, were manifested differently from what is known today.

This chapter is thus concerned with the description and tentative identification of epidemics recorded as having occurred in central Mexico during the sixteenth century. Close attention will be paid to Indian testimony, in the anticipation that such evidence may state

whether or not a given illness was common during preconquest times. Establishing the antiquity of disease
outbreaks is of decisive importance for the analysis of
epidemics with regard to their intensity and impact.
Hitherto, native sources have been afforded little attention.

The Epidemic of 1520–1521

The first reported epidemic of Old World origin falls
chronologically into the turbulent time of the conquest.
It preceded Spanish military *entradas* and fact-finding
expeditions, reaching areas that had not yet been penetrated by any European. Despite its being the first, and
notwithstanding the general uncertainty of identification already referred to, it is remarkable that we can determine precisely what the epidemic was.

Contemporary Spanish sources speak uniformly of
viruelas, which we know to be smallpox (López de Gómara 1966:191; Díaz del Castillo 1960, 1:378; Motolinía
1971:21; Mendieta 1945, 3:173; Sahagún 1956, 3:355–
56; Muñoz Camargo 1892:f. 35v). These sources attribute the infection to a specific person, a black member of
the contingent led by Pánfilo de Narváez. Smallpox
identification is supported by a detailed and vivid description of the illness that Sahagún (1956, 4:136–37,
195–96; 12:81; 8:4, 22) received from Indian informants
who lived through the epidemic. The direct connection
between the density with which smallpox pustules appear in one concrete case, and the chance of survival of
the afflicted, is especially clear in this description. Even
common complications—the incidence of postinfection
blindness, as well as the pockmarks left after recovery—are accurately described. Nahuatl sources also report this epidemic and refer to it as *huey zahuatl*, or "big
rash" (*Anales de Tecamachalco* 1903:7). Other sources
(*Codex Aubin*, f. 44v; *Anales de Cuauhtitlán* 1938, par. 685)
speak of *totomonaliztli*.

No one on either side, given when and under what

circumstances smallpox first appeared, was in a position to present credible testimony about the number of dead. Mortality rates can only be guessed, for available evidence must be considered crude and impressionistic. Motolinía, not an eyewitness, says that in some regions of Mexico one-half the population died, in other parts somewhat less (Motolinía 1971:21; Mendieta 1945, 3:173; López de Gómara 1966:191). The assessment of Motolinía, followed verbatim by Mendieta, may nonetheless not depart greatly from actual conditions.

Research conducted in parts of Europe long exposed to smallpox suggests that, among an unimmunized population, mortality can be of the order of 30 percent. Among previously unexposed populations, the situation in which native peoples in the New World found themselves, mortality can be considerably higher (Dixon 1962:317, 325). Convincing evidence of the latter exists in relation to the experience of Indian groups in eastern North America, among whom Duffy (1953: 244) records mortality levels from smallpox epidemics in the eighteenth century ranging from 55 to 80 percent. Of importance here for estimating overall mortality is not only mortality among the sick but also the likelihood of becoming ill. There must have been a higher probability of contracting the disease among a New World population first exposed to it than among a previously exposed population in Europe. During a smallpox epidemic in England at the end of the nineteenth century, for example, the probability of becoming sick through contact within a household lay between 75 percent among young adults and children and less than 50 percent among older adults. Mortality among the afflicted, the likelihood of becoming ill, and levels of age-specific mortality varied from epidemic to epidemic. Given the operation of such distinct variables, it would be desirable to differentiate in assertions about the demographic consequences of the 1520–21 epidemic. Lack of evidence, however, prevents this from being done. The average epidemic mortality rate might well have been in the order of 50 percent, a figure Joralemon (1982:122) arrived at for Peru. During a smallpox epidemic in Arequipa in 1589, about seventy years after native Peruvians first came in contact with the disease, Joralemon qualifies as "conservative" an estimated rate of infection of 80 percent, a designation that can likewise be applied to his estimated mortality rate of 30 percent.

Because smallpox spread quickly from central Mexico to regions at that time neither conquered nor even known about, information regarding the area affected by the epidemic must be incomplete. That the epidemic spread to the west and south (Tudela 1977:345; Recinos and Goetz 1953:115) seems certain. Dobyns (1963:496) argues that this same sickness extended, presumably partly by sea, even into the Andean region. There, between 1524 and 1526, it caused great population decline, killing the Inca ruler and his heirs and precipitating social upheaval well before the arrival of Pizarro. Against this interpretation, however, lie unanswered questions. How could the epidemic maintain its virulence for such a long period of time? Where, between Guatemala and the northern ranges of the Andes, lived a sufficient reservoir of disease carriers, among whom smallpox could have been passed and maintained for the necessary period of at least three years? On the other hand, the speed at which smallpox epidemics move even in densely settled areas should not be overestimated. It took five months, after all, from the beginning of May until early October, for smallpox to spread in 1520 from the Gulf Coast to the central Mexican highlands. The Indian informants of Sahagún (1950–69, 12:81) stated that the epidemic lasted about sixty days in Tenochtitlán, but it could have lasted considerably longer.

While the descriptions of Spanish and Indian sources clearly identify smallpox in central Mexico, the same cannot be said with equal certainty of outlying regions.

It is indeed possible that descriptions of smallpox outside the Aztec core are veiled by the appearance of accompanying infections. Such might be the case, for instance, in Michoacán, where bloody diarrhea is noted and, at the same time, smallpox is mentioned (Tudela 1977:345). In Guatemala the epidemic could have coincided with another illness, one perhaps of indigenous origin. Disease there, moreover, might be related to earlier contact with Europeans on the coast of Yucatán. The description of the 1519 epidemic in Guatemala mentions such symptoms as coughing, nosebleeds, and illness of the bladder (Recinos and Goetz, 1953:115). Here one must also take into account the difficulty of accurate translation and a reference to bleeding from the urinary tract occurring frequently during smallpox infection.

The Epidemic of 1531

While the majority of descriptions, as well as an explicit designation, allows for clear identification of the 1521 epidemic, considerably less so is the case of the epidemic that began in 1531. Motolinía (1971:22), the source whom others (Mendieta 1945, 4:174) copied, speaks distinctly of *sarampión* and names an infected Spaniard who was said to have brought the disease to Mexico. A description of the symptoms, however, is not given. The sickness was referred to by the Indians as "small skin rash," as opposed to the "big rash" of the preceding smallpox epidemic. Sources in the Aztec language do not report this epidemic, with the exception of Chimalpahin (1965:7, 8), who uses the same term he employed for smallpox, namely *zahuatl*. His information, nonetheless, is quite remarkable, for he speaks of a "thin" or "light" rash and stresses that it was mostly children who died. The *Codex Aubin* (f. 46v) reports only the illness, not the death, of one person. Alone, this information is obviously an insufficient basis for precise diagnosis, but perhaps it permits the elimination of alternatives.

In modern dictionaries, *sarampión* is translated as "measles" and described accordingly (Real Academia Española 1956:1178). However, the older *Diccionario de Autoridades*, dating from the first half of the eighteenth century, furnishes a description of *sarampión* that does not correspond to how measles is described today. The *Diccionario de Autoridades* (1716–39, 6:47) emphasizes that *sarampión* strikes mostly children, that it sets in with high fevers, and that subsequently the entire body is covered by a rash of small red grains. For a Latin name, *papulae, vel pus[t]ulae rubentes*, is cited. Descriptions of symptoms, upon which diagnosis may be based, speak of a precipitous rise of temperature and the appearance of vesicles, or a pustule-forming skin eruption, also repeated in Latin. This wording causes one to think less of measles, as the disease generally is accompanied only by a flat skin appearance. It is possible, as will be argued again later, that this set of symptoms might reflect the presence of several infections.

We can only speculate, on the basis of limited testimony, about the mortality rate of the epidemic. Motolinía (1971:22), by 1531 a resident of Mexico for several years and an eyewitness of this particular epidemic, commented that the number of dead was smaller than during the first epidemic. The exceptionally high child mortality that Chimalpahin talks about has been already pointed out.

Correlating *sarampión* with measles only makes sense if no clear reference to other diseases exists. We must, therefore, consider a more explicit evaluation of the epidemic. The account of symptoms and the Nahuatl designation, "small skin rash," which can also be translated as "little pox," opens up the possibility of identifying the disease as chicken pox. Today, however, chicken pox registers negligible mortality rates of less than 0.1 percent (Grumbach and Kikuth 1971, 1:1946), a figure that runs counter to the mortality referred to in the sources. We can never determine whether past outbreaks of chicken pox among unexposed populations resulted in exceptionally high mortality, for medical science only distinguished between smallpox and chicken pox with the advent of Jenner's experiments with smallpox vaccine (Ackerknecht 1963:60). Chicken pox did not exist as a distinct disease in the contemporary mind, cautioning against identification of the 1531 epidemic as such. We must also remember that Spanish sources refer to *sarampión* rather than *viruelas*, a different disease altogether. This point should not be taken lightly in view of the imprecise and therefore troublesome terminology of early colonial writers.

The definition of *sarampión* in the *Diccionario de Autoridades*, but not the sources scrutinized here, also allows it to be identified as scarlet fever, in conjunction with a streptococci infection manifested as impetigo. The fact that Tolhausen's dictionary, published in 1892, translates scarlet fever as *tabardillo* and *tabardete*, a disease that will be discussed later, should not be taken as a strong counter argument, for the *Diccionario de Autoridades* cites under its *sarampión* entry a seventeenth-century author who used *sarampión* and *tabardillo* interchangeably in his story of the life of a saint. Identification as scarlet fever would help explain high child mortality.

Arguments against an identification as measles certainly exist. It has already been pointed out that the description of blistery skin elevations does not correspond to the usual appearance of modern-day measles. Flare ups of impetigo, however, are not uncommon during measles and in the Middle Ages gave rise to confusion with smallpox (Mayer, in Gsell and Mohr 1965, 1 (1): 479).

If the argument of inapplicable skin appearance is discarded, during an outbreak of measles among a population never before exposed to it we must assume that almost everyone would be stricken (Bonin, in Grumbach and Kikuth 1971:1449). Such an incidence is documented for Fiji, where in 1875 measles broke out on the islands for the first time in seventy years. In this case more than 20 percent of the population died within four months (Ashburn 1947:90). Measles epidemics under these conditions affect the entire population, not just children, so long as adolescents and adults have not acquired immunity through previous contact with the disease. Without this prerequisite, it seems unlikely that high mortality during outbreaks of measles is restricted only to children.

Chimalpahin's mention of high child mortality is therefore the most concrete argument against identifying the 1531 epidemic as measles, which is generally labeled as such in the literature. If we rule out measles, so also must we dismiss designations of smallpox, chicken pox, and scarlet fever. What, then, the epidemic of 1531 precisely was, available sources do not allow us to determine.

The Epidemic of 1532

Only Indian sources report an epidemic for the year 1532 (Chimalpahin 1965:8; *Codex Mexicanus*, planch 79; *Anales antiguos de México*, no. 179). The name chosen for the illness, *zahuatl*, was similarly applied to both preceding epidemics, suggesting that infection may simply have lingered. An additional term chosen by Chimalpahin, *totomonaliztli*, was also supplied by Sahagún's informants for the 1520 epidemic. It is therefore not surprising that, in the secondary literature, smallpox is again held responsible for this wave of disease.

Other information from the same sources, however, undermines this designation. Illness is reported by the *Anales antiguos de México* to have stricken the entire population, including children, and Chimalpahin and the *Codex Mexicanus* state that mortality was general. Many old people were said to have died (the Nahuatl verb *miqui* is employed) in Tlalmanalco in particular. If the disease had again been smallpox, precisely the older members of the population, who had survived the 1520 smallpox epidemic and, as survivors, had acquired immunity, in theory should have been spared a new outbreak. Furthermore, while children had been born during the twelve years since the first pestilence, they would presumably have formed too small a reservoir to engender another outbreak.

If smallpox is ruled out as the cause of the 1532 epidemic, we are again left with the problem of not knowing what the sickness actually was. Chimalpahin's designation of *zahuatl totomonaliztli* provides but a brief description of an illness that produced pock-like pustules on the skin. All kinds of infections that had been confused with smallpox for centuries fall within the range of possibilities. Measles comes first to mind, as a continuation of the 1531 epidemic. Only imprecise comments can be made about the territorial extent of the sickness. Chimalpahin speaks of the presence of the epidemic in his homeland, Chalco, as well as in all of Mexico.

The Epidemic of 1538

One source (*Códice Telleriano-Remensis,* pl. 32) tells of an epidemic in this year, describing it as an outbreak of smallpox that caused numerous deaths. Because this epidemic is not reported by other central Mexican sources, the sickness may have occurred only in a mild form over a small area, or the person who compiled the codex was guilty of a chronological or factual error. Dobyns (1983:262–64) argues that the epidemic may have reached the area we know today as the southeastern United States, but evidence is incomplete.

The Epidemic of 1545–48

The epidemic of 1545–48, probably the most disastrous ever to hit central Mexico, is reported by a large number of predominantly Indian sources. It is thus all the more remarkable that only a few of these sources provide a name for the disease. We must therefore conclude that the sickness was so widespread and had so little in common with what was known in Mesoamerica during pre-Columbian times that the existing terms were inapplicable, whether as equivalents or inferences. Spanish writers who witnessed the epidemic were struck by the enormous number of dead. Perhaps they were so shocked by the enormity of death that they failed to make any statements about the symptoms (Motolinía 1971:413; Sahagún 1956, 3:356; Domingo de Betanzos, in CDHM 2:200; Antonio de Mendoza, in AAP-SI-209). The same failure holds also for those authors who reported about the epidemic secondhand (*Cartas de Indias* 1877:331; Torquemada 1723, 1:615, 642; Muñoz Camargo 1892:266; *Relación geográfica de Tepeaca*, in PNE 5:19). Only Mendieta (1945, 3:174), according to the concepts of his time, names the cause of the epidemic as "full bloodiness," by which he presumably means blood flowing from the nose. Fever accompanied the illness. Several Indian sources describe victims bleeding from the mucous membranes of the mouth, nose, eyes, and anus (Chimalpahin 1965:13, 76; *Anales de Tecamachalco* 1903:11; *Codex Aubin*:f. 47v; Sahagún 1950–69, 8:5; *Anales de Tlatelolco* 1948:51, 64). Other Indian sources speak of a great epidemic, either inscribed in stone (*Códice Telleriano-Remensis*, pl. 34; *Anales de San Gregorio Acapulco* 1952:110; *Anales antiguos de México*, nos. 17, 23) or portrayed pictographically (*Tira de Tepechpán*; *Códice en Cruz*, vol. 3; *Codex Mexicanus*, planch 81).

Because of its severity and its striking symptoms, the epidemic of 1545 has been given a fair amount of attention on the part of scholars preoccupied with identification. Humboldt (1966:45, 513), concerned with the origins of yellow fever, established a certain similarity with this disease and defined it as a typhus-like illness. Later authors, Sticker (1932:205) among them, identified it as typhus exanthematicus, today simply called typhus. This identification is based on a comparison of the 1545 epidemic with later ones, especially those of 1576 and 1736. There are three arguments against making such a comparison. First, the epidemics of 1576 and 1736 (and many others) were called *matlaltotonqui* by some of the same Indian sources that were unable to provide a name for the 1545–48 sickness. Humboldt refers, above all, to *matlazáhuatl*, which is not documented for this time, and which could simply be a corrupted form of *matlalzáhuatl*. Second, according to each Indian source, every element of the population, nobles and commoners alike, were struck down by the disease. Children are singled out by the *Anales de Tecamachalco* (1903:11). According to Martín Enríquez (*Cartas de Indias* 1877:331), who was not an eyewitness, the epidemic did not affect people of European origin. This assertion, however, is somewhat contradicted by a statement by Sahagún (1956, 3:356) that he himself became seriously ill towards the end of the epidemic. Sahagún also makes the point that during the epidemic of 1576, allegedly the same as the one of 1545–48, blacks as well as Spaniards fell sick. A third argument against identification as typhus is the fact that no source, when discussing this epidemic, refers to the word *tabardillo*, the usual term employed for typhus in later years.

There is unanimous agreement that the epidemic of 1545–48 was the most devastating of all. The number of dead must have varied from region to region, but according to all reports, mortality was high. The eyewitness Motolinía (1971:413) speaks of a death rate of between 60 and 90 percent throughout New Spain. Torquemada (1723, 1:642) estimated the total number of deaths at 800,000. At Tlaxcala, 150,000 were reported dead, a toll of up to 1,000 each day. Cholula was said to have experienced 100,000 deaths, some 400 to 900 each day. Huejotzingo's dead numbered 400 to 900 (Mendieta 1945, 3:174; Domingo de Betanzos, in CDHM 2:200).

For Tlatelolco, Sahagún (1956, 3:356) claims that he buried more than 10,000 people. These reports fluctuate too widely to permit close correlation, and even gross reckoning indicates that they often are not compatible. It is, however, unreasonable to imagine that at a time of such crisis, anyone could have compiled a basis for more exact data.

Following Humboldt and Sticker, Zinsser (1949:249) refers to the epidemic as typhus. Other scholars, including McNeill (1976:185) and Dobyns (1963:499), appear more skeptical, the latter pointing out that in the Andean region this epidemic was coupled with one that broke out among animals as well. Once again, even though typhus remains the most satisfactory explanation, doubts persist.

Much clearer, and therefore easier to comment on, are the demographic consequences of the epidemic. The sources indicate that the intensity or rate of death exceeded that of the smallpox epidemic of 1520. If that sickness cut population in half, then the 1545–48 epidemic must have had a similar or even greater proportionate impact. What increase in the rate of death might be feasible? One quarter more than the 50-percent mortality of 1520 puts us in the range of Motolinía's estimates. The nature of the testimony prevents any calculation of age-specific mortality.

The Epidemic of 1550

In 1550 many deaths in New Spain were caused by an outbreak of *paperas* (*Códice Telleriano-Remensis*, pl. 36). At this time *paperas* appears to have applied to all kinds of swelling in the face and the throat. Mumps comes immediately to mind (Gibson 1964, 448). Sources in the native language allow the same conjecture. They speak of *quechpozahualiztli*, or "swellings in the neck" (Sahagún 1950–69, 8:8; *Anales de Tlatelolco* 1948:51, 64; Chimalpahin 1965:14, 171). The *Codex Aubin* (f. 47v) tells in slightly more detail of painful growths in the neck area and high fever. The reported cases of death were probably due to complications. The frequency and the nature of complications can only be guessed.

It is undoubtedly a sign of the severity of the sickness that all relevant sources talk about a large number of deaths. Settling for a diagnosis of mumps requires consideration of an important demographic factor. Among adult males, who in a hitherto unexposed population surely did not contract the disease in small numbers, mumps is associated with inflammation of the testicles, which can lead to sterility in as many as one-third of those affected. Severe inflammation of the testicles causes great pain and may lead to pancreatitis, which can be fatal.

The Epidemic of 1559–60

Native sources report that harvests during 1559–60 were ruined by locust invasions, which, in combination with unusually severe frosts, caused deaths from starvation (*Códice Telleriano-Remensis*, pl. 38). It is possible, therefore, that such conditions brought on a mild repetition of the sickness that struck in 1545–48. If this was the case, disease in 1559 and 1560 appears to have had only a slight impact and is only mentioned by Martín Enríquez, a viceroy who at that time was not yet resident in Mexico (*Cartas de Indias* 1877:331). If such comparison is correct, then uncertainty regarding the identification of the 1545–48 epidemic applies to the 1559–60 one as well. The viceroy's comparison, however, was prompted by a rather superficial similarity of symptoms, which he could have known only from hearsay.

Epidemics are reported for the year 1560 from both the Gulf Coast and Guatemala. In each case the name of the sickness is missing, but descriptions are quite detailed. For Guatemala, the *Annals of the Cakchiquels* (Recinos and Goetz 1953:143) record nosebleeds, followed by a gradually worsening cough. Finally, the skin was covered by large and small abscesses, and stiffness in the neck set in. All members of the population were affected. For the Gulf Coast, the *Relación geográfica de Tuztla* (PNE 5:6) describes vomiting of bile, the constriction or blockage of air passages, and death within six hours. The illness lasted in Guatemala until 1562, but for how long on the Gulf Coast we cannot tell. These two reports, therefore, do not necessarily deal with the same epidemic.

The symptoms described above suggest a correlation with the plague epidemic that swept through Europe at the same time. But the European plague, which presumably would have been quickly recognized and thus diagnosed by contemporary observers, was not recorded as having occurred in the New World. Other identifications in the literature are likewise less than satisfactory. Based primarily on evidence of catarrh and nosebleeds, McBryde (1940:297–98) deduced that the sickness was an American offshoot of the influenza epidemic that had been present in Mediterranean lands since 1557. This identification was taken as definitive and so is mentioned as established fact in subsequent literature (McNeill 1976:209). Dobyns (1963:500–501) pronounced himself skeptical of scattered and unreliable secondary literature, but later suggested (1983:269–70) that it was influenza, which appeared in the colonies along with smallpox. The Guatemalan source, however, which specifically names the disease four years later, makes no mention of smallpox. Furthermore, identification as diphtheria, based on the symptoms manifest on the Gulf Coast, is also possible.

Very little can be said about the number of deaths caused by this epidemic. While many people were said to have died in Guatemala, for central Mexico all we have is an unsatisfactory statement that the sickness was less severe than during the epidemic of 1545–48. Given the fact that most sources record nothing about the epidemic, we must conclude, for central Mexico, that we are likely dealing with the viceroy's incorrect information or a less than spectacular cluster of illnesses.

The Epidemic of 1563–64

The next wave of pestilence was also paid scant attention. Only Mendieta (1945, 3:174) and Valderrama (Scholes and Adams 1961:45) report that an epidemic took place. The latter, undertaking a tour of inspection at the time, names *sarampión* as the cause. Native sources add to the confusion. Chimalpahin (1965:18) speaks of *matlaltotonqui*, which translates as "green fever." The *Relación geográfica de Tepoztlán* (PNE 6:245), in a short but exceptionally clear text, lists *tabardete* as the Spanish equivalent and in addition mentions a spotted rash that covered the whole body. In connection with this statement, Chimalpahin's designation stands in contrast to other sources of Indian origin, which again adopt the term *zahuatl* (*Anales de Tecamachalco* 1903:34; *Codex Aubin*:f. 53v) along with the Spanish *sarampión* (*Codex Aubin*:f. 53v; *Anales de San Gregorio Acapulco* 1952:113).

That a disease called *sarampión* in the sixteenth century does not necessarily correlate with measles already has been established. When *sarampión* and *zahuatl* are simultaneously used for the epidemic of 1563, it indicates that it must have been an illness characterized by a blistery rash. This interpretation is supported by another testimony, which speaks of *xaltic zahuatl* (*Anales de Tecamachalco* 1903:34), a term that can be translated as a "sandy, pock-forming rash." The word "sandy" presumably refers to the texture of the eruptions. It must be repeated, however, that during outbreaks of measles, under certain conditions the skin can acquire a complexion best described as sandy. As stated earlier, this feature in the Middle Ages made distinguishing between measles and smallpox quite difficult.

Diagnosis, then, is again problematical. Measles

seems a good possibility as the predominant disease, though not without reservations. Chimalpahin's designation as *mutlaltotonqui*, the strongest argument against a correlation with measles, is an isolated exception among the available evidence. It should perhaps be rejected as being confused with *matlazáhuatl*, a disease that the *Relación geográfica de Tepoztlán* (PNE 6:245) lists as the equivalent of *sarampión*. Statements about mortality are not consistent. While Chimalpahin (1965:18) speaks of many deaths at all social levels, Spanish sources make the epidemic appear less grave. Mendieta (1945, 3:174) mentions cases of death only vaguely. Writing on February 28, 1564, Martín Cortés (Scholes and Adams 1961:340) says that although many were stricken by the disease, only a few died. This is not true, however, of Chalco, where almost half the population is said to have perished in a year and a half (ENE 10:59). Other sources are silent on this point. The epidemic seems to have spread from Chalco across much of central Mexico. In Guatemala, deaths from smallpox are also recorded for 1564 (Recinos and Goetz 1953:145).

After this epidemic, apart from a minor episode of sickness reported only in one Indian source (Gibson 1964:449) for 1566, a decade's respite appears to have set in, during which time no major outbreaks of disease or food shortages are recorded. The ten years or so between 1566 and 1576 therefore must have had a recuperative effect on the native population.

The Epidemic of 1576–80

If one chose to measure the importance of an event based on the number of authors who wrote about it, then the epidemic of 1576–80, without doubt, would be among the most significant in the history of colonial Mexico. For various reasons, a considerable number of reports were compiled around the time of this epidemic, and so mention of it is common. Graphic commentary, especially that contained in the *Relaciones geográficas*, written shortly after the disease first broke out, conveys its devastating impact and frightening effects on contemporaries and those born later. While many sources (*Tira de Tepechpán*; *Codex Mexicanus*, planch 86; *Anales antiguos de México*, no. 16) report the epidemic, only two call the sickness by a specific name. Chimalpahin (1965:26) ascribes the same designation he employed for the epidemic of 1563, namely *matlaltotonqui*, but he also adds a detailed description of the symptoms. The second source, Mendieta (1945, 3:174), speaks of *tabardillo*. According to the *Relación geográfica de Tepoztlán*, the terms are equivalent. Designation as *viruelas*, employed by Robles (1972, 1:239–40), is inconsistent with the above nomenclature. It is possible, however, that in the course of its exceptionally long duration, the epidemic was characterized by the interplay of several different diseases.

Indian sources report unanimously that, as in the sickness of 1545–48, the most striking symptom of the epidemic was bleeding from the mouth and nose, in addition to hemorrhaging from the ears, eyes, and vagina, as well as bouts of bloody diarrhea (Chimalpahin 1965:26; *Anales mexicanos Azcapotzalco* 1900:72; *Anales de Tecamachalco*, 1903:66–67; *Codex Aubin*:f. 60v; Torquemada 1723, 1:642). Throughout these harrowing descriptions, laconic native prose takes on the quality of a named illness: *eztli toyacacpa quiz*, "blood came from our noses." By contrast, Spanish sources ignore symptoms and report exclusively about Indian mortality (ENE, 12:20, 56; Sahagún 1956, 3:356; Muñoz Camargo 1892:277). Only one eyewitness provides useful descriptive information, which might actually refer to the manifestation of another disease within the whole complex of the epidemic. The *Relación geográfica de Ocopetlayuca* (PNE 6:258) states: "It is the nature of this illness that it causes great pain at the 'mouth of the stomach' and is accompanied by a high fever in all parts of the body. Death sets in after six or seven days . . . the sick who survive this time become healthy. At the same time, there are cases of relapse with deadly consequences. No medicinal plant is effective against this disease."

In the secondary literature, there is general agreement that the epidemic of 1576–80, like the ones preceding and following it, was an outbreak of typhus. Recently, however, Malvido and Viesca (1985) have argued for identification as plague, which the sources they scrutinize call *cocoliztli*. It is worth observing that only the eyewitness Mendieta, by naming the disease *tabardillo*, points to an illness characterized by a fever and a rash. From the mid-sixteenth century on, Spaniards employed the word *tabardillo* to mean typhus.

No other source mentions a rash, which, on a pigmented skin, might not have been very conspicuous. More troublesome is the fact that the most striking and frequently described symptom, bleeding from body orifices, does not figure among presently known symptoms of typhus. Writing in the sixteenth century, however, Fracastorius (Major 1945:165) describes heavy nosebleeds occurring shortly before death of typhus victims, an observation that other contemporary writers did not make. Conversely, Sticker (1932:202) attributes the cause of these bleedings to a highland climate, which should influence the appearance of such phenomena in a wide variety of disease outbreaks. Sticker's explanation, therefore, renders the testimony about bleedings suspect and consequently makes accurate diagnosis problematical. Moreover, correlating the Spanish *tabardillo* with the Nahuatl *matlaltotonqui* is something Charles Gibson (1964:448) regards as not very sound. He put forward the unconvincing idea that the epidemic might have been pleurisy. We cannot, then, rule out typhus, although the statement "death sets in after six or seven days" suggests too short a time span for typhus. On the other hand, such a brief period might be realistic in view of the widespread malnutrition brought on by poor harvests of that year.

If identification as typhus is to be promoted seriously, then we must determine whether carriers of the disease were indigenous to Mexico or whether they were a post-conquest introduction. Epidemic typhus is caused by the microorganism *Rickettsia prowazekii* and is transmitted from person to person by means of the body louse, *Pediculus humanus*. Man is most commonly infected after lice carried by rats deposit feces on human skin. Scratching results in abrasion and the onset of sickness (Anderson and Arnstein 1956:449–51). If early Nahuatl dictionaries or the zoological survey undertaken by Sahagún (1950–69:11) contain an autochthonous term for a species of rat, our analysis must assume the preconquest existence of this type of rodent. While review of the sources yields evidence of different kinds of mice, such is not the case with respect to rats. Human lice, however, are represented by at least four aboriginal terms (A. de Molina 1944:1/Piojo). That lice existed before the conquest seems certain, a conclusion strengthened by Zinsser (1949:172), recording the presence of head lice in the hair of pre-Hispanic mummies. After *Rickettsia* organisms were introduced, therefore, they encountered at their disposal an indigenous, widespread vector for the transmission of typhus (Zinsser 1949:216–39).

Statements about total losses are also revealed by the sources. Differences in estimated number of deaths may be attributed to the point in time when, in the course of the epidemic, pronouncements were made: the earlier the testimony, the lower the estimate. After two months, the archbishop of Mexico reported 100,000 dead throughout New Spain (ENE 12:20). Near the end of the epidemic, Torquemada (1723, 1:642) put the number of dead at over two million. Writing to the King on October 26, 1583, the archbishop of Mexico reckoned that more than half the Indian population had perished (ENE 12:86). The tolls for single places are quite staggering: 60,000 dead in the city of Tepeaca alone (*Relación geográfica de Tepeaca*, PNE 5:19) and 50-percent mortality at Temazcaltepec (*Relación geográfica de Temazcaltepec*, PNE 7:22). Attention to detail on the part of most writers, especially Chimalpahin (1965:26), allows us to reconstruct a chronology for the epidemic. The first cases of sickness are reported to have occurred in August 1576. By October of that year the disease seems to have abated, but it flared up again at the beginning of 1577 and raged until April. The year 1578 was apparently free of the disease, but it returned in 1579, possibly along with other illnesses (Robles 1972, 1:240). Its intermittent course meant that the epidemic, as Gibson (1964:499) correctly argued, lasted longer in some areas than in others. Only a few statements were made about the spatial range of sickness. It seems clear, however, that the epidemic spread all over New Spain and south into Guatemala (Chimalpahin 1965:26; Recinos and Goetz 1953:149). Although victims of the epidemic were predominantly Indians, there is for the first time mention of the fact that blacks and some Spaniards also fell ill (Chimalpahin 1965:26).

The "Hunger Epidemic" of 1587

Numerous cases of illness are reported for 1587 and may be linked to the presence of widespread famine. Only the vague term *cocoliztli* is offered as a designation, mentioned in the *Actas de Cabildo* of September 9 that same year. Other sources (Mendieta 1945, 3:174; *Tira de Tepechpán*; *Codex Aubin*:f. 65v; *Anales antiguos de México*, no. 17) speak of sickness but offer no descriptions of symptoms. Both the *Actas de Cabildo* and Mendieta attribute increased mortality and sickness to a lack of food.

The Epidemic of 1595

Mendieta (1945, 3:174) relates that, in the course of writing his book, an epidemic broke out that he considered to be the combination of three diseases: *sarampión*, *tabardillo*, and *paperas*, the last surely being mumps. Around this time, *sarampión* was also named by other sources (*Anales de Tlatelolco* 1948:53; *Codex Aubin*:f. 68v; *Anales antiguos de México*, no. 17). Identification as measles, based on descriptions of skin eruptions, seems most likely, but smallpox may also have been present.

Epidemic Outbreaks, 1604–27

Between 1604 and 1627 outbreaks of sickness certainly occurred but appear not to have been as severe as previous episodes (Mendieta 1945, 3:174). The epidemic of 1595 flared up again in 1604, when *sarampión* and *paperas* are reported, this time in conjunction with diarrhea (Chimalpahin 1965:35). Smallpox, once again, should not be ruled out (*Anales antiguos de México*, no. 17). There is no mention of mortality for the 1604 sickness, but Gibson (1964:449) mentions a high rate of death. Illness also prevailed during 1613 and from 1615 to 1616, when *sarampión* and *viruelas* reappeared. In 1622, reports for the Puebla region speak of a coughing sickness that caused discomfort and, in many cases, death. An illness called *mal de lutos* is reported for 1623 (*Anales antiguos de México*, no. 17), and in 1627 sickness broke out in Mexico City following a period of heavy rains and flooding (Gibson 1964:449).

Conclusion

Both Spanish and Indian sources extant for the study of disease outbreaks in sixteenth-century Mexico exhibit awareness of, if not alarm at, the high rate of mortality that sickness brought about, exceptional even by the standards and perceptions of the time. Awareness of

Table 1.1. Symptoms and diagnoses of disease outbreaks in
sixteenth-century Mexico

Fever	"calenturas" "calenturas tercianas" "calenturas quartanas"
Fever with rash	"viruelas" "tabardillo" "sarampión" "sarna"
Upper respiratory disorders	"romadizo" "tos" "dolor de costado"
Swelling of glands	"hinchazones (de la garganta)" "paperas" "landres" (swelling of the lymph gland)
Bloody secretions	"flujo de sangre" "cámaras de sangre" (bloody stools) "pujamiento de sangre"

death was one thing, description and analysis of its cause quite another. Although considerable attention was paid to the ravages of disease, the knowledge necessary for exact pronouncements regarding its nature and effects was lacking. We can roughly classify the then utilized designations according to symptoms (Table 1.1).

Within these groups, names were often employed synonymously by people not medically trained. Mendieta (1945, 3:174), for example, classified the sickness of 1596 "as a mixed epidemic of measles, mumps and typhus." Mention of several disease names during an outbreak of sickness does not necessarily mean the presence of several illnesses carefully distinguished by the recording eyewitness. While various designations can be applied throughout to a single disease, a single name, used on different occasions or by different authors, may also conceal more than one illness. Such ambiguity obviously presents great difficulties to the proper identification of the epidemics.

The impact of disease outbreaks is described only summarily. In Nahuatl, the expression *micohua* (they died) occurs with numbing regularity. In Spanish-language sources one reads the equivalent *mortandad*, indicating general mortality. It is impossible to arrive at any quantitative assessment on the basis of such statements, for they reflect only the subjective perceptions of contemporary observers. Reports stating that one-quarter, one-third, or one-half of the population died as a result of sickness are only slightly better. Apart from the possibility that, knowingly or unknowingly, writers slanted their depictions according to the purpose of their report (tribute collectors preferred low death tolls, clergy with humanitarian concerns high ones), reliable estimates are rare. Burial numbers furnish approximate evidence and provide us only with a lower limit of death figures. Other statistics about levels of mortality which require careful handling include estimates of the number of empty houses following an epidemic (*Relación geográfica de Itepexi*, PNE 4:13) and the number of tributaries removed from local registers.

An indirect measure of the seriousness of particular epidemics may be surmised from their being mentioned independently by several good, tightly composed sources. Three severe and widespread outbreaks of sickness that decimated the population occurred between the time of the conquest and Philip II's call for *relaciones geográficas* to be compiled: the first pandemic dates to 1520, the second between 1545 and 1548, the third from 1576 to 1580. Evidence of these three major bouts of sickness is often supplemented by remarks that, since the arrival of the Spaniards, numerous hitherto unknown diseases also appeared, in greater or lesser severity. Smallpox and measles, it is clear, soon became diseases that especially endangered children. The overall impression, from the *relaciones geográficas* in particular, is that diseases which caused a severe epidemic then remained endemic and led relatively quickly to renewed and extensive outbreaks. Some of these diseases bestowed considerable or even lifelong immunity on the survivors. Like smallpox and measles, they essentially took on the status of "children's diseases," which, it seems, later would strike and prune only new generations of the very young. This reasoning, by no means incontestable, permits us also to venture that, after a while, severe epidemics are caused by diseases that either have not appeared for a long time, so that a large reservoir of susceptible people awaits infection, or that do not provide long-lasting immunity. Repeated outbreaks, therefore, are possible. Such diseases could have triggered only one pandemic, as in the case of measles.

The same is true, to a lesser degree, of smallpox. In spite of being highly contagious, smallpox did not result in a complete infection of all Indians (Dixon 1962:317), for there always remained, even among adults, a population pool susceptible to renewed outbreaks. Smallpox generally produces a lifelong immunity, although not always. One must reckon, then, with the frequent recurrence of smallpox epidemics of varying magnitude.

The situation is similar with typhus, which does produce a lifelong immunity (Gsell and Mohr 1965:40). Incomplete infection of the population during one outbreak is therefore a prerequisite for subsequent reappearance, even though this is contradicted by testimony in the sources speaking of general affliction. Outbreaks of typhus, it would appear, could only have recurred at intervals that allowed the growth of a sufficiently large susceptible population. A span of thirty years seems sufficient, otherwise the sources would have spoken of an intervening outbreak in which mostly children were stricken.

There is good reason to think that most epidemics were accompanied, to a greater or lesser extent, by gastrointestinal infections, as evidenced by frequent reference to *cámaras de sangre*. These illnesses, most probably involving amoebiasis, occurred almost all the time, even between the major epidemics, although with seasonal fluctuations (*Relación geográfica de Tepeaca*, PNE 5:32). Given the presence of hunger, other diseases, and new cultural mores impairing general well-being, gastrointestinal infections must have reached extremes. Disorders of the upper respiratory system also existed, to which Spaniards as well as Indians were prone. Both types of sickness presumably were native and widespread in Mexico before the conquest (*Relación geográfica de Coatepec-Chalco*, PNE 6:58; *Anales de Cuauhtitlán* 1938:515; Cook 1945). In addition, the change in settlement patterns brought about by *congregación*, a policy whereby formerly scattered native populations were regrouped in compact clusters, surely caused a deterioration in sanitary conditions, which in turn created an even worse situation for Indians when disease broke out (Gerhard 1977; MacLeod 1973).

What Woodrow Borah, in his introduction, calls "compound epidemics" occurred frequently, certainly more often than clear-cut cases of sickness brought on by a single disease. Only the very earliest epidemics, if any, may be attributed to one specific pathogen. In later years, epidemics triggered by one sickness were joined by other illnesses latent in the population. Working in

Table 1.2. Principal causes of disease-related death in central Mexico, 1521–1595

Year	Epidemic
1521	Smallpox
1531	Measles
1545	Typhus (?)
1550	Mumps
1563	Measles (?)
1576	Typhus (?)
1595	Measles

unison, the impact of a combination of disease agents could be, and was, disastrous.

Care must be exercised, therefore, when compiling disease chronologies, especially for the first decades after contact, that focus on single epidemic episodes (Sánchez-Albornoz 1974:60–63). Correlating diverse descriptions with a single disease cannot always be done, however neat we would like the connection to be. What can be advanced, as in Table 1.2, are identifications of the leading disease in a lethal conglomerate.

A striking feature of these identifications is that outbreaks of measles and typhus occur almost exactly thirty years apart. The timing of these particular outbreaks, if identification is correct, fits nicely into the argument made earlier, that whenever a sufficiently large, susceptible population was present, among whom an epidemic could flare up, its effects were correspondingly grave. In terms of numbers of deaths, the smallpox epidemic of 1521 ranks first, followed by typhus and measles. Population decline could not have taken the gradually increasing course assumed earlier by Cook and Borah. Rather, depopulation must have set in abruptly, soon after the arrival of smallpox, to lessen in intensity later on, interrupted always by periodic outbreaks of other grave sickness.

DISEASE AND DEPOPULATION IN EARLY COLONIAL GUATEMALA

W. George Lovell

A Constant Cough (*Florentine Codex*)

In discussions of Latin American historiography, few debates generate such persistent controversy as that concerning the magnitude and intensity of native population decline following contact with, and conquest by, imperial Spain. That the central issue in this debate may no longer be "How many Indians were there?" but "What caused so many to perish so quickly?" represents an important step forward. We will, it seems safe to assert, continue to count differently, some higher, some lower than others. Of late, however, our scholarly energies appear to be channelled more towards clarification of historical determinants than involvement in academic arithmetic, crucial though the latter enterprise

NOTE: The research upon which this chapter is based was made possible by support from the Killam Program of the Canada Council, the Social Sciences and Humanities Research Council of Canada, and Queen's University Advisory Research Committee. The author thanks Christopher H. Lutz for advice and direction. Wendy Kramer helped in the gathering of archival data, and Armando J. Alfonzo and Heidi Fielder in organizing information in tabular form. The trace of the late William R. Swezey runs throughout.

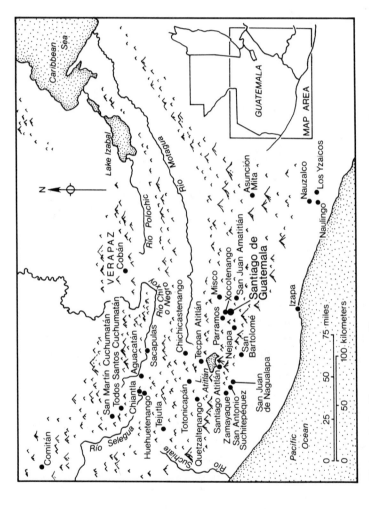

Figure 2.1. Colonial Guatemala

always will be. In the final analysis, addressing the meaning of a process is what really matters.

This intellectual shift may be discerned in the contribution of numerous scholars, but it seems appropriate to illustrate the point with reference to work in the two languages most resorted to for purposes of discourse. A recent essay by Linda Newson (1985) reflects the progress made in English-language scholarship since publication of the collection edited by William Denevan (1976) and the bibliographic synthesis undertaken by Henry Dobyns (1976[b]). With a specific focus on the colonial Maya, Cristina García Bernal (1978) and Elías Zamora Acosta (1985) exemplify the more balanced and insightful direction Spanish-language scholarship has taken since the time of Francisco de Solano (1974). Much remains to be done,[1] but advances have been made. Even though the bickering continues, we walk across more common ground than before.

What, then, do we think caused widespread and precipitous depopulation among Native Americans in the wake of European penetration of the New World? The reasons, not surprisingly, are ones that require careful explanation, but the disease factor (without in any way failing to observe that warfare, disruption, exploitation, and culture shock must also be reckoned with) now emerges in most discussions as a key demographic variable. Old World diseases introduced by European invaders and their African slaves brought dreadful destruction to indigenous New World populations, whose immune systems never before had to deal with such a virulent range of infections (Crosby 1976[a]; Joralemon 1982). If the role disease played in native population decline is to be given prominence, if its lethal passage is to be used to persuade champions of lower estimates of aboriginal numbers to think higher, links obviously must be made between reports of epidemic outbreaks and accounts of Indian depopulation. It is to the forging of such a link, in the context of early colonial Guatemala, that this chapter is directed.

The Sources

The sources upon which a case may be built connecting depopulation in early colonial Guatemala with sickness and death are not nearly as rich as those that exist for Mexico (Gibson 1964:448–51; Cook and Borah 1971, 1974, 1979; Florescano and Malvido 1980). They are, however, considerably more abundant than the few shreds of evidence available for sixteenth-century America north of the Rio Grande (Sauer 1971:302–4; Snow and Lanphear 1988:15–20). Given the intense scrutiny David Henige (1985-86; 1986; 1989) has afforded the work of Henry Dobyns (1983; 1989a), it is imperative that interpretation of the sources be tight, measured, and properly contextualized, that little be asserted without a grounded, documentary basis. Inaccuracies and imperfections, of course, are inevitable, but these may be minimized by keeping as close to first-hand, contemporary testimony as the act of interpretation permits.

Reports of native depopulation in Guatemala from 1539 to 1617 are summarized in Table 2.1. All of these reports come from unpublished manuscripts housed in the Archivo General de Indias (AGI) in Seville, a more complete source of sixteenth-century materials than the Archivo General de Centroamérica (AGCA) in Guatemala City. A range of estimates of the Indian population in the sixteenth century is presented in Table 2.2. Table 2.3 outlines widespread (pandemic) outbreaks of disease, while Table 2.4 documents more localized (epidemic) occurrences. A brief discussion of native depopulation will be followed by a more detailed analysis of disease outbreaks, especially those which can be considered more pandemic than epidemic in nature.

Native Depopulation

In the documentation summarized in Table 2.1, there is repeated mention that the native population is in a state of accelerated decline. No reference is made, however, to the presence of sickness or disease as an underlying cause. About half of these episodes deal with petitions lodged by privileged Spaniards who complain that revenues generated by the tribute paid to them by Indians has dropped considerably. A fall in income, they rightly conclude, is related to a fall in the number of those who are supposed to pay tribute. The *encomienda* (Indian tributary grant) of Mita, for example, was declared around 1562 to be worth "almost nothing" because "many Indians have died."[1] For similar reasons, in 1568 Alonso Páez (AGI, Patronato 68-2-3) anticipated an income of less than 100 pesos from towns that were worth much more when his father held them in *encomienda* some thirty years previously. Cristóbal Aceituno grumbled that his share of San Juan de Nahualapa "does not amount, in each year, to 400 *tostones*, on account of the losses incurred by the great decrease of tribute payers."[2] He bemoaned the fact that all he could expect were "eight *cargas* (loads) of cacao, from which one cannot support oneself two months of the year."[3]

Other cases relate not to the private concerns of *encomenderos*, people who held Indian towns in *encomienda*, but to the more collective preoccupations of church and state. Thus on March 8, 1575, a Franciscan cleric wrote to the king to "let Your Majesty know about what is go-

---

[1] Archivo General de las Indias (hereafter AGI), Patronato 65-1-15. The Spanish text reads "por averse muerto muchos indios no rentan casi nada."

[2] AGI, Patronato 57-3-1. The Spanish text reads "no me vale ni me renta en cada un año 400 tostones por las bajas que se an hecho respeto a la gran diminución de los tributarios."

[3] AGI, Patronato 57-3-1. The Spanish text reads "ocho cargas de cacao que no se puede sustentar dos meses del año."

Table 2.1. Reports of native depopulation in early colonial Guatemala, 1539–1617

Year	Place	Summary	Source
Ca. 1539	Towns held in *encomienda* by Diego Díaz in Totonicapán and Huehuetenango	"se an muerto o despoblado"	AGI, AG 110
Ca. 1546	San Juan de Nagualpa	"gran diminución de los tributarios"; "a venido a tanta baja y diminución"	AGI, Patronato 57-3-1
Ca. 1552	Aguacatán, Comitán, Los Anaucos, Xicalapa, Xocotenango	"gran descrecimiento y diminución"	AGI, Justicia 286
Ca. 1555	Santiago Atitlán and subject towns	"enferman y mueren gran parte"	AGI, Justicia 283
Ca. 1555	Numerous towns	"los pobres indios se an muerto en gran cantidad y otros se an despoblado y se an ido a meter a tierras de guerra"	AGI, AG 41
Ca. 1556	Yzalcos and surrounding towns	"que se an muerto y mueren de mil personas arriba en ellos"	AGI, AG 52
Ca. 1557–59	Santiago Atitlán	"por ser muy poca la gente y averse muerto muchos vecinos no tienen bienes ni haciendas"	AGI, Justicia 302
Ca. 1558	Tacuscalco and other towns held in *encomienda* by Francisco de Calderón	"los indios han venido en mucha diminución"	AGI, Patronato 61-2-8

Date	Place	Quotation	Source
Ca. 1562	(Asunción) Mita	"por averse muerto muchos indios han venido en tanta diminución"; "mucha diminución a causa de muertes de indios"	AGI, Patronato 65-1-15
Ca. 1568	Aguacatán, Istapalatenango, Miahuatlán, and Sacapulas	"aber venido los indios en diminución"	AGI, Patronato 68-2-3
Ca. 1573	Throughout Guatemala	"an fallecido muchas personas"	AGI, AG 169
Ca. 1575	Throughout Guatemala	"los naturales son cada día menos, los españoles cada día más y así hay grandísimas necesidades"	AGI, AG 169
Ca. 1577	Throughout Guatemala	"los naturales cada día vienen a ser menos y se van acabando"	AGI, AG 170
Ca. 1580	Tecpán Yzalco	"tanta diminución"	AGI, AG 170
Ca. 1581	Verapaz	"más de 13,000 tributarios ayan venido a tanta diminución"	AGI, AG 163
Ca. 1582	Chiantla and Huehuetenango	"los indios a venido en diminución, a venido a menos"	AGI, Patronato 61-2-4
Ca. 1583	Nauzalco	"mucha diminución"	AGI, Patronato 77-2-2

Table 2.1. continued

Year	Place	Summary	Source
Ca. 1585	Naulingo	"mucha diminución"	AGI, Patronato 62-1-14
Ca. 1588	Towns in Chiapas held in *encomienda* by Luis de Mazariegos	"mucha diminución por averse diminuido los indios"	AGI, Patronato 85-3-3
Ca. 1589	Mixco, Nejapa, Parramos, and Tejutla	"an venido en diminución como an hecho otros pueblos"	AGI. Patronato 80-1-3
Ca. 1598	Verapaz	"los pocos naturales cada día ir en diminución"	AGI, AG 163
Ca. 1600	Nextalapa (Chiapas?)	"están los indios casi acabados"	AGI, Patronato 82-3-6
Ca. 1603	Throughout Guatemala	"mucha diminución"	AGI, AG 156
Ca. 1611	Yzalco	"aver venido en diminución el pueblo y los tributos"	AGI, Patronato 86-1-1
Ca. 1614	Izapa	"aver venido el pueblo a menos"	AGI, Patronato 56-4-3
Ca. 1614	San Antonio Suchitepéquez	"aver venido el pueblo en diminución de tributarios"; "mucha diminución"	AGI, Patronato 56-4-3, 82-1-5
Ca. 1617	Zalpatagua and (?) Esculco	"diminución por aver habido mucha mortandad"	AGI, Patronato 87-1-3

ing on in this land."[4] He pointed out that "each day the Indians become fewer in number, while Spaniards increase, and this is a matter of some urgency. If the Indians perish within two generations then the sons and grandsons of those who conquered in Your Majesty's name will suffer great hardships."[5] This tone of alarm was reinforced two years later when another Franciscan, Fray Gonzalo Méndez, warned the king that "the Indians continue to die out, this much is evident, for since records were begun eight years ago there have been many more deaths than baptisms. In a few years all will be lost, in the same manner as were lost the Indians of the islands of Santo Domingo."[6] Fray Gonzalo followed up this missive with another, his fifth letter to the king over a period of ten years. Writing from Santiago de Guatemala on March 24, 1579, the tenacious friar listed no fewer than twenty-one reasons why the king and the Council of the Indies should be concerned about Indian survival, highlighting the economic consequences of depopulation while at the same time respectfully reminding the king of his moral obligations. That someone in authority actually read what Méndez wrote seems likely, for on the back of his letter (AGI, Guatemala 170) is penned "vista, no ai responder." These four words—"noted, no reply needed"—serve as a fitting epitaph for an empire Spain was destined to lose. The Crown, certainly by the late sixteenth century, was acutely aware that all was not well in the Indies,

---

[4] AGI, Guatemala 169. The Spanish text reads "dar quenta a VM [Vuestra Majestad] de lo que por acá pasa esta tierra."

[5] AGI, Guatemala 169. The Spanish text reads "los naturales son cada día menos, los españoles cada día más y así ay grandísimas necesidades y si los indios no duran más de dos vidas padescerán los hijos y nietos de los conquistadores que a ganado a Vuestra Majestad toda esta tierra mucha necesidad."

[6] AGI, Guatemala 170. The Spanish text reads "los naturales van acabando y esto por cosa clara por que ocho años que empezó a tener cuenta son de continuo cada año más mucho los que mueren que se bautiza y en pocos años más se vienen acabar todos como se acabaron los yndios de las yslas de Santo Domingo." The letter is dated March 15, 1577.

that its native subjects there were fast dying off and had in certain instances (Sauer 1966) already disappeared. How to redress the situation, to legislate successfully against the human factors that helped propel it, was something never to be resolved.

Depopulation and the Role of Disease

The contemporary testimony discussed above indicates quite unequivocally that the native population of Guatemala declined sharply in the course of the sixteenth century. Estimates of the numbers involved in this process of decline vary markedly, as Table 2.2 illustrates. All those whose work is reflected in this table, however, concur that a decline did take place, a decline of major dimensions. Even Francisco de Solano, whose figures are the lowest of the group, acknowledges that his estimates deal with a "massive collapse," although he goes on to kindle the flame of the Black Legend by

Table 2.2. Estimates of Maya depopulation in early colonial Guatemala, 1520–1600 (in thousands)

Year	Denevan (1976)[a]	Lovell, Lutz, and Swezey (1984)[b]	Sanders and Murdy (1982)[c]	Solano (1974)[d]	Zamora Acosta (1985)[e]
Ca. 1520	2,000	2,000	500–800	300	315
Ca. 1550		427.85		157	121
Ca. 1575				148	75
Ca. 1600				195	64

Sources: See Bibliography.
[a] Estimate is for the territory of the present-day republic of Guatemala.
[b] Estimate is for southern Guatemala, defined as the area of the present-day republic of Guatemala excluding the northern department of El Petén, with some overspill west into the Mexican state of Chiapas and east into the republic of El Salvador.
[c] Estimate is for highland Guatemala only.
[d] Spatial basis of estimate unclear.
[e] Estimate is for western Guatemala, specifically the colonial jurisdiction known as the *alcaldía mayor* of Zapotitlán y Suchitepéquez. Neither eastern Guatemala nor the northern Petén district is included in these estimates.

Table 2.3. Widespread (pandemic) outbreaks of disease in early colonial Guatemala, 1519–1632

Year	Place	Sickness or Symptoms	Source
1519–21	Among the Cakchiquel and Tzutuhil Maya	Smallpox, measles, influenza, or pulmonary plague; "tos, sangre de narices y de mal de orina"	Recinos (1950:119–20); *Descripcion de San Bartolomé* (1965:216)
1533	Throughout Guatemala	"Sarampión" and "viruelas"	AGI, AG 9A, 50; Fuentes y Guzmán (1932–33, 1:338)
1545	Throughout Guatemala	"Gucumatz"; "tabardillo"; "fríos y calenturas"; "enfermedades y pestes." Pulmonary plague (?)	Fuentes y Guzmán (1932–33, 3:425–26); *Isagoge Histórica* (1934:290)
1558–63	Throughout Guatemala	"Sarampión"; "viruela"; "tabardillo"; frío intenso y fiebre"; "sangre de la nariz"; "tos"; "les brotaban llagas pequeñas y grandes"	Vázquez (1937–44, 1:154); AGI, AG 9; Recinos (1950:146–47)
1576–78	Throughout Guatemala	"Viruela"; "tabardete"; "sarampión"; "sangre de narices"; "bubas"; "catarros"; "enfermedades y pestes"	AGI, AG 10, 156; *Isagoge Histórica* (1934:290)
1607–8	Throughout Guatemala	"Tabardillo"; "sangre de narices"; "enfermedad general"	AGI, AG 12, 419
1620s	Throughout Guatemala	"Viruela"; "peste general"	AGI, AG 867
1631–32	Throughout Guatemala	"Tabardillo"	Gage (1928:201); Molina (1943:24–25)

declaring members of the Berkeley School to be driven by "a secret passion," the objective of which is "to blame Spanish action as the direct cause" of native depopulation (Solano 1974:61). Disease, not "Spanish action" in the form of slaughter or slavery, most scholars now accept was the critical factor, the allegations of Solano notwithstanding.

That said, care must be taken not to focus exclusively on the disease factor, for in so doing we eliminate other nonbiological variables from the analysis, variables which played an important role in shaping the colonial Indian experience (Newson 1985). Thus we can concur with Zamora Acosta (1985:131) that disease must be considered "the fundamental cause" but express reservation at its being designated the "almost single" reason behind native population decline.

These observations aside, reconstruction of pandemic or epidemic chronologies remains a vital task if the link between disease and depopulation is to be effectively and convincingly made. Table 2.3 lists eight disease outbreaks, which, in all likelihood, constitute pandemic occurrences. Table 2.4 may be considered a record of twenty-five episodes relating to more local, epidemic outbreaks of disease. Because of their greater impact, the pandemic outbreaks will now be looked at one by one, with the epidemic occurrences treated jointly afterwards in more summary fashion.

The Sickness of 1519–21

A well-known passage from the *Annals of the Cakchiquels* (Recinos and Goetz 1953:115–16) provides us with the following description of a "great and mortal epidemic," which appeared in Guatemala some five years before the *entrada* led by Pedro de Alvarado in 1524:

It happened that during the twenty-fifth year [1519] the plague began, oh, my sons! First they became ill of a cough, they suffered from nosebleeds and illness of the bladder. It was truly terrible, the number of dead there were in that period. The prince Vakaki Ahmak died then. Little by little

heavy shadows and black night enveloped our fathers and grandfathers and us also, oh, my sons!
It was in truth terrible, the number of dead among the people. The people could not in any way control the sickness.
Great was the stench of the dead. After our fathers and grandfathers succumbed, half of the people fled to the fields. The dogs and the vultures devoured the bodies. The mortality was terrible. Your grandfathers died, and with them died the son of the king and his brothers and kinsmen. So it was that we became orphans, oh, my sons! So we became when we were young. All of us were thus. We were born to die!

Controversy, however, exists over identification of this sickness. It is therefore important to observe that an earlier English translation (Brinton 1885:171) renders the Cakchiquel text as follows:

In the course of the fifth year the pestilence began, O my children. First there was a cough, then the blood was corrupted, and the urine became yellow. The number of deaths at this time was truly terrible. The Chief Vakaki Ahmak died, and we ourselves were plunged in great darkness and great grief, our fathers and ancestors having contracted the plague, O my children.
Truly the number of deaths among the people was terrible, nor did the people escape from the pestilence.
The ancients and the fathers died alike, and the stench was such that men died of it alone. Then perished our fathers and ancestors. Half the people threw themselves into the ravines, and the dogs and foxes lived on the bodies of the men. The fear of death destroyed the old people, and the oldest son of the king at the same time as his young brother. Thus did we become poor, O my children, and thus did we survive, being but a little child—and we were all that remained.

While we must be thankful that such a poignant and graphic description has survived, problems exist, for medical and nonmedical opinion is divided as to what this disease might have been. Most commentators, among them Recinos and Goetz (1953:115), Solano (1974:70), Veblen (1977:490), and Zamora Acosta (1985:

Table 2.4. Local (epidemic) outbreaks of disease in early colonial Guatemala, 1555–1618

Year	Place	Summary	Source
Ca. 1555	Zamayaque	"muertes y enfermedades"	AGI, AG 111
Ca. 1562	Chichicastenango	"grandes enfermedades y pestilencias"; "gran mortandad"; "mucha diminución y muertes"	AGI, Patronato 59-3-2
Ca. 1562	Zalquitlán and Yzalcos	"pestilencias y enfermedades"; "tributo en diminución"; "han muerto muchos indios"	AGI, Patronato 75-1-2
1564	Cakchiquel communities	"Se propagó la enfermedad de la viruela, de la cual murió mucha gente"	Recinos (1950:149)
Ca. 1571	Towns in Chiapas close to Guatemala	"grandes enfermedades y muertes"	AGI, Patronato 76-2-2
1572	Numerous "pueblos de indios"	"pestes"	AGCA, A1, 1512:f 416
1576	Cakchiquel communities	"También en el mes de septiembre hubo una peste de bubas que atacó y mató a la gente. Todos los pueblos sufrieron la enfermedad"	Recinos (1950:155)
Ca. 1578	Verapaz	"muchos de los naturales se an muerto de enfermedad"	AGI, AG 51

			Relación de Santiago Atitlán (1964:85)
Before 1585	Santiago Atitlán	"mucha disminución"; "viruelas y sarampión e tabardete e sangre que les salía de las narizes"; "otras pestilencias"	
1585	Quezaltenango	"grande enfermedad"	AGI, Contaduría 968
1588	Cakchiquel communities	"Comenzó entonces una epidemia de erupciones entre los niños, de la que no morían los viejos"	Recinos (1950:171)
1590	Cakchiquel communities	"El día 3 de enero comenzó una enfermedad de tos, fríos y calenturas de que moría la gente"	Recinos (1950:174)
1600	Towns in Chiapas	"enfermedades prolixas y largas que an llevada mucha gente"; "los pobres naturales son muchos los que se an muerto"; "a esta causa a habido hambres"	AGI, AG 161
1601	Cakchiquel communities	"En el mes de octubre comenzó la mortandad a causa de una epidemia que atacaba la garganta de mujeres y hombres [que morían] en dos días"	Recinos (1950:193)

Table 2.4. continued

Year	Place	Summary	Source
Before 1604	Towns held in *encomienda* by Juan de Aguilar	"ha muchos años que con enfermedades y pestilencias se an consumido los naturales"	AGI, Patronato 64-1-1
1607–8	Ysguatán and Coylpitán, in Chiapas	"los indios se habían muerto de pestilencia"	AGI, Patronato 64-1-1
Ca. 1608	San Juan Amatitlán	"se an muerto en una peste mucha cantidad de indios"	AGI, AG 111
Ca. 1610	Mixco, Nejapa, Parramos, and Tejutla, held in *encomienda* by Alvaro de Paz	"los indios se an disminuido y muerto con las pestes que a avido"	AGI, Patronato 85-3-3
Ca. 1610	Valley of Guatemala	"pestes"; "mortandad entre los indios"	AGI, AG 13
1612	Numerous towns	"peste"; "para que los indios no mueren en tiempo de hambre"	AGI, AG 13
Ca. 1613	Todos Santos Cuchumatán	"falta de tributarios"; "indios viejos y enfermos"	AGI, Patronato 58-1-4
1614	Santiago de Guatemala	"peste general"	AGCA, A1, 1772, 11766
1617	San Martín Cuchumatán	"indios enfermos"	AGI, Patronato 58-1-4
1618	Towns in Chiapas	"diminuciones por enfermedades y muertes de los naturales"; "falta de indios"	AGI, AG 161

126), believe the Cakchiquel account to refer to small-pox. On the other hand, Daniel Brinton (1885:207), a physician as well as the first person to translate the *Annals of the Cakchiquels* into English, considered the description diagnostic of a malignant outbreak of measles. Brinton is supported in this assessment by the more recent work of Villacorta Cifuentes (1976:50–57), also a physician. Villacorta derives much of his evidence for designation as measles from the earlier study of another Guatemalan doctor, Horacio Figueroa Marroquín (1983), whose *Enfermedades de los conquistadores* first appeared in 1955. Figueroa Marroquín (1983:45–61) provides a fairly convincing argument in favor of measles.

George Shattuck (1938:41), who taught at the Harvard School of Public Health, considered the identity of the epidemic to be "not certainly known because of the vagueness of the terms used by the annalist to describe it." He suggests, however, that "probably it was smallpox which came from Mexico," adding that quite possibly "more than one disease was epidemic at about that time." MacLeod (1973:19) also regards the outbreak as smallpox but concurs with Shattuck's suggestion that likely more than one disease was involved. He contends, specifically, that "the descriptions of the disease found in the Guatemalan Indian annals resemble those of pulmonary plague." Carlos Martínez Durán (1941: 44), professor of the history of medicine at the Universidad de San Carlos de Guatemala, shied away from categorical designation, but suggested influenza, measles, or exanthematic typhus. He was adamant, however, that the disease could not have been smallpox, for the Cakchiquel chronicler (Diego Hernández Xahil) would then, as for an outbreak of sickness in 1564, have employed the term *viruela* or *viruelas*. Martínez Durán (1941:69) correlates the Cakchiquel word for the pestilence, *chaac*, with the Nahuatl term for exanthematic typhus, *matlatzáhuatl*. Brinton (1885:207) tells us that Brasseur de Bourbourg erroneously translated *chaac* as "la maladie syphilitique" and states that the word "applied to any eruptive disease, to the whole class of exanthemata."

Felix Webster McBryde (1940:296–97), observing that influenza was widespread in Europe during the early sixteenth century, advanced the notion that the symptoms best fit "those of the great pandemic of influenza in 1918–19," a notion MacLeod (1973:399) considers an "unconvincing argument." Sherburne F. Cook, well trained in the natural and medical sciences before embarking on pioneering studies of historical demography in Mexico and California, seems not to have been as dismissive as MacLeod of the influenza designation, for he is acknowledged by McBryde (1946:301) "for critically reading the manuscript of this article." Crosby (1972:58) thinks that, indeed, the disease "may have been influenza" because it "was apparently not smallpox, for the accounts do not mention pustules." Orellana (1987:141) points out that while the Spanish word *viruelas* almost always is translated as smallpox, the term in fact refers to the "pimpled pustuled appearance" of the disease, and not to the illness itself. *Viruelas* as a manifestation or symptom may have been employed by contemporary Spaniards to apply also to "measles, chicken pox, or even typhus," although the designation (Crosby 1967: 43) usually did mean smallpox. Orellana (1987:142) suggests that the sickness might have been a malignant form of smallpox. The balance of commentary thus may favor smallpox, but not unanimously so. What seems worthy of observation is that medical doctors who analyze the native text are more inclined to diagnose measles than smallpox.

What would help determine more accurate diagnosis, obviously, are other descriptive sources relating to disease outbreaks at this time. Unfortunately, very little is available. Later on in the *Annals of the Cakchiquels* (Recinos and Goetz 1953:143) there is reference to an outbreak in 1560 of "the plague which had lashed the people long ago," with the observation that "small and large sores broke out on them." If the sores were pustules, and the 1560 outbreak the same disease as that which occurred in 1519–21, then the case for smallpox could be strengthened. It is disappointing that no other native document of the many available (Carmack 1973:11–79) can be turned to for assistance or corroboration. In the *Descripción de San Bartolomé*, a *relación geográfica* compiled in 1585, it is stated that "before the Spaniards arrived in this land there was an incurable outbreak of smallpox."[7] It may therefore be possible, as indeed Zamora Acosta (1985:126) has done, to correlate the smallpox reference in the *Descripción de San Bartolomé* with the outbreak recorded for 1519–21 in the *Annals of the Cakchiquels*.

Diagnosis, then, is problematical. Decidedly not, however, is the clear reference to high mortality, social disruption, fear, and panic that this sickness brought to the Cakchiquel Maya. The source (Recinos and Goetz 1953:115) also distinguishes between 1519, when "the plague raged," and 1520 and 1521, when "the plague spread." Even if the Cakchiquel were the sole diligent recorders of the sickness, it surely must also have affected their Tzutuhil, Quiché, and Mam neighbors. Referring to the outbreaks of sickness that preceded Alvarado's arrival as "the shock troops of the conquest," MacLeod (1973:40–41) is in no doubt as to the profound consequences of this disease:

Given present-day knowledge of the impact of smallpox or plague on people without previous immunities, it is safe, indeed conservative, to say that a third of the Guatemalan highland populations died during this holocaust. Knowledge of past epidemics in Europe and of the aftermath of smallpox

---

[7] *Descripción de San Bartolomé*, p. 267. The Spanish text reads "antes que los españoles viniesen a esta tierra les subcedió una pestilencia de viruelas yncurables."

and plague can also lead us to assert that those who survived were left at least for a year or so in a weakened condition, with greatly lowered resistance to the minor ills, colds, bronchitis, pneumonia, and influenza which carry off so many invalids.

When, in 1524, Pedro de Alvarado led the first Spanish *entrada* into Guatemala, he was therefore confronted in battle by native warriors whose peoples had already been weakened by the presence among them of a new strain, or strains, of disease.

The Sickness of 1533

Citing three contemporary sources, MacLeod (1973: 98) records measles as having had a "general" pandemic presence in Central America between 1532 and 1534. That measles devastated Honduras and Nicaragua around this time seems fairly certain, for in addition to MacLeod's sources we have those consulted by Linda Newson (1986:128–29; 1987:120). We also have the first-hand testimony of Pedro de los Ríos, a royal treasurer who resided in León. Writing to the king on June 22, 1533, Ríos observed that the shortage of Indians in Nicaragua to pan for gold was related directly to "many sicknesses which have struck them, especially one recently of *sarampión*."[8] The extent to which this outbreak of measles also affected Guatemala is less clear, for our sources are again rather scant. Fuentes y Guzmán (1932–33, 1:338) mentions an early but undated outbreak, one he describes as arriving in Guatemala, along with smallpox, from neighboring Mexico. Measles and smallpox, the chronicler asserts, spread "like fire in dry grass, laying waste to entire towns of several thousand inhabitants."[9] Asturias (1958:87), citing the Do-

---

[8] AGI, Guatemala 50. The Spanish text reads "muchas enfermedades que les a dado especialmente una que nuevamente les a dado de sarampión." Another letter (AGI, Guatemala 9A) dated May 1, 1533, written to the king by Licenciado Francisco Castañeda, also mentions *sarampión*, which he says has killed "más de seis mil indios."

[9] The Spanish text reads "como el activo y cebado fuego de los campos secos, pueblos enteros de innumerables y crecidos millares de habitadores."

minican chronicler Antonio de Remesal, also refers to smallpox in Guatemala at this time. Of measles specifically, Fuentes y Guzmán (1932–33, 1:338) quotes Pedro de Alvarado as having declared: "Because measles has struck the Indians I order those who hold *encomiendas* and *repartimientos*, on punishment of forfeiting them lest they not comply, to care for and cure their charges without engaging them in any activity, for experience has shown in other similar epidemics that much territory has been depopulated."[10]

Fuentes y Guzmán may not always be a reliable source (Carmack 1973:183–187) but his credibility on this occasion is enhanced when he makes it clear that he is quoting directly from Pedro de Alvarado, someone not widely regarded as a responsible overseer of Indian welfare (Sherman 1983:173–75). If the rapacious Alvarado thought it prudent to desist, albeit temporarily, from enforcement of *encomienda* and *repartimiento* obligations, then he likely had good reason for doing so. Fuentes y Guzmán (1932–33, 1:339) goes on to point out, directly after quoting Alvarado, that by overlooking or ignoring the presence of disease, the connection Las Casas insisted on making between Indian population decline and Spanish cruelty is inaccurate and misplaced.

Confidence in using Fuentes y Guzmán as a source for this outbreak of sickness was bolstered when an examination of early colonial correspondence (AGI, Guatemala 9A) disclosed the existence of an important letter. Writing to King Charles V on September 1, 1532, from Santiago de Guatemala, Pedro de Alvarado concludes a detailed report about various affairs of state with the following remark:

---

[10]The Spanish text reads "por cuanto ha caido peste de sarampión sobre los indios, mando que los que los tuviesen encomendados, y repartimiento de ellos, pena de perdimiento de los tales indios encomendados, los cuiden y curen sin ocuparlos en servicio alguno; porque se ha visto por experiencia que con otras semejantes pestilencias se han despoblado muchas tierras."

All that remains for me to tell Your Majesty is that, throughout New Spain, there passed a sickness that they say is
sarampión, one which struck the Indians and swept the land,
leaving it totally empty. It arrived in this province some
three months ago and, on my instructions, arrangements
were made so that the Indians would be better cared for, so
that they would not die in such great numbers as in all other
parts. It was not possible to act before many died, so in these
parts also there has been a very great loss, for many indeed
are dead.[11]

Alvarado goes on to state, as Fuentes y Guzmán
claimed, that he ordered restrictions to be placed on the
use of Indian labor. In an effort to reduce mortality, specific mention is made of "slaves who were taken from
the mines" being "treated and cured," as well as "other
Indians who were relieved of their duties."[12] Alvarado,
never one to lose an opportunity to make himself look
good, hoped that the king understood and agreed with
his actions. Because of the emergency, Alvarado mentions also that "gold was not melted down in as great a
quantity as we had hoped" and so takes care to warn
the king that, in consequence, "Your Majesty's share is
diminished."[13]

While Spaniards in the sixteenth century appear to
have employed the term *sarampión* quite freely, Shattuck
(1938:42–43) remarks rather skeptically that using the
word as "evidence for the occurrence of epidemics of
measles is unsatisfactory," not least because "measles

[11] AGI, Guatemala 9A. The Spanish text reads "solamente me queda de
decir que en toda la Nueva España vino una pestilencia por los naturales que
dicen sarampión, la qual acalado toda la tierra sin dejar cosa ninguna en ella
y llegó a esta provincia abra tres meses y puesto que por mi parte fueron
hechas muchas diligencias para que los naturales fueron mejor curados y no
se diese lugar a que muriessen en tanta cantidad como en todas las otras
partes no pudo tanto preservarse que no haber muerto muchas y haber sido
en estas partes muy gran pérdida a si por los muchos que son muertos."
[12] AGI, Guatemala 9A. The Spanish text reads "mandé luego que todos los
esclavos que fueron sacados de las minas y tratados y curados . . . y que los
otros naturales en sus servicios fueron relevados."
[13] AGI, Guatemala 9A. The Spanish text reads "no se fundió oro en tanta
cantidad como esperabamos y Vuestra Majestad perdió de su parte."

was not recognized in Europe as a separate entity before the eighteenth century." Figueroa Marroquín (1983: 48) makes the same simple point. We must therefore await further evidence before a final conclusion can be reached.

The Sickness of 1545–1548

Indians in Mexico suffered dreadfully between 1545 and 1548 from a disease that native chroniclers referred to as *cocoliztli* or *hueycocoliztli* (Gibson 1964:448; Gerhard 1972:23–24; Malvido and Viesca 1985:27). The term *cocoliztli* translates simply as "sickness" or "pestilence," *hueycocoliztli* as "great sickness" or "great pestilence" (Alonso de Molina 1970:235, 155r). That *cocoliztli* spread south from Mexico and infected Guatemala, where it was known as *gucumatz* (MacLeod 1973:19), is evident from a number of sources. Explicit mention is made in the *Isagoge Histórica* (1935:290) that in 1545 and again in 1576 "great plagues and heavy Indian mortality" occurred throughout "all the provinces of Guatemala."[14] Many "populous and famous towns," it is stated, were "destroyed totally" by diseases that "reached these provinces from Mexico."[15] Around the time of the earlier outbreak, testimony from the *encomendero* Gonzalo de Ortíz mentions that "God sent down such sickness upon the Indians that three out of every four of them perished."[16] Ortíz stated bluntly that "because of this, all is now lost in Mexico, and here also."[17]

Contrary to the above observations, the Audiencia of Guatemala wrote to the king on December 31, 1545,

[14]The Spanish text reads "debe entenderse también de todas estas provincias del reino de Guatemala . . . hubo grandísimas pestes y mortandades de indios."
[15]The Spanish text reads "las enfermedades y pestes se extienden muchísimos pueblos de los más numerosos y famosos se han destruido totalmente."
[16]AGI, Justicia 299. The Spanish text reads "envió Dios tal enfermedad sobre ellos que de quatro partes de indios que avia se llevó las tres."
[17]AGI, Justicia 299. The Spanish text reads "a esta causa está todo perdido lo de México y lo de aquí."

when it was based at Gracias a Dios and not Santiago, alleging that "the pestilence that has afflicted Indians in New Spain has not reached Guatemala."[18] This statement appears to have been more wishful than responsible thinking on the *audiencia's* part, possibly because a capital base in western Honduras meant that Crown officials were somewhat removed from events and circumstances in Guatemala itself. The *audiencia*, however, offered "prayers to God" that the sickness "not reach here" and that, if it did, "many fewer die than have died in Mexico."[19]

The supplication of the *audiencia* notwithstanding, *gucumatz* must be recognized as having been present in Guatemala between 1545 and 1548, with disastrous results. What exactly the sickness was once again is more problematical. Fuentes y Guzmán (1932–33, 3:426) makes reference around this time to "typhus or colds and fevers, a common epidemic of coastal parts."[20] MacLeod (1973:19) concludes that "while awaiting more evidence," *gucumatz* "was none other than the old enemy, pulmonary plague," an extremely fatal contagion that develops when bubonic plague attacks the lungs and respiratory system. Orellana (1987:143, 146) concurs with MacLeod that the Quiché term *k'ucumatz* correlates with the pneumonic form of plague, an illness marked by great lassitude, fever, thirst, and the swelling of glands.

The Sickness of 1558–1562

The years between 1558 and 1562 saw Guatemala struck by a wave of sickness that left many dead and their survivors hungry. Several sources facilitate a re-

---

[18] AGI, Guatemala 69. The Spanish text reads "la pestilencia que ha avido entre los indios en la Nueva España no ha llegado en Guatemala."
[19] AGI, Guatemala 69. The Spanish text reads "plega a Dios que no llegue por acá que a morir muchos menos que ha muerto en México."
[20] The Spanish text reads "tabardillo o fríos y calenturas, epidemia ordinaria de la costa."

construction. The chronicler Francisco Vázquez (1937–44, 1:154) recorded that in 1558 "the kingdom was almost destroyed" by a disease from which "a great number of people died because there was no cure."[21] He described the sickness as one in which the afflicted suffered nosebleeds. On June 30, 1560, and again on February 7, 1561, the *audiencia* informed King Philip II that all over Guatemala "everyone is sick and ridden with pestilence" and "a very great number of Indians have perished."[22] Arrangements were made to help those in need, for if disease did not kill them, hunger would. Furthermore, the *audiencia* pointed out, if Indians died because of a lack of assistance, then tribute would decline, and Spanish recipients would soon become impoverished (AGI, Guatemala 9). It seems likely that the sickness the *audiencia* and Vázquez wrote about was the same one recorded in the *Annals of the Cakchiquels* (Recinos and Goetz 1953:143–44):

In the sixth month after the arrival [1560] of the Lord President [Juan Núñez de Valdecho] in Pangan, the plague which had lashed the people long ago began here. Little by little it arrived here. In truth a fearful death fell on our heads by the will of our powerful God. Many families [succumbed] to the plague. Now the people were overcome by intense cold and fever, blood came out of their noses, then came a cough growing worse and worse, the neck was twisted, and small and large sores broke out on them. The disease attacked everyone here. On the day of Circumcision [January 1, 1560], a Monday, while I was writing, I was attacked by the epidemic.

One month and five days after Christmas my mother died, and a little later death took my father. We buried my mother, and six days later we buried my father. At the same time, on the day II Akbal, doña Catalina, the wife of don Jorge, died.

---

[21] The Spanish text reads "fue señaladísima la sangre de narices que hubo el año 1558, en que murieron sin que nadie pudiese hallar remedio, muchísimas gentes . . . casi destruyó el reino."

[22] AGI, Guatemala 9. The Spanish text reads "toda está enferma y con pestilencia . . . se han muerto muy gran cantidad de indios."

Seven days after Christmas the epidemic broke out. Truly
it was impossible to count the number of men, women, and
children who died this year. My mother, my father, my
younger brother, and my sister, all died. Everyone suffered
nosebleeds. Sickness and death were still rampant at the end
of the sixty-third year after the revolution [May 18, 1562].

Once again, because of differences in how the Cakchiquel original is rendered into English, it is important
to note how Brinton (1885:194) translated this passage:

Six months after the arrival of the President at Pangan, began
here again the pestilence which had formerly raged among
the people. It came from a distance. It was truly terrible when
this death was sent among us by the great God. Many families bowed their heads before it. The people were seized with
a chill and then a fever; blood issued from the nose; there was
a cough, and the throat and nose were swollen, both in the
lesser and the greater pestilence. All here were soon attacked.
These maladies began, O my children, on the day of the Circumcision, a Monday, and as I was writing, we also were attacked with the disease.

Identification in this case, because the Cakchiquel
text clearly associates this sickness with an earlier one,
might on first appearance benefit from comparative
analysis. But if, as seems likely, the "greater pestilence"
of Brinton's translation is the sickness of 1519–21, then
diagnosis of this "lesser" one is riddled with the same
difficulties as before. Designation as smallpox is perhaps best supported by mention in the Recinos and
Goetz translation of "small and large sores." Brinton,
however, makes no references to such eruptions, nor
do two other Spanish translations (Villacorta Calderón
1934:281; Reynaud, Asturias, and González de Mendoza 1946:160–61). What all versions speak of is an illness that saw people come down with fever, suffer
nosebleeds, and develop a cough. These symptoms, according to Figueroa Marroquín (1983:58), are complications that may exacerbate an outbreak of smallpox but
in fact form part of the clinical diagnosis of measles. Fi-

gueroa Marroquín (1983:52) goes so far as to state, after scrutinizing three different Spanish translations (Villacorta Calderón 1934; Reynaud, Asturias, and González de Mendoza 1946; Recinos 1950) of the Cakchiquel text, that the descriptions "leave no doubt" that the sickness was measles. Villacorta Cifuentes (1976:53–54) accepts the argument made by Figueroa Marroquín and also settles for measles, as does Orellana (1987:146). Martínez Durán (1941:69) suggests exanthematic typhus but does not rule measles out. That the sickness might have been a combination of diseases is again quite possible, as a popular Spanish rhyme (Figueroa Marroquín 1983:45) light-heartedly reveals:

Sarampión toca la puerta,	Measles knocks the door
Viruela dice: Quién es?	Smallpox asks: Who's there?
y Escarlatina contesta:	And Scarlet Fever replies:
Aquí estamos los tres!	All three of us are here!

By 1563, crisis conditions still prevailed, for sickness lingered (Batres 1920, 2:318), and "hunger and food shortages, brought on by drought, meant that there was neither wheat, nor corn, nor even recourse to eating bananas and roots" (Vázquez 1937–44, 1:154). An outbreak of smallpox among the Cakchiquel a year later (Recinos and Goetz 1953:145) only added to their suffering.

The Sickness of 1576–1577

During 1576 and 1577, Guatemala was hit by another wave of pestilence sweeping south from Mexico. A recent study by Malvido and Viesca (1985) has diagnosed the *cocoliztli* mentioned in Mexican sources around this time as an epidemic of plague. The Mexican sources also refer to this sickness as *matlazáhuatl*, which may have been typhus exanthematicus (S. F. Cook 1946: 321). Documentation for Guatemala certainly can be correlated with the *cocoliztli* of Mexico (*Isagoge Histórica* 1935:290), but reference is made also to smallpox, typhus, colds, and other unspecified sicknesses. To these, Martínez Durán (1941:71) adds "bubas, sarampión y peste de flujo de narices." Writing to the king on March 15, 1577, President Pedro de Villalobos stated that "from Mexico has entered, to this country, a plague of smallpox and typhus, from which have died, and die daily still, a great many Indians, especially young children."[23] Two days previously, a royal accountant had notified the king that "the outbreak of smallpox among the Indians has been contagious and widespread."[24] The same accountant, Eugenio de Salazar, one year later informed the king that, owing to the impact of the epidemic, tribute payments were considerably in arrears. He argued that it made sense to "relieve from the responsibility of paying tribute those Indians who have been sick and who are still in great hardship."[25] President Villalobos, in another letter to the king dated March 17, 1578, stated further that "at present there is a shortage of corn" because the sick had been unable to tend to their fields.[26]

By the time Villalobos handed over the presidency of the *audiencia* to Diego García de Valverde in November 1578, the epidemic had run the worst of its course. Documents relating to Valverde's presidency, however, are littered with references to the sickness of 1576–77 because it was during the years of his *audiencia* (1578–89) that many of the social and economic consequences of the epidemic had to be dealt with. Foremost of all, Valverde attempted to compile new tribute assessments (MacLeod 1973:130–31) that would reflect the demo-

[23] AGI, Guatemala 10. The Spanish text reads "de México vino a esta tierra una pestilencia de viruela y tabardete de que han muerto y de cada día mueren mucha cantidad de yndios en especial niños de poca edad."
[24] AGI, Guatemala 10. The Spanish text reads "la enfermedad de las viruelas entre los yndios ha sido contagiosa y general."
[25] AGI, Guatemala 10. The letter is dated March 15, 1578, and the Spanish text reads "ha sido justo descargarse las deste cargo por los yndios con las enfermedades . . . han estado y están tan necesitados."
[26] AGI, Guatemala 10. The Spanish text reads "hay de presente falta de maíz por no haber podido sembrar los indios."

graphic reality of the 1580s, not more populous times a decade or two earlier.[27] Legitimate, long-overdue reassessment, Valverde must have thought, was at last being carried out when a sharply worded command reached Guatemala. In it (Simpson 1950:154) Valverde was ordered by the Crown to undertake the following:

To investigate and correct the abuses reportedly committed by *encomenderos, corregidores*, and *alcaldes mayores* against the Indians, [among them]: (1) collecting tributes on ancient population counts, when the actual number of Indians had diminished by as much as two-thirds; (2) collecting tributes for dead or absent Indians; (3) selling *encomienda* Indians to one another; (4) using Indians as slaves; (5) beating them; (6) loading them excessively; (7) making them sleep in the fields, where they died from the bites of poisonous reptiles; (8) mistreating them so badly that mothers killed their children rather than have them serve the Spaniards; (9) causing the Indians to starve themselves to death, or to hang themselves, for the same reason; (10) causing them generally to hate the name of Christian.

Valverde was astounded by these allegations and moved quickly to defend himself. What he was accused of tolerating, Valverde insisted, were precisely the kinds of things he had encountered upon arrival in Guatemala and had set out immediately to redress. The president had heard that the king and the Council of the Indies had been deliberately misinformed by a Dominican friar, one Bernardo de Almarsa, with whom Valverde apparently had clashed and who was known to harbor a personal grudge (AGI, Guatemala 10). Valverde called upon several prominent citizens and clergymen to put the record straight. Among them, the testimony of Pedro de Liévano attributes Indian depopulation morally to "secret judgments of God beyond the reach of man" before turning to "three or four pestilences that came

---

[27] AGI, Guatemala 10, *Razón de las tasaciones que se han hecho después que el presidente vino a esta audiencia, de pueblos de su distrito con lo que antes tributaban.*

from Mexico" as decidedly more worldly, objective explanations of divine retribution.[28]

The Sickness of 1607–1608

On November 30, 1608, the president of the Audiencia of Guatemala, Alonso Criado de Castilla, informed the king that "Indians in this country have been afflicted by a general sickness for more than a year."[29] He went on to describe how, "with great abruptness, in two or three days, and sometimes even sooner, these miserable Indians die without any cure or remedy," and observed that the sick experienced "a flow of blood running from their noses, which one is seldom able to stop."[30] Criado de Castilla mentioned specifically that the above symptoms "occur, among some people, along with typhus."[31] The *audiencia* used certain funds at its disposal to help those communities most severely affected. This course of action, however, was done without beforehand obtaining formal permission from the Council of the Indies. In a retroactive order of 1613, the king bestowed his approval on the *audiencia*'s decision to assist the Indians. The "great sickness and pestilence of 1607 and 1608," the king commented, obviously called for some form of government intervention, but he instructed the *audiencia* not to behave in the future with such disregard for proper administrative procedure.[32]

---

[28] AGI, Guatemala 10. The Spanish text reads "en lo que toca a morirse los indios e ir en dimunición son juicios secretos de Dios que los hombres no los ascanzan y lo que este testigo ha visto en el tiempo que ha estado en estas provincias es que desde la provincia de México han venido tres o cuatro pestilencias con las cuales ha venido la tierra en grandísima disminución . . . ."

[29] AGI, Guatemala 12. The Spanish text reads "la enfermedad general que los naturales desta tierra an tenido de mas de un año."

[30] AGI, Guatemala 12. The Spanish text reads "con mucha brevedad en dos o tres días y algunas veces de repente morían estos yndios miseros sin que admitiese remedios ni se pudiese entender la cura della . . . dándoles un flujo de sangre de narizes que pocas veces se podía restanar."

[31] AGI, Guatemala 12. The Spanish text reads "y en algunos con mezcla de tabardillo."

[32] AGI, Guatemala 419. The Spanish text reads "los años de 1607 y 1608 que hubo grandes enfermedades de peste en esa provincia."

The Sickness of the 1620s

For some time before 1623, but apparently after the typhus outbreaks of 1607 and 1608, Guatemala was again infected by a pestilence that may have been smallpox. Our most precise source for this outbreak is a letter written by the city council of Santiago on October 9, 1623, in which the king was informed that "since the beginning of August the sickness that hitherto had been general throughout the country has ceased."[33] The city council wished expressly to assure the king that tribute payments ought not to be affected "because those who died in greatest number were children and young people," not adults.[34] In Santiago itself, this sickness may have been the same that contaminated the capital in 1614. On August 2 of that year the city council agreed to ask the Mercedarian convent to organize a procession through the streets of Santiago, a procession in which images of the Virgin would be carried in the hope of convincing her to intervene and help stop "the general sickness."[35]

The Sickness of 1631–32

Yet another outbreak of typhus devastated Guatemala in the years 1631 and 1632. Antonio de Molina (1943:24–25), a Dominican friar and seventeenth-century chronicler, recorded that "in 1631 there was, in this city [Santiago], a very great sickness that carried off a great number of people," a sickness that also prevailed "in surrounding towns and in all the provinces."[36] Mor-

[33] AGI, Guatemala 967. The Spanish text reads "desde principio de agosto [de este] año cesó la peste general que hubo en este reyno."
[34] AGI, Guatemala 967. The Spanish text reads "según la noticia que esta tiene en los pueblos de indios ay poca diminución de tributarios porque los que fallecieron en mayor numero eran niños y muchachos."
[35] AGCA, A1, legajo 1772, expediente 11766. The reference to sickness reads "la peste general."
[36] The Spanish text reads "el año de 1631 hubo en esta ciudad de Guatemala una peste muy grande en que murió muchísima gente y en los pueblos de la comarca y en todas las provincias de Guatemala."

tality in the capital, Molina wrote, "was terrible."[37] On April 27 the following year, the city council of Santiago again requested that a religious procession be organized to entice divine or saintly intervention that would bid the sickness cease (AGCA, A1, legajo 1772, expediente 11766). Neither Molina nor the city's council mention precisely what contagion was at large, but the observant Thomas Gage (1928:291) provides us with a fairly definitive diagnosis of typhus:

The next year following, all that country was generally infected with a kind of contagious sickness, almost as infectious as the plague, which they call *tabardillo*, and was a fever in the very inward parts and bowels, which scarce continued to the seventh day but commonly took them away from the world to a grave the third or fifth day. The filthy smell and stench which came from them which lay sick of this disease was enough to infect the rest of the house, and all that came to see them. It rotted their mouths and tongues, and made them as black as coal before they died. Very few Spaniards were infected with this contagion; but the Indians generally were taken with it. It was reported to have begun about Mexico, and to have spread from town to town, till it came to Guatemala, and went on forwards; and so likewise did the locusts the year before, marching as it were from Mexico over all the country. I visited many that died of this infection, using no other antidote against it save only a handkerchief dipped in vinegar to smell into, and I thank God I escaped where many died. In Mixco I buried ninety young and old, and in Pinola above a hundred; and for all these that were eight years old, or upwards, I received two crowns for a Mass for their soul's delivery out of Purgatory. But think not that because so many died, therefore the towns growing less my offerings for the future were lessened. The *encomenderos* or lords of the two towns took care for that, who, that they might not lose any part of that tribute which was formerly paid unto them, presently after the sickness was ceased,

[37]The Spanish text reads "fue terrible la mortandad que hubo en la ciudad."

caused them to be numbered, and forced to marriage all that were twelve years and upwards of age.

Gage (1928:292) also recorded that, as was often the case, crisis conditions were exacerbated by inclement weather:

The judgements ceased not here in that country in my time; but after this contagion there was such an inundation of rain that the husbandmen feared again the loss of all their corn. At noon time the dark clouds for a month together began to thicken and cover the face of the heavens, pouring down such stormy showers as swept away much corn, and many poor cottages of Indians; besides the rain, the fiery thunderbolts breaking through the clouds threatened a doleful judgement to all the country.

Along with smallpox, typhus was to be a scourge for Indians in Guatemala for the remainder of the colonial period and well into the nineteenth century (Lovell 1988).

Local Epidemic Outbreaks, 1555–1618

If the eight disease outbreaks discussed above, because of their extensive treatment in the sources, can be considered pandemic in scope and impact, then the documentation referred to in Table 2.4 collectively relates to more localized bouts of sickness. Disease must have broken out at the local level far more often than the twenty-five occurrences here tabulated, but only further archival foraging and systematic integration of the findings of community and regional studies will elaborate the record.

Several of the episodes referred to in Table 2.4 undoubtedly concern the manifestation, at one town or in a handful of settlements comprising a parish or *encomienda*, of a contagion that prevailed more generally. Thus the "gran mortandad" listed for Chichicastenango around 1562, and the "pestilencias y enfermedades" re-

corded for Zalquitlán at this same time, likely represent
the occurrence in these places of the pandemic that may
have been measles, smallpox, or typhus. Similarly, the
"epidemic of buboes which attacked and killed the
people" living in Cakchiquel communities in 1576, and
the sickness that had carried off "many of the natives"
in the Verapaz by 1578, can be correlated with the second of the two waves of *cocoliztli* that swept across Guatemala from Mexico. In the same fashion, the typhus
pandemic of 1607 and 1608 seems the most probable explanation of disease-related death recorded during
these years for the towns of Ysguatán, Coylpitán, San
Juan Amatitlán, and those held in *encomienda* by Álvaro
de Paz.

Other disease outbreaks, conversely, are difficult to
link to a pandemic occurrence and are thus best inter-
preted as sickness that apparently had only a limited
radius of infection. The epidemics of 1588, 1590, and
1601 among the Cakchiquel illustrate this local dynamic
quite well, as does the "grande enfermedad" in 1585 in
Quezaltenango and ten or so other instances summarized in Table 2.4. As later evidence for the Sierra de los
Cuchumatanes suggests (Lovell 1985:170–71; 1990:167–
194), the spatial impact of sickness could be highly localized, with disease occurring in some communities
without necessarily reaching and infecting adjacent or
surrounding ones.

Conclusion

On the basis of evidence presented here, much of it
drawn from archival material complementing better-
known and more readily available printed sources, an
argument has been made that draws a direct connection
between disease outbreaks and Indian depopulation in
early colonial Guatemala. Contemporary testimony between 1539 and 1617 of ongoing diminution among native inhabitants (Table 2.1) may be related to general
(Table 2.3) or local (Table 2.4) outbreaks of sickness. As

many as eight pandemics swept across Guatemala between 1519 and 1632, and localized episodes of sickness
occurred even more frequently over the same period of
time. The documents we have at hand, it must be re-
membered, are written records that survived, down
through the years, flood, fire, earthquake, negligence,
and theft, whether they remained in Guatemala or were
shipped off to the king and the Council of the Indies in
Spain. Furthermore, not all disease outbreaks necessarily would have been chronicled. If anything, the historical record downplays rather than accentuates the tragic
consequence of empire that claimed, long ago, count-
less thousands of Maya lives.

Old World Epidemics
in Early Colonial Ecuador
Linda A. Newson

Fever (*Florentine Codex*)

In pre-Columbian Ecuador diseases were far less prevalent than they were in the Old World, and epidemics
were almost nonexistent. Although population densities had been reached that could sustain human-to-
human disease chains indefinitely, such infections had
not become established. Most crowd infections origi-
nate as transfers from animal herds to human populations, and so their failure to develop in the New World
can be explained in part by the absence there of large animal herds, particularly of domesticated species (McNeill
1976:45; Way 1981:261). Although domesticated came-
lids were present in the Andean area, they did not form
concentrated herds capable of sustaining diseases. Furthermore, these animals were generally herded in the
puna, above settlements located at intermediate elevations. In the case of Ecuador, the wetter climate of the
páramo was unsuitable for raising llamas and alpacas,

NOTE: The author would like to thank the British Academy, the Central
Research Fund of the University of London, and the Wellcome Trust for financial support to undertake archival research in Ecuador and Spain.

whose introduction to the region was almost certainly associated with Inca conquest and whose distribution was limited to drier valleys and small herds owned by Inca and local chiefs (Oberem 1978:54). In pre-Columbian times the only possible source of infection from domesticated animals was the guinea pig, which was raised in most households for ritual purposes and food (Salomon 1978:120).

Diseases native to the Andean area were either spread by arthropods or were parasitic, and they were chronic and endemic, rather than acute and epidemic. They included intestinal and respiratory infections such as dysentery and tuberculosis, bartonellosis (Carrion's disease in the form of Oroya fever and *verruga peruana*), leishmaniasis, Chagas's disease, pinta, and syphilis (Way 1981:253–91).[1] In most cases these diseases would not have been fatal, but they would have had debilitating effects. The presence of typhus, which may have been more deadly, is not proven, although conditions for its propagation existed. Head and body lice, which act as vectors for the disease, are common throughout the area (Zinsser 1935:175–77; Busvine 1976:43–44). They were noted by Cieza de León (1984, 1:169, 219) and have been found in Andean mummies in the Pasto region. The typhus organism, as well as plague, may be carried by guinea pigs, from which it may be transferred to humans by arthropod vectors (Browne 1984:27). Browne suggests (1984:27–28) that the Inca made the connection between fleas and typhus in that "a plague of fleas" was taken to be a sign of approaching death.[2] Many accounts from the sixteenth century, particularly the *relaciones geográficas*, which commented on

---

[1] Tuberculosis has been identified in the lung tissue of Peruvian mummies (Allison 1982:8, 11). Allison also suggests that the bone lesions encountered were probably the result of syphilis.

[2] Browne argues that Poma de Ayala (1980, 1:255) confused smallpox and measles with typhus, which produces a similar rash. Whether the association of fleas with death predated Spanish conquest is open to debate.

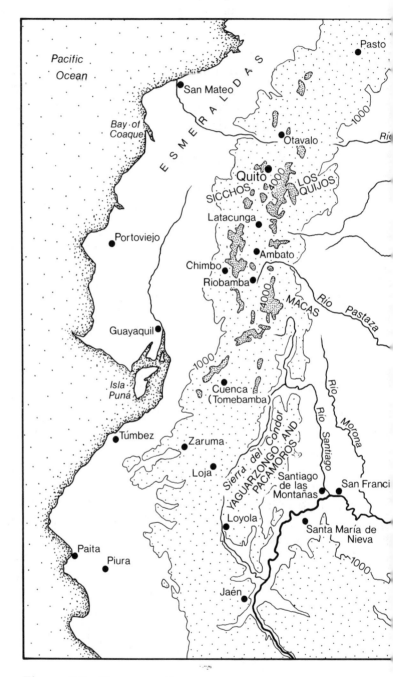

Figure 3.1. COLONIAL ECUADOR

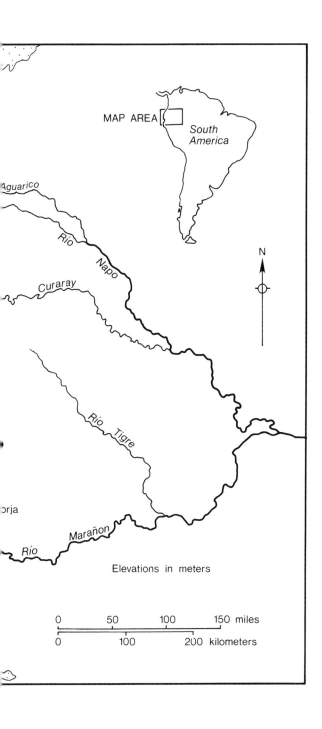

MAP AREA

South America

Aguarico

Río

Napo

Curaray

N

Río Tigre

orja

Marañon

Río

Elevations in meters

| 0 | 50 | 100 | 150 miles |
| 0 | 100 | 200 | kilometers |

the diseases that had existed prior to Spanish conquest, indicated that in Ecuador the major illnesses among the Indians had been intestinal and respiratory disorders. Headaches and fevers were less commonly mentioned, but none included any reference to *tabardillo* or *tabardete* (typhus) before the arrival of the Spaniards.[3] Not only were diseases less developed in pre-Columbian times, but the isolation of the American continent meant that its inhabitants possessed no immunity to Old World diseases. Consequently, in the New World, common European and African childhood diseases became first-rank killers, and deadly diseases became even more fatal.

The First Wave

The earliest Old World disease to strike the Inca empire arrived between 1524 and 1527. Sarmiento de Gamboa (1960:265) states that Huayna Capac died in Quito in 1524 of "fever, though others say it was smallpox and measles." Cieza de León (1984, 1:219) notes that Huayna Capac contracted the disease in the same year that "Francisco Pizarro and thirteen Christians moved along the coast," which would place it between 1526 and 1527. Lastres (1951, 1:149) suggests that Huayna Capac died in 1525.

Cieza de León (1984, 1:219) maintains that the disease was *viruelas* (smallpox), which was "so contagious that more than 200,000 souls died." Similarly, Cobo (1956, lib. 12, cap. 17:93) suggests that the disease was smallpox, of which "many died." Cabello de Balboa (1951:393) refers to the death of Huayna Capac from "a deadly fever," recording that at the same time "a widespread

[3]RGI 1965, 2:206, La Cibdad de San Francisco del Quito 1573; RGI 1965, 2:266, Pablos 20.9.1582; RGI 1965, 2:273, Pereira 1.10.1582; RGI 1965, 2:292, Salinas Loyola, n.d.; RGI 1965, 2:286, Ytaliano 4.5.1582; RGI 1965, 3:126, no author, n.d.; CDI 1864–84, 9:452–503, Descripción de la villa del Villar Don Pardo 1605. The lack of reference to *tabardillo* is perhaps not surprising since the disease was not known by that name until after an outbreak of typhus in Spain in 1577, when the disease was studied by doctors (L. A. León 1951:5).

and incurable pestilence" was raging in Cuzco. Garcilaso de la Vega also focuses on the fever symptoms of the disease, relating it to a chill that Huayna Capac caught after bathing in a lake. The chronicler tells us that Huayna Capac "came out with a chill, which the Indians call *chuccu*, which is trembling, and as it was followed by a fever, which they call *rupa* (a soft *r*), that is to burn, and the next day and on the following he felt worse, and believed that his illness was fatal" (Garcilaso de la Vega 1960, 2:354). Santa Cruz Pachacuti Yamqui (1968:311), however, identifies the epidemic as measles, which resulted in the skin being covered with scabs. Poma de Ayala (1980, 1:93, 260) calls the disease "sarampión, birgoelas [sic]," and later "sarampión y birguelas," or measles and smallpox. From these descriptions it is clear that the disease, accompanied by high fevers and skin eruptions, was highly infectious, and resulted in heavy mortality. A few authors (Hermida Piedra 1951:13; Madero 1955:25; Arcos 1979:94) have suggested that it was malaria or more possibly exanthematic typhus, but there is considerable doubt as to whether either was present in the New World at that time.[4] Other writers (Polo 1913:5–6; Lastres 1951, 1:150; Dobyns 1963:497; Crosby 1972:52–53) argue that the epidemic was probably smallpox. The disease may have been accompanied by measles, but more likely it was hemorrhagic smallpox, where the smallpox virus infects the blood, causing a prodromal rash on the skin that might be confused with measles. Hemorrhagic smallpox afflicts nonimmune populations in which infected persons die, before they can pass on the infection. Not all victims die, however, and once skin spots have developed, the disease may be passed on through the inhalation of droplets expelled by the victims, or

---

[4]Madero (1955), citing Herrera, says that Huayna Capac contracted malaria while he was in the island of Puna punishing the Indians there for their betrayal, but Herrera's account refers to "una grande enfermedad general de viruelas" (Herrera y Tordesillas 1934, 10 dec. 5, lib. 3, cap. 17:258).

else the virus may contaminate clothing or floor dust as the spots break down and scabs are shed (Christie 1977.255–63).

Circumstantial evidence also points to smallpox. The disease first struck Mexico between 1519 and 1520. From there it spread south to Guatemala and by 1527 had hit Indian populations in Honduras and Panama (Newson 1982:278). Whether the disease had passed to Panama from Mesoamerica or whether it had arrived directly from the Greater Antilles is unknown, but clearly the area was hit in the 1520s. Panama was used as a base from which the Pacific coasts of Colombia and Ecuador were explored. In 1522 Pascual de Andagoya explored 200 miles of the Pacific coast of Colombia, and in 1524 Francisco Pizarro and Diego de Almagro explored the same coast as far south as Puerto de la Hambre. It was not until 1526 to 1527 that Bartolomé Ruiz and Francisco Pizarro explored the Ecuadorian and Peruvian coasts as far south as the Santa River. The most obvious source of the first disease to strike the Inca Empire were the latter expeditions. When Spaniards reached Ecuador and Peru, however, seafaring crews had not been in contact with Panama for some time, and there is no evidence that they were suffering from any infections. It is possible that the virus was carried in clothing or dust, in which condition it may survive for up to eighteen months, but the spread of the disease by this means is not common (Christie 1977:259–60). The normal channel of infection is direct, face-to-face contact. An alternative source of the infection could have been one of the earlier expeditions that touched the coast of Colombia, from where it could have spread overland or along the coast from group to group.

Towards the end of 1524, Huayna Capac died of smallpox in Quito some time after a number of his relatives had died in a similar epidemic in Cuzco. This has prompted suggestions, such as made by Borah in his introduction to this volume, that the disease spread from south to north, that it may have been introduced overland through the Río de la Plata region rather than through the Pacific coast. While the timing of the outbreaks is not in dispute, it seems unnecessary to propose an introduction from Río de la Plata to explain this pattern of occurrence. The source of infection for both outbreaks may have been the southern coast of Ecuador. Huayna Capac died in Quito immediately after he had returned from the coast, where he had been punishing the Huancavilca and Puna for their treachery. This suggests (Sarmiento de Gamboa 1960:265) that he may have contracted the disease on the coast. At that time the Inca were trying to extend their dominion over the coast, having established a fort at Túmbez. Some of those involved in coastal campaigns came from the sierra (Cieza de León 1984:77–78), and it is possible that the disease was carried back to Cuzco by soldiers some time before Huayna Capac arrived on the coast to seek his revenge.

Other diseases that are likely to have struck the Inca Empire prior to Spanish conquest include plague and measles. Both were probably present in Nicaragua and Panama in the early 1530s. Elsewhere I have suggested (Newson 1982:279–80) that there was an outbreak of bubonic plague in Nicaragua early in 1531, followed by an epidemic of measles in 1533. Although Dobyns (1963:498) suggests that there was an epidemic of measles in Panama in 1531, the references he cites make no specific reference to measles. In fact the "pestilencia" to which he refers could equally well have been bubonic plague. I concur with Chamberlain (1953:28) that the date of the measles epidemic in Central America was 1533. The dates of the epidemics are significant, for during this period expeditions were being mounted to Peru. Francisco Pizarro's third expedition embarked for Peru in December 1530, but in 1532 he was reinforced by troops and supplies brought from Nicaragua by Sebastián de Benalcázar. In early 1533 expeditions led by

Diego de Almagro from Panama and Francisco de Godoy from Nicaragua also arrived in Ecuadorian waters (Estete 1918:17–19; Cieza de León 1984:259, 262, 280). There was therefore contact with Central America when epidemics were raging there, but this does not prove that the diseases entered Ecuador and Peru at that time. Lizárraga (1968:40) noted that Indians near Lima claimed that they failed to resist Spanish rule because "a few years before" they had suffered an epidemic of *romadizo* and *dolor de costado,* "which carried off the greater part of them." Pains in the side and the chest are often a symptom of plague, which, with the presence of a respiratory infection referred to as *romadizo,* suggests that the disease may have been pneumonic plague. The date of the epidemic is vague, however, and the symptoms described could equally well have been the result of pneumonia or another respiratory complication associated with smallpox.

When Pizarro's third expedition reached the coast of Ecuador south of the Bay of Coaque in 1531, some Spaniards became ill, according to Fray Pedro Ruiz Navarro, from "attacks of smallpox and buboes, from which some died and from which others were left disfigured and exceptionally ugly."[5] Other accounts (Zárate 1913:465; Estete 1918:17; López de Gomara 1918:226; Cieza de León 1984:68, 260) also stress the disfiguring character of the disease, which resulted in "some reddish boils with the texture of nuts, which form on the face and the nose and in other places." In some cases victims tried to excise the swellings, with the result that they bled to death. Although the "bubas" referred to might be symptoms of plague, more likely they were the result of a form of Carrion's disease called *verruga peruana.* This is also suggested by the tendency towards severe hem-

---

[5] CDIE 1842–95, 26:238, Fray Pedro Ruiz Navarro, n.d.; and Madero (1955:31). Fray Pedro's text in Spanish reads "achaques de viruelas y bubas de que murieron algunos, y otros quedaron hoyosos los rostros y sumamente feos."

orrhaging. The disease was probably a native disease, for it was said to be worse among Spaniards who had no knowledge of how to cure it. Arce (Madero 1955: 29–30) suggests that it was probably *pian*, the appearance of which is very similar to *verruga peruana*, and which is related to syphilis though not necessarily transmitted venereally. He argues that the disease could not have been *verruga peruana*, since it is not suited to the climate of the Ecuadorian coast and is not mentioned again in that area. The latter is contradicted, however, by the fact that *verruga peruana* was also contracted by Girolamo Benzoni (1967:256) on his visit to the province of Portoviejo in 1546.

Although it seems likely that measles did spread to the Andean area before Spanish conquest, possibly from Central America, where an epidemic occurred in 1533, the only reference to it relates to the death of Huayna Capac. It has already been argued, however, that his death was probably due to smallpox rather than measles. There are few precise details on the impact of epidemics before Spanish conquest. Cieza de León (1984: 219) recorded that the epidemic of smallpox that killed Huayna Capac was "general" and so contagious that "more than 200,000 souls died." Others (RGI 1965, 2:267; Morúa 1962–64, 1:104) stress the large numbers killed in terms of "infinite thousands" and "innumerable people." Lizárraga (1968:40) reported Indian claims that they would not have been defeated by the Spaniards if an epidemic had not "consumed the greater part of them." He refers, however, to the epidemic as "*romadizo* and *dolor de costado*," possibly plague, not smallpox. The epidemics were not only devastating, but widespread. As already noted (Sarmiento de Gamboa 1960: 264), Huayna Capac's relatives died of a "great pestilence" in Cuzco, while he himself died of smallpox in Quito, and his successor, Ninan Cuyoche, died of the same sickness in Tomebamba (Cuenca). This epidemic was significant not only in the numbers it killed, but also because it precipitated the Inca dynastic wars and facilitated Spanish conquest.

Mid-Century Epidemics

For over a decade there is no evidence of new epidemics in Ecuador. In 1539 there was an epidemic in Popayán described by Cieza de León (1984:127) as "a pestilence in the houses," which, together with a famine that raged at the same time, resulted in 100,000 deaths and an increase in cannibalism. Herrera y Tordesillas (1934, 13 dec. 6, lib. 6, cap. 1:12) refers to the epidemic as "peste" and says it resulted in sudden death.[6] At the same time, another epidemic in the province of Cartagena was identified (Friede 1955–60, 5:148) as "measles and smallpox," but it may have been a distinct disease. The epidemic in Popayán was not recorded further south, though the region was pacified from Quito between 1536 and 1540. Thus, contacts between the two areas could have spread an infection (Larraín Barros 1980, 2:83). The reference to the disease being in the houses suggests that it may have been associated with rats and may therefore have been typhus or plague.

According to Cieza de León (1984:26), in 1546 a "general pestilence" ran throughout the kingdom of Peru. He made this comment in describing the province of Quimbaya in central Colombia. It is assumed, therefore, that the epidemic affected that region and was also present in the interposed province of Ecuador. No documentary evidence has come to light to support this assertion, but this may reflect the turmoil prevailing in the Quito region during the civil wars. The epidemic was described as causing a headache and a very high fever, the pain passing to the left ear and the victim dying within two or three days (Herrera y Tordesillas 1934,

---

[6] Herrera y Tordesillas (1934) says that 50,000 died of hunger and being eaten, and 100,000 of the *peste*.

16 dec. 8, lib. 2, cap. 16:162). Dobyns (1963:499) has suggested that the epidemic may have been an Andean phase of the *matlazáhuatl* that devastated New Spain in 1545. This disease has not been properly identified, but it might have been typhus or pneumonic plague (Zinsser 1935:183, 256–58; McNeill 1976:185; MacLeod 1973: 119; N. D. Cook 1981:68, 71). Typhus generally has a rash associated with it, and for this reason it is sometimes mistaken for smallpox or measles. While the term *matlazáhuatl* does imply the presence of a rash, there is no mention of a rash associated with the Andean epidemic. Indeed the symptoms of intense headache and fever followed by rapid death suggest that more likely it was an epidemic of pneumonic plague. Furthermore, Polo (1913:9) noted that llamas and sheep contracted a disease at the same time, and it is known that during a plague epidemic these animals may also be attacked.[7] On the other hand, the typhus organism, *Rickettsia* sp., appears to infect only monkeys and guinea pigs (Manson-Bahr 1941:255, 281). The absence of buboes and the occurrence of rapid death indicate that if plague was present it was manifest in pneumonic rather than bubonic form. The greater infectiousness of the former, not dependent on a reservoir of infected rats but spread by coughing and sneezing, means that the epidemic would have spread quickly. Since the disease is

[7] In 1547 Benzoni noted that there had been two epidemics of *lepra*, which killed llamas. The first killed a large number of them, but the other *lepra de los españoles* had more or less destroyed them (Benzoni 1967:262). While in the account of the latter epidemic there is a suggestion of a link between llamas and humans, the source of the infection is not clear. The first epidemic may have been that which occurred among livestock in Peru in 1544 and 1545. It apparently killed two-thirds of the livestock, including *guanacos* and *vicuñas*, but it was said to have been less devastating among the wild animals because they inhabited colder regions and did not go around in herds as large as those of domesticated stock (Polo 1913:8; Garcilaso de la Vega 1960, 2:314–15). On the basis of the description of the symptoms, Browne (1984: 53) has suggested that it could not have been anthrax or rinderpest; more likely it was sheep pox. In 1548 a similar epidemic was said to have extended to *zorras*.

normally fatal, it would have resulted in heavy mortality.[8] The observation of Cieza de León (1984) that "innumerable people died" would fit with its diagnosis as pneumonic plague. If the disease was pneumonic plague, then the overall mortality rate of 20 percent assigned to the epidemic by N. D. Cook (1981:68, 70–71) on the assumption that it was typhus would have to be raised. The next pandemic in the viceroyalty of Peru broke out in 1558. Several sources refer to it as smallpox and measles (RGI 1965, 2:292; Montesinos 1906, 1:254; Cobo 1956, 2:447; Zinsser 1935:256). The virus was said to have been introduced from Hispaniola by Negro slaves purchased by the bishop of Santa Fe, and in Nueva Granada it was said to have killed over 40,000 people.[9] For Ecuador a number of sources indicate that the epidemic was accompanied by catarrh, which occurred mainly at the beginning and end of the summer and which killed both Spaniards and Indians (RGI 1965, 2:205, 292; Herrera 1916:50). Browne (1984:54) suggests that the catarrh was a secondary infection, associated with smallpox and measles, which frequently attacks recuperating victims. Influenza was present in Europe (Dobyns 1963: 500–501), including Spain, in 1557. It was probably this disease that struck. If influenza occurred in combination with smallpox and measles, it must have caused considerable mortality. In 1562 the remaining Indians around

---

[8]Bubonic plague is normally contracted through the bite of a flea that has obtained the disease from an infected rat. The presence of the disease thus depends on a reservoir of infected rats, and its spread tends to be slow and sporadic. Pneumonic plague, however, can be spread from person to person through the inhalation of droplets expelled into the air by the coughing or sneezing of an infected person, and its spread, therefore, tends to be more rapid. The origin of pneumonic plague is uncertain, but it has been suggested that it develops when a person suffering from a respiratory infection—a high possibility in the Andean area—contracts bubonic plague. Plague flourishes between 10 and 30 degrees C. Pneumonic plague is found at the lower end of the temperature range and bubonic plague at the higher end of the range, although not over 30 degrees C or in dry conditions (Pollitzer 1954:418, 483, 510–13, 535–38).

[9]AGI, ASF 188:226r–229rff., Penagos 15.9.1559.

Cuenca were described as "still some or nearly all ill with smallpox." Whether this was the tailend of the 1558 epidemic or a separate local outbreak is uncertain.[10]

For a period of over twenty years there is no evidence of epidemics in Ecuador. There may have been an epidemic of smallpox in Almaguer, in the southern highlands of Colombia, in 1566. The same epidemic possibly afflicted parts of eastern Colombia in 1568 and 1569. So far, however, there is no concrete documentary evidence to support these suggestions (Aguado 1956–57, 1:426; Romoli de Avery 1962:258; Colmenares 1975: 83–84). An account of the Cuenca region by Hernando Pablos in 1582 noted that smallpox and measles were occurring "according to their seasons," thereby suggesting that they had become endemic. In that same year "a terrible peste," probably smallpox, ravaged villages in the Cuenca region (RGI 1965, 2:266; Albornoz 1948:111; Hermida Piedra 1951:76). The latter epidemic was probably a local outbreak, for had it been more widespread, it would have been recorded by other authors of the *relaciones geográficas* compiled in that year.

The Crisis of 1585–1591

From 1585 to 1591, the peoples of the Andes were hit by successive waves of epidemics. It seems likely, as Dobyns (1963:501–2) suggests, that there were in fact two major epidemics during this period, emanating from different regions. One probably spread north to Quito from Cuzco and Lima, while another clearly moved south through Ecuador. Between 1585 and 1586, the cities of Lima and Cuzco were struck by epidemics of smallpox, measles, and possibly mumps, which appear to have resulted in high levels of mortality, comparable to those experienced in New Spain. An epidemic of "high fevers, smallpox and measles" hit Quito, and within three months, 4,000 people died, especially chil-

---

[10] AMQLC 16:364–65, Cabildo of Cuenca 10.6.1562.

dren (Polo 1913:11–12; Madero 1955:66). The epidemic
in Ecuador has been variously dated between 1586 and
1589. The second epidemic was accompanied by spots
similar to smallpox and measles. It appears to have been
introduced from the Cape Verde Islands through two
possible channels. In 1585 Drake's fleet touched the
Cape Verde Islands. Subsequently several hundred of
his crew died. Following the capture of Cartagena,
Drake's fleet remained there for six weeks in early 1586,
by which time the expedition was so weakened by disease that it returned to England. Other sources suggest
that the disease was introduced by Negro slaves through
Cartagena. From there it spread inland to Mariguita,
and subsequently throughout the Andean region. It appears to have arrived in Quito in 1587, from where it
spread to Cuenca, Loja, Paita, and Trujillo (AGI, Lima
32, Conde de Villar 19.4.1589; RGI 1965, 3:70; Simón
1882–92, 3:271; Polo 1913:15–20; Herrera and Enríquez
1916:57; Castellanos 1955, 3:733–35; Dobyns 1963:504–
5; Colmenares 1975:84). In Lima the epidemic claimed
3,000 victims in three months. The Jesuit provincial, Father Arriaga, described the epidemic there (Polo 1913:
16–18) as resulting in boils, which covered all the body
and blocked the throat, preventing the victims from eating or breathing and thereby causing many deaths. Boils
were common around the eyes, causing those affected
to lose one or both eyes and become so disfigured that
they could only be identified by their names. They also
gave off a fetid smell. Dobyns (1963:504–5) argues that
the disease could not have been smallpox or measles
because it would have afflicted a larger proportion of
Drake's crew. He suggests that the prolonged mortality
on the expedition argues in favor of a disease spread
by a vector, but probably not bubonic plague, since it
would have been easily identified as the Black Death.
More likely it was typhus (AGI, Lima 32, Conde de Villar 19.4.1589; RGI 1965, 3:70). This suggestion is backed
by references to the presence of a "tabardete pesti-

lencial," from which no one could escape, along with smallpox and measles (AGI, Lima 32, Conde de Villar 19.4.1589; RGI 1965, 3:70). The combined effect of these diseases was clearly devastating, not only for Indians, but also for some creoles. In 1614 the *tabardete* epidemic of 1590 was still alive in the minds of members of the city council of Quito; a year earlier, in 1589, an epidemic of influenza broke out in Potosí, but by that time at least it had not spread farther north.[11] There is no mention of it in Ecuador.

It is clear that between 1587 and 1591 several epidemics afflicted Ecuador, often occurring simultaneously or in the wake of different diseases, which conferred no immunity and thereby made their impact more deadly. Velasco (1977–79, 3:137) claims that in Quito these epidemics carried off 30,000 of the city's 80,000 inhabitants.[12] Sickness also devastated the "provinces of Otavalo, Latucunga, Puruayes, Chimbo, Sichos, Riobamba, the city of Pasto and its subject towns, Cuenca, Loja, Zaruma, Zamora, and the jurisdiction of Yaguarsongo" (RGI 1965, 3:70). Of these parts, the southern sierra seems to have been especially affected. Here overwork and ill treatment of the Indians, particularly in mining, combined with disease to produce high levels of mortality. In the early 1590s, Indians around Cuenca and Loja were said to have been "consumed and finished off" as a result of smallpox, measles, and dysentery (AGI, Patronato 240). It was said that around Zaruma at this time there had been 20,000 Indians, but work in the mines and the aforementioned diseases left only 500 Indians of all ages (RGI 1965, 2:208–309). Farther south, in the province of Jaén, the "sickness of smallpox" had effectively reduced a population of 30,000 Indians to only 1,000. Yaguarsongo and Pacamoros had also been

[11] AMQLC 26:394–95, Cabildo of Quito 28.7.1614; AGI, AL 32, Conde de Villar 19.4.1589. It is described as "romadizo con calentura."
[12] Velasco's writings have been heavily criticized for their lack of historical accuracy. These figures do appear to be exaggerated.

devastated (AGI, Quito 8, Barros 28.2.1591; AGI, Quito 23, informe 10.3.1591).

Some of these epidemics appear to have spread east to the hinterlands of Loyola and Santiago de las Montañas, where between 1585 and 1586 diseases only vaguely described as "pestilencia" and "enfermedades" resulted in a marked reduction in the population—in the case of Cangasa, a reduction of more than one-third (Anda Aguirre 1980:181–88). The coast also suffered from epidemics at this time. Campos (1894:46) maintains that it was the 1589 epidemic that resulted in the extinction of the Huancavilca, though even before 1574 they had been reduced to a quarter of their size by diseases variously referred to as "pestes," "enfermedades," and "pestilencias" (AGI, Patronato 118). Early seventeenth-century references to Indian villages around Portoviejo attributed population decline in the region to epidemics of measles and typhus (CDI 1864–84, 9:247–309). These were probably the epidemics that occurred between 1585 and 1591.

The Period 1597–1618

In 1597 there was an outbreak of measles and "pains in the side" in Lima (AGI, Lima 33, lib. 1:25–29ff., Velasco 16.9.1597). Although this epidemic may have spread north, there is no evidence of it reaching Ecuador. In 1604 the city council of Quito (AMQLC 20:98, 5.2.1604) requested a doctor from Lima to cope with the many sick that there were at the time, but it did not specify the disease responsible. Two years later there was an outbreak of *garrotillo* (diphtheria), which was general throughout the district of Quito. Many people died (AGI, Quito 19, Aguirre de Ugarte 24.4.1607). Diphtheria was followed in 1611 by an outbreak of typhus and measles in Quito (AMQ, LC 26:107, Cabildo 10.11.1611; Herrera and Enríquez 1916:73–74; Arcos 1979:108). Arcos suggests the latter two diseases were also present in 1612, along with *escarlatina* (scarlet fever), and that in

1614 typhus reappeared, again accompanied by diphtheria (AMQLC 26:394, Cabildo 28.7.1614; Herrera 1916: 76–77; Arcos 1979:76–77). Unfortunately, Arcos gives no sources for his assertions. While in 1614 there was an outbreak of diphtheria in the Cuzco region (Dobyns 1963:508–9), the only epidemics occurring in Quito in 1618 were measles and "valley sickness" (*mal del valle*), which was described as particularly devastating among children (AGI, Quito 10, Morga 20.4.1618). These frequent recurrences of diseases and their impact on children suggest that they were gradually becoming endemic.

General Considerations

There is doubt that malaria and yellow fever, both tropical diseases, were present in Ecuador at the time of Spanish conquest. Malaria is presently found in warm, humid climates throughout the West Indies and South America. In Ecuador, the anopheles mosquito, which acts as a vector for the parasite, is found at altitudes up to 2,400 m (Paredes Borja 1963:305). It now seems certain, however, that malaria was introduced to America from the Old World. The late arrival of malaria is suggested because, unlike Old World populations, Indians in the New World do not produce polymorphisms resistant to malaria. Furthermore, in the New World, malarial parasites are relatively unspecialized and have a restricted range of hosts, again suggesting their more recent appearance (Dunn 1965:385–404; Wood 1975: 93–104).

Similarly, yellow fever is now considered to be an introduction from the Old World. The first identifiable epidemic of yellow fever occurred in Yucatán and Cuba in 1648. Ashburn (1947:30–34) argues convincingly that the yellow skin coloration often observed in the sixteenth century was the result of starvation rather than yellow fever (see also Duffy 1972:140; McNeill 1976: 187–189). Recent zoological and historical research sug-

gests that sylvan yellow fever may have been present in
Latin America in pre-Colombian times (Denevan 1976:
5). Yellow fever, however, is a very distinctive disease.
The first epidemic to be identified in Ecuador occurred
in Guayaquil in 1740, followed quickly by another in
1743 (Paredes Borja 1963:383).
Evidence from the accounts of early visitors to the
coast of Ecuador are contradictory. Some suggest that
three diseases were endemic: fevers, dysentery, and
"bubas," the latter cured with sarsaparilla, which suggests that it may have been syphilis (CDI 1864–84, 9:
247–309; "Sobre los tributos de los indios de Yaguachi
(1579)" 1972:81). Although fevers were common on
the coast, those experienced on early expeditions probably resulted from malnutrition induced by inadequate
provisions and the necessity to live off the land. Arcos (1979:93) suggests that malaria attacked Alvarado's
troops on the Ecuadorian coast in 1534, but Paredes
Borja (1963:187) points out that Alvarado's accounts
make no mention of a specific disease. He argues that
the fevers they experienced were probably due to shortages of food and changes in climate.
   Apart from the epidemics found in the highlands,
which in some cases also affected the lowlands, the
coast was generally considered to be healthy even into
the seventeenth century (AGI, Quito 25, Hernán González 11.4.1600; CDI 1864–84, 9:247–309; Rumazo González 1948–49, 4:40–75; Cabello Balboa 1945, 1:11).
"Mosquitos" were reported in parts of Esmeraldas in
the territories occupied by the Cayapa and Malaba. In
1600, Hernán González, a citizen of Quito who had
been involved with the conversion of Indians in Esmeraldas, said that there were "no mosquitoes of any kind
except on the seashore" (AGI, Quito 25, Hernán González 11.4.1600). Similarly, a soldier accompanying missionaries in 1611 noted that there were no mosquitoes
to be found inland and only "very small" ones on the
beach (AGI, Quito 9, 11.4.1611). Another observer, how-

ever, commented that there were small mosquitoes that bit in the night. The nocturnal habit of the insects suggests the presence of anopheles mosquitoes, but this habit is common to other insects also, most notably sand flies. Mosquitoes and sand flies are similar in appearance, but the latter are much smaller and hence would fit the soldiers' accounts more precisely. Sand flies (*Phlebotomus* sp.) may induce fevers and headaches. They may also be responsible for the transmission of the leishmaniasis parasite and possibly the virus associated with Oroya fever and *verruga peruana*, both of which are known to have been present on the coast in pre-Colombian times (Manson-Bahr 1941:208, 997). Sand flies could therefore have been responsible for some of the fevers recorded in the region. According to Cieza de León (1984–85:240), soldiers on Francisco Pizarro's second expedition who embarked at San Mateo were bothered by "so many mosquitoes" that to escape from them they had to bury themselves in the sand up to their eyes. Despite this measure, Spaniards died each day from the "plaga contagiosa" of mosquitoes. While the disease may have been malaria, more likely it was Oroya fever spread by sand flies.

It is clear that the use of the term "mosquito" in documentary sources cannot be used as definitive evidence for the presence of the anopheles variety, for the term was applied to a whole range of insects. Lizárraga (1968: 5–6), for example, identified three types of "mosquito" around Guayaquil: "zancudos [long-beaked mosquitoes],which buzz all night, are most infectious, and prohibit sleep"; "rodadores," which bit only during the day and could not fly; and the smallest and worst, "jejenes" or "comejenes," which attacked the eyes.[13] A similar distinction between "mosquitos zancudos" and other smaller insects found around the Desaguadero was

---

[13]Some earlier editions of this work describe *zancudos* as "infintísimos" rather than "infectísimos."

made by Oidor Villasante (RGI 1965, 1:129). The latter insects were regarded as far worse since they caused the skin to swell and induced great pains so that victims felt as though they had been poisoned. These symptoms suggest the harmful effects of sand flies rather than mosquitoes (Manson-Bahr 1941:404–5). It is worth observing that in Esmeraldas, the Mercedarian friar Pedro Romero distinguished between mosquitoes and "other *sabandijas*." He described the latter as more harmful (AGI, Quito 9, Fr. Romero 9.4.1611). From the above descriptions, only the *zancudos* as described by Lizárraga could refer to mosquitoes proper. It is interesting to note that, as in other accounts, they were not regarded as the most harmful. In summary, evidence suggests that mosquitoes were present on the coast. During the sixteenth century, however, they were not carrying the malaria plasmodium. The fevers described by the Spaniards were probably spread by other insects, most likely sand flies.

Nonetheless, it would be disingenuous to ignore the few accounts that describe the coast as unhealthy. These accounts were generally written to the Crown by Spanish bureaucrats, not missionaries or soldiers with first-hand knowledge of the region. The accounts usually refer to Esmeraldas only, and their authors may have used the unhealthiness of the coast to justify in part their lack of political or economic interest in the region and their failure to colonize it effectively (AGI, Quito 8, Auncibay 18.2.1587; ANHQ, cedulario 1:165v–166vff., real cédula 6.11.1589).

Epidemic Disease in the Eastern Lowlands

The presence and impact of epidemic disease in the Amazon region of Ecuador is less well documented. In pre-Columbian times, this area appears to have been relatively free of disease, and it was probably completely free of epidemics. The unhealthiness of the region today derives in large part from the prevalence of malaria and yellow fever. Early missionaries described it as healthy, even though they often commented on the abundance of insects (Figueroa 1904:227). Equally telling is the fact that the two major expeditions that traversed the Amazon region in the sixteenth century apparently were not struck by fevers. Accounts of the expeditions of Francisco de Orellana (1541–42) and Pedro de Ursúa and Lope de Aguirre (1560–61) make no comment about the unhealthiness of the region. There is no evidence that members of these expeditions suffered from fevers, although they were bothered by insects. If malaria had been present it would almost certainly have afflicted the Spaniards during their long journeys across the continent (Vázquez 1909:431; Carvajal 1958:28, 33; Ashburn 1947:112–14). The absence of fevers can again be linked to the absence of domesticated animals and to the fact that, in Amazonia, population clusters were too small and too dispersed to maintain acute infections (Black 1975:515–18; Neel 1977: 160–61). Both of these conditions changed with the arrival of the Spaniards. Missionaries introduced domesticated animals as well as rats and other vectors, and congregated the Indians into large, permanent settlements.

During the sixteenth century, Spanish control was extended, albeit tenuously, over areas immediately to the east of the Andes, including Los Quijos, Macas, and Yaguarsongo and Pacamoros. In pre-Columbian times, Los Quijos had trading links and even kinship ties with Indian groups around Quito and Latacunga, while Indians in Yaguarsongo and Pacamoros had contacts with groups in Cuenca and Loja. These patterns of contact were paralleled during the colonial period, when the eastern regions were pacified from neighboring areas in the highlands. From 1538 on, Spanish expeditions penetrated Los Quijos, but the only reference to an epidemic there comes from Conde de Lemus y Andrade. He noted in 1608 that the region had been affected by

"malignant smallpox" (RGI 1965, 1:77, Conde de Lemus y Andrade 16.2.1608). This account was probably
referring to the epidemics of the late 1580s, which afflicted other eastern regions further south. Expeditions
to Los Quijos, which culminated in the founding of
Baeza in 1559, had left Quito the previous year, when
smallpox was raging. The virus could therefore have
been introduced at that time. On the other hand, it was
not until the 1570s that Licentiate Diego de Ortegón
conducted a program of resettlement in the region. Previously, nucleated populations may have been too small
to maintain the disease, even if it had already been introduced (AGI, Quito 82, Ortegón 1.2.1577). When, farther south in 1557, don Juan de Salinas Loyola founded
the town of Santiago de las Montañas, he had with him
"many sick people" (RGI 1965, 3:199, Salinas Loyola
10.6.1571). This sickness could be related to the smallpox epidemic of 1558, although the date is rather early.
Alternately, the sickness could have been associated
with the arduous journey across the Sierra del Condor.
Even if there was no epidemic at that time, as already
indicated, the Yaguarsongo and Pacamoros region was
hit by disease in the 1580s. Here the towns of Santiago
de las Montañas and Santa María de Nieva were used
as bases for slave raids into Maina territory to the east.
It is possible that these raids carried diseases further
into the interior (Figueroa 1904: 14). The first definite
outbreak of smallpox among the Maina occurred in San
Francisco de Borja in 1642, where some *encomiendas* lost
200 or 300 Indians. Children were the worst hit, suggesting that the population had been affected previously. Figueroa (1908:15, 346) attributed to *pestes* Indian
population decline in San Francisco de Borja between
1619, when it was founded, and 1642. This is the earliest
evidence available for epidemics in the Amazon headwaters. The most notable epidemic effects followed
concerted missionary efforts to convert the Indians be-

ginning in the mid-seventeenth century (Sweet 1969: 45–48, 131–45).

Levels of Epidemic Mortality

Early accounts of the impact of Old World diseases suggest that they often resulted in the death of one-third to one-half of those affected (Crosby 1972:35–63). The devastating impact of these diseases on previously noninfected populations has been corroborated by more recent epidemics (Dobyns 1966:410–11; Jacobs 1974:130–32; McNeill 1976:189–90; N. D. Cook 1981:63–66). In developing a disease mortality model for estimating the size of the aboriginal population of Peru, Cook has associated various mortality levels with different pandemics in Peru. For example, the first epidemic of smallpox (1524–26), he suggests, claimed between 33 and 50 percent of the population, and the epidemics of the late 1580s between 30 and 60 percent (N. D. Cook 1981:70). The mortality rates that Cook associates with different epidemics are reasonable, and his model produces an estimate of between 3.5 to 8 million for the Peruvian coast and sierra in 1520, which falls within the general outlines for aboriginal population estimates for the region.[14] Cook's model, nonetheless, does make a number of assumptions that are worthy of comment. First, it is debatable whether areas as extensive as a province or an *audiencia* lost such large proportions of their populations. Second, given that the model produces population estimates that accord with the documentary and other evidence, the implied assumption must be that mortality associated with disease was the overriding factor in population decline, when it is clear that many other factors were also involved.

[14]N. D. Cook (1981:70–74): smallpox (1524–26), 33 to 50 percent; smallpox and measles (1530–32), 25 to 30 percent; plague or typhus (1546), 20 percent; influenza and smallpox (1558–60), 18 to 20 percent; smallpox, measles and the like (1585–91), 30 to 60 percent; and diphtheria (1614–15), 10 percent.

Although high levels of disease-related mortality are generally accepted, most of the documented accounts of their impact, and especially the more recent ones, relate to relatively small areas and limited populations. It is doubtful whether conditions favoring the spread of these diseases would have prevailed over extensive areas. The impact of particular diseases is likely to have depended on a variety of factors, including climate, altitude, population density, the degree of interpersonal contact, subsistence patterns, sanitation, and immunity. Conditions on the coast, in the highlands, and in the Amazon headwaters of Ecuador were environmentally and culturally quite distinct. Furthermore, there would have been additional variation within these vast regions. Certainly observers noted differences in demographic change between the lowlands and the highlands. In 1582 one commentator noted that the population of the hot, coastal lowlands around Guayaquil and Portoviejo was declining, whereas that of the cold, temperate sierra was increasing (RGI 1965, 2:183, "Relación de las cibdades" 1582). In fact, other evidence suggests that the population of the sierra was also declining, but the distinction between the two areas in terms of their different demographic experiences was probably valid. It is interesting to note that no reason was given for the decline on the coast, but the remedy was seen to lie in relieving Indians from excessive labor. What is clear is that different parts of the country, including regions within the broad areas identified, did have different demographic experiences for very complex reasons, some of which were related to the impact of disease.

While there is evidence for early Andean pandemics being manifest in Ecuador, not all regions, or places within them, were affected by every epidemic. Diseases might travel more easily with people, troops, and supplies along the inter-Andean corridor, but contacts to the west and east were less intense. It would therefore have been possible for Indian communities there to es-

cape major epidemics. Even within the Ecuadorian sierra, the rugged topography, comprised of basins sepa-
rated by transverse mountain *nudos* (knots), would have
discouraged contact so that not all communities would
have been hit by every epidemic. Indeed, Shea (1976:
161) has suggested that the lower population decline
generally noted for the Andean area following contact
might be attributable in part to the slower spread of disease, since valleys were isolated from each other by
high mountain ranges. He compares conditions in the
Andean area with those in central Mexico, where he argues that diseases could spread more easily in a radial
fashion, thereby resulting in a higher level of decline.
The effect of the settlement pattern on the spread of disease was even noted by contemporary observers, who
saw the positive benefits of dispersed settlement patterns and nuclear rather than extended family resi-
dences (RGI 1965, 2:286, 326). In this context the reset-
tlements ordered by Viceroy Toledo in 1570, although
incomplete in Ecuador, are likely to have had adverse
effects on disease mortality. Altogether, the spatial impact of disease was not uniform, and the large proportions of natives reported to have died as a result of epidemics were probably local maxima.

Epidemics and Fertility

Although Old World diseases were a major factor in native population decline throughout the Americas, other
factors were also involved, among them death in battle,
enslavement, overwork, ill treatment, food shortages,
and famines, to say nothing of the decline induced by
lower fertility or disguised by migration and miscege-
nation. Interest in the demographic impact of epidemics has focused almost exclusively on mortality rates,
while little account has been taken of their impact on
fertility and the ability of Indian populations to recover.
The most immediate impact of a number of diseases
on fertility, including smallpox, influenza, and malaria,

would have been to induce high levels of pregnancy loss (McFalls and McFalls 1984:60–61, 130, 533). An epidemic that results in pregnancy loss or the death of a child might be compensated for within a short time, perhaps within less than a year, but the loss of a spouse usually has a greater impact on fertility since it requires a longer period of adjustment until a new partner can be found. This process might be prolonged, in some cases indefinitely, if there are cultural restrictions on the suitability of marriage partners and remarriage. The situation may be exacerbated further by imbalances in the sex ratio induced by the greater susceptibility of pregnant women to certain diseases, such as smallpox and influenza, and the lesser chance of their survival. The problem of acquiring a new marriage partner was probably most acute in small communities where suitable new spouses were not always available. In such cases, valuable reproductive years might be lost and the fertility rate reduced. Once conjugal unions had been formed, the fertility rate would have continued to be low due to male infertility induced by a number of diseases, notably smallpox and mumps, which may continue through life (McFalls and McFalls 1984:534). Furthermore, the direct psychological impact of an epidemic involving the emotional stress associated with the loss of loved ones, and in some cases the disfiguring effects of a disease, might combine with other economic and social stresses associated with colonial rule to induce lower fertility. The importance of the impact of disease on fertility has been underestimated, not only in general terms, but also in explaining the failure of some groups, particularly small tribal groups, to recover.

Conclusion

The epidemic history of early colonial Ecuador, quite significantly, parallels that of neighboring Peru. Major epidemics occurred between 1524 and 1527, from 1531 to 1533, in 1546, between 1558 and 1560, and from 1585

Table 3.1. Old World epidemics in Ecuador, 1524–1618

1524–27	Smallpox epidemic (Huayna Capac falls victim)
1531–33	Possibly plague and measles introduced from Central America
1531	Oroya fever and *verruga peruana* among Pizarro's troops on the coast
[1539]	Smallpox epidemic in Popayán, Colombia
1546	Pneumonic plague, or possibly typhus, in Peru and southern Columbia and hence probably in Ecuador
1558	Smallpox, measles, and possibly influenza
1562	Smallpox in Cuenca
[1566]	Smallpox epidemic in Almaguer, southern Colombia
1582	Epidemic in Cuenca, possibly smallpox
1585–91	Smallpox, measles, and possibly mumps spreading north from Cuzco; typhus moving south from Cartagena
[1589]	Influenza epidemic in Potosí
[1597]	Outbreak of measles and "pains in the side" in Lima
1604	Unidentified epidemic in Quito
1606	Diphtheria in Quito
1611	Measles and typhus in Quito
1612	Scarlet fever appears, with measles and typhus
1614	Typhus and diphtheria present in Quito
[1614]	Diphtheria present in Cuzco
1618	Epidemics of measles and *mal del valle* in the province of Quito

Sources: Evidence for each epidemic is given in the text. The epidemics in brackets occurred in neighboring regions but so far have not been identified in Ecuador.

to 1591. There were also a number of more localized outbreaks. A summary is presented in Table 3.1. The identification of some of the epidemics differs from those suggested by earlier researchers. There is no evidence for the penetration of Old World diseases into the Amazon region before the seventeenth century. Neither is there any evidence for the presence of malaria or yellow fever before that time. Fevers noted on the coast of Ecuador were probably the result of starvation or Oroya fever spread by sand flies. In assessing the overall impact of epidemics, account should be taken not only of the mortality it induced, but also the way it affected fertility. There are also likely to have been very considerable spatial variations in the impact of disease outbreaks.

Epidemic Disease in the Sabana de Bogota, 1536–1810

*Juan A. Villamarín
and Judith E. Villamarín*

Pustules (*Florentine Codex*)

Although much recent work has been done on the historical demography of Colombia, a sequence of epidemics based on documentary evidence has yet to be reconstructed. Epidemic disease was an important factor in the almost continuous decline of the native population throughout the colonial period, in the Sabana de Bogotá and in Colombia generally (Table 4.1). Reconstructing the history of epidemic disease is crucial for any analysis of the relationship between outbreaks of sickness and population decline. It also furthers our knowledge of the ecology of infectious disease, establishing a sequence of disease spread and examining its variation in terms of local adaptation, complications, and secondary infections, which might have varied from one area to another.

This chapter provides an outline of epidemics in the Sabana de Bogotá of Colombia between 1537 and 1810. Documentary evidence, including letters, petitions from Indian communities, parish registers, and reports of

Table 4.1. Major epidemics in the Sabana de Bogotá, 1558–1803

Dates	Epidemic	Comments
1558	Smallpox	High mortality among Indians, "murió gran cantidad" (AGI, Santa Fe 188:f. 234r–235r, Oidor Grajeda to the king, October 1559). Little impact on Spaniards (Aguado [1581?] 1956–57, 1:424).
1568–69	Influenza	"Murieron muchas gentes," especially Indians (Aguado [1581?] 1956–57, 1:426).
1588	Smallpox	"Destruyó, así naturales como españoles, más de la tercera parte de la gente" (Simón [1626] 1882–92, 3:271–72).
1617–18	Measles	Killed more than one-fifth of the Indians. Affected other populations too, but not Spaniards born in Spain (Simón [1626] 1882–92, 3:272).
1621	Smallpox	Much greater impact on Indians than Spaniards (Lucena 1965:385, President Borja to the king, June 1625).
1630–33	Typhus (*tabardillo*)	Killed about one-third of the Indians in districts of Santa Fe and Tunja. Significant mortality in all other groups as well (AGI, Santa Fe 61, Cabildo of Santa Fe to Crown, October 1633).
1651	Smallpox	Primary impact on Indians (AHNC, Caciques e Indios 72:f. 916r–924v).
1667–68	Smallpox	Heavy death toll reported in some Indian communities (AHNC, Visitas de Cundinamarca 11:f. 496r; AHNC, Miscelánea 112:r. 188r; AHNC, Caciques e Indios 57:f. 641r).

Table 4.1. continued

Dates	Epidemic	Comments
1692–93	Measles (92) Smallpox (93)	Contributed to 30-percent decline in tributary population (Villamarín and Villamarín 1981:80, 66–78). Strong impact (measles) on Spaniards and others also (Pacheco 1959– 62, 2:125).
1729	Measles	Most Indian communities affected (AHNC, Miscelánea 22:f. 443r, 390r–451v). Spaniards and others affected too (Vargas Jurado [1780?] 1902:13).
1756	Smallpox	Outbreak in the city and rural areas (AGI, Santa Fe 575, Viceroy Solís, December 1760).
1781–83	Smallpox	High mortality in all groups, Indian and others. In Santa Fe alone 5,000–7,000 people died (Caballero [1813] 1902:93; Posada and Ibáñez 1910:464, 469).
1801–03	Smallpox	Prevention efforts concentrated in city; no steps taken in rural Indian communities (See text and Posada and Ibáñez 1910:463– 72).

presidents and viceroys, are the primary sources we have at hand. These sources have been supplemented by chronicler's accounts, diarist's records, and secondary works based on archival data. We also deal, briefly, with certain instances in which the evidence is too fragmentary to identify the illness or to say definitively whether or not an epidemic was in progress. A concluding section discusses one of the best-documented epidemic periods, 1801–1803, and pieces together the steps that were taken to contain an outbreak of smallpox in the capital, Santa Fe, and the surrounding Sabana. Data pertaining to one specific community, Chía, in the late eighteenth and early nineteenth centuries are also presented, not so much to document the course of a single epidemic as to point out the quality of locally available information. The case particulars of Chía, in summary form, highlight the difficulties investigators confront when dealing with data relating to areas outside the capital, especially data as fragmentary as surviving parish registers.

The Setting

The Sabana de Bogotá and Valley of Ubaté are made up of highland basins ranging in elevation from about 2,550 to 2,650 meters. The basins are surrounded by mountains that ascend to 3,000 meters. The study area (Figure 4.1) is slightly over 6,000 square kilometers and contains three major river systems: the Bogotá, the Suárez, and the Ubaté. The soil is lacustrine and fertile. Rainfall is seasonal; the driest time falls between December and March. A series of microclimates exists, known to prehispanic as well as modern cultivators. Agriculture is also affected by frost, which can occur at any time of the year but is most intense from December to February. Other communities in the province were situated at elevations of 1,000 to 2,000 meters in warmer lands (*tierra templada*) with different resource potential. The Chibcha, who lived there when the Spaniards arrived in 1537, were a sedentary agricultural people with local, ranked political hierarchies and incipient state formation. After the conquest, the Spaniards immediately drew on Chibcha Indians for labor, goods, and services but did not make a complete and reliable count of them in the Sabana region until over half a century later, by which time there had already been great population loss (Villamarín and Villamarín 1979:27–29; 1981:45–47).

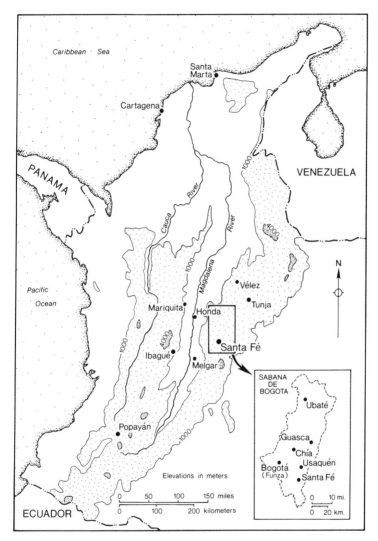

Figure 4.1. COLOMBIA AND THE SABANA DE BOGOTA

Precontact Epidemic Outbreaks

Several scholars have raised the question of whether or not native peoples in the Americas were affected by newly introduced diseases before actual contact with Europeans. There were a number of epidemics on the coast of South America before the Chibcha had contact with the Spaniards in 1537. Before the Europeans arrived, the Chibcha traded with neighboring communities along the Magdalena River and had indirect contact with groups on the coast. New infectious diseases could therefore have been brought back to the Sabana as a result of these associations, but until now no archival or chronicler's accounts have been found to that effect.[1]

Sixteenth-Century Epidemics

Three well-documented epidemics occurred in the sixteenth century, two of smallpox and one, not readily identifiable, which may have been influenza.

1558 (smallpox). An epidemic of smallpox struck New Granada in 1558.[2] The *alcalde mayor* of New Granada, Juan de Penagos, said that it originated among slaves purchased by Bishop Juan de los Barrios of Santa Fe. These slaves had been brought to New Granada from Hispaniola. Penagos stated that more than 40,000 Indians died during this epidemic.[3] According to Fray Pedro Aguado, 15,000 Indians died. Aguado also noted that the disease, although very contagious among the Indi-

---

[1] Castellanos ([1601] 1955, 1:236); Simón ([1626] 1882–92, 2:306–8). Dobyns (1963:494) has also pointed out the importance of investigating evidence for precontact disease introductions from Europe.

[2] Aguado ([1581?] 1956–57, 1:424) described the epidemic thus: "Viruelas . . . contajiosa y pegajosa . . . La demostración de esta enfermedad era viruelas; pero a los que daba se hinchaban y paraban adamascados y se henchían de gusanos y queresas que les metían por las narices y por la boca y otras partes del cuerpo . . . y era tanta la mortandad."

[3] AGI, Santa Fe 188:f. 226r–229r, Alcalde Mayor Penagos to the king, September 1559.

ans, did not have much impact on the Spaniards. Similar observations were made by local officials.[4] The epidemic was also widespread throughout Central and South America.[5]

1568–1569 (influenza?). The second epidemic cannot be identified, nor can a place of origin be designated. There are some indications that the disease may have been influenza.[6] The epidemic occurred during 1568 and 1569 and affected both Spaniards and Indians. Aguado reported a substantial number of deaths among the Indians.[7]

1588 (smallpox). A third epidemic, smallpox, occurred in 1588, affecting both Spaniards and Indians.[8] Castella-

---

[4]Aguado ([1581?] 1956–57, 1:424). Alcalde Mayor Penagos noted that the disease was still rampant in some of the provinces (AGI, Santa Fe 188:f. 226r–229r, Penagos to the king, September 1559). Oidor Grajeda spoke of a great plague of smallpox among the natives, as a result of which a great many died (AGI, Santa Fe 188:f. 234r–235r, Grajeda to the king, October 1559). Two Crown officials stated: "Que por pecados de los que en esta tierra estamos dionos Nuestro Señor un castigo entre los naturales de pestilencia de viruelas de tal arte que un faltado muchos naturales" (AGI, Santa Fe 188:f. 240r–243v, San Miguel and Colmenares to the king, October 1559).

[5]Dobyns (1963:500) notes that in Peru the epidemic was referred to as "smallpox and measles," which he thinks was probably hemorrhagic smallpox, possibly with an influenza component. Sánchez-Albornoz (1974:63) refers to an epidemic of virtual continental extent. On pox virus varieties and infections in humans and animals, see Fenner et al. (1988); on smallpox and its history, Hopkins (1983) and Alden and Miller (1987:199, 215); and on infectious disease, Burnet (1953).

[6]Aguado ([1581?] 1956–57, 1:426) stated that the disease, ". . . dio en los naturales y españoles generalmente una enfermedad muy variable, que daba en muchas maneras: a unos en romadizo, a otros en dolor de costado, a otros en dolor de oido."

[7] Aguado ([1581?] 1956–57, 1:426) wrote that many people died, including Oidor Diego de Villafañe. Licenciado Latorre said that Villafañe died soon after becoming sick in December of 1568, but he did not mention a concurrent epidemic (AGI, Santa Fe 188:f. 728r–729r, Latorre to the king, April, 1569). In 1571 President Venero de Leyva stated that New Granada's Indians had been affected during the preceding fifteen years by smallpox, measles, and fevers, as well as by "modorras, dolores de costado, landres tras los oidos, hinchazones, and cámaras de sangre" (AGI, Justicia 645:f. 186v–202r). See also Eugenio Martínez (1977:220).

[8]The epidemic is described as a "plaga de viruelas" by Castellanos ([1601] 1955, 3:733).

nos stated that the disease came from the coast via a black woman slave who had been brought to Mariquita. Fray Pedro Simón said that the outbreak lasted for six months.[9] All reports indicated that it took a heavy toll, especially among the Indians.[10] During a tour of inspection in the 1590s, native officials in the Sabana complained that the tribute levies included all those Indians who had died of smallpox in the late 1580s. Their testimony indicates that people continued to die even after the epidemic had ended. Many survivors, weakened by the illness, succumbed to other infections.[11] Castellanos wrote that the epidemic spread southward to Popayán, Quito, and Lima, while Simón mentioned its passing to Peru, Chile, and Venezuela.[12] The epidemic in New Granada was part of a smallpox pandemic in the Americas.[13] Zamora wrote, mistakenly,

[9] Castellanos ([1601] 1955, 3:735); Simón ([1626] 1882–92, 3:271).

[10] Castellanos ([1601] 1955, 3:733) refers to a great mortality rate among young people, "mozos, mozas, jóvenes." Simón ([1626] 1882–92, 3:271–72) said that the epidemic killed more than one-third of the population, both Indians and Spaniards, and that 100 to 200 hundred cadavers at a time were buried in common graves. He states that the epidemic of 1588 was "uno de los más desgraciados de que tienen noticia los naturales," the most severe since the arrival of the Spaniards. A document of 1588 reports that the community of Bogotá suffered "mucha mortandad . . . ha sido tan general que a arruinado este pueblo y toda la tierra y los convalecientes no están para poder trabajar" (AHNC, Testamentarías de Cundinamarca 23:f. 862v–863r).

[11] A captain of Tibabuyes reported in 1594 that "los yndios de este pueblo eran muchos," but that many had died seven or eight years previously in the smallpox epidemic, and also during the times of *romadizo* (AHNC, Visitas de Boyacá 17:f. 235v). A *cacique* of Simijaca stated that many of his people had died "así en tiempo de las viruelas como en otras enfermedades" (AHNC, Visitas de Boyacá 17:f. 534r). A *cacique* from Suta said in 1594 that many Indians died of smallpox and other illnesses, particularly in the previous seven years (AHNC, Visitas de Boyacá 17:f. 303v). One of the *caciques* of Ubaté stated in 1594 that there was difficulty in paying tribute because of illness and Indian emigration (AHNC, Visitas de Cundinamarca 5:f. 213v–214r). Also in 1594, the *cacique* of Cucunubá said that many Indians had died of smallpox there (AHNC, Visitas de Cundinamarca 4:f. 27v–28r).

[12] Castellanos ([1601] 1955, 3:735); Simón ([1626] 1882–92, 3:271).

[13] Dobyns (1963: 501–8) states that at least two diseases may have been involved in the epidemic period of 1585–91, the smallpox component going

that the epidemic occurred in 1587, and his statement has been passed on by scholars to the present, as has his exaggerated view that the epidemic killed almost the entire highland Indian population, with deaths numbering in the "millions".[14] Modern estimates, based on reconstructed population figures for the central highlands, indicate that there is no evidence to support Zamora's inflated population estimates, nor that the population loss from all causes was so high.[15]

---

northward from Cuzco, and another, possibly typhus, coming southward from Cartagena, having originated in the Cape Verde Islands and arriving via Drake's expedition. He notes that others believe that black slaves from the Cape Verde Islands, who were brought to Panama, introduced the southward-moving disease (Sánchez-Albornoz 1974:62–63). In June 1618 (AGI, Santa Fe 68, no. 69) Crown officials in Santa Fe mentioned the passage of a measles epidemic thirty years before, that is, about 1588.

[14]Zamora ([1701] 1930:303) wrote that smallpox began in 1587, and was "tan persistente en su contagio, que duró hasta . . . 1590. Cundió por toda la tierra, con tal estrago de los indios, que reducidos a número, se contaban por millones los muertos. Se asolaron grandes y famosos pueblos, sin que pareciera después más rastro de sus asientos, que las paredes de las iglesias." Ibáñez (1913–23, 1:61) gives the date of the epidemic as 1587 and says (without citation): "Pues mató hasta el 90 por 100 de la raza indígena." Dobyns (1963:503) also refers to the 1587 date and says that up to 90 percent of the native population in Santa Fe was killed (citing Ibáñez). Hopkins (1983:213) refers to the smallpox epidemic of 1587–90, saying that it "allegedly killed 90% of the Indians around Bogotá." Sánchez-Albornoz (1974:62), in referring to the area around Bogotá, claims that "the Indian inhabitants were literally decimated." Soriano (1966:51) states that the epidemic started in 1587 and continued until 1600. He wrote that "la mortalidad entre los indígenas fue enorme, terminándose casi completamente la población de ellos, especialmente en la provincia de Tunja. Se calcula que las dos últimas epidemias produjeron una mortandad entre los indígenas del 90 al 95%."

[15]Colmenares (1970:61, 68) says that tributaries, men between the ages of seventeen and fifty-four, dropped in Tunja from 38,495 in 1572 to 16,680 in 1596, a decline of 57 percent, and that Tunja's total population dropped from 123,184 to 53,376, also a decline of 57 percent (all figures calculated by him on the basis of partial censuses). Eugenio Martínez (1977:212–13, 223) gives a tributary decline for Tunja of 28 percent between 1572 and 1602, from 28,914 to 20,843. There was a 43-percent drop between the same dates, from 23,366 to 13,307, in a sample of seventy-four communities. Early demographic material for the Sabana is scarce, with no censuses for individual communities before the 1590s. The population in the area was probably smaller than that of Tunja at the time of conquest, but its demographic decline probably paralleled that of Tunja. Other authors, such as Eugenio Mar-

Castellanos blamed the spread of the epidemic on the "great carelessness" of Crown officials, who failed to impose and thereafter enforce travel restrictions. He wrote that it was possible to control the spread of infection by not permitting transit of people or goods from one infected place to another, giving as proof the case of Pamplona, where, by virtue of the *corregidor*'s strict enforcement of such regulations, the disease apparently never struck.[16]

Unconfirmed sixteenth-century epidemics. According to Zamora, the year 1566 witnessed "an extremely serious plague of smallpox throughout New Granada." Many Spaniards died, and there was "great loss of life" among the Indians. No documentary evidence or reports by early chroniclers have yet been found to support Zamora's statements regarding this epidemic.[17]

Seventeenth-Century Epidemics

At least seven major epidemics occurred during this period, four of smallpox, two of measles, and one of typhus.

1617–1618 (measles). An epidemic that local officials identified as measles broke out in 1617 and lasted through-

---

tínez (1977:214, 223), believe that the rate of decline in the Sabana was much lower, by at least 20.5 percent for the second half of the sixteenth century. She notes that her figures come from estimated figures reported at different times, and not from censuses.

[16]Castellanos ([1601] 1955, 3:735). Control measures were adopted in later years (see AHNC, Miscelánea 33:f. 360r–376v). It was prohibited for people, clothing, or goods to be taken out of Cartagena, where there was an epidemic of smallpox.

[17]Zamora [1701] 1930:243. Ibáñez (1913–23, 1:47) apparently refers to this epidemic when he speaks of one occurring during the government of Venero de Leiva. Ibáñez claims that it was the first to strike Santa Fe. Soriano (1966:48) states that in 1566 there was an epidemic of smallpox that lasted for three years, affecting Santa Fe in particular, and causing a heavy death toll. No reference is given.

out 1618.[18] The epidemic was preceded by a general
failure of crops as a result of locust infestation and a
consequent scarcity of food in New Granada.[19] Indians
were stricken more severely than others; some sources
estimate that up to one-fifth of them died.[20] This epidemic may have been a regional manifestation of a
hemispheric pandemic.[21]

1621 (smallpox). There is little information on this epidemic. It appears to have affected the Indians more than
other sectors of society[22] and was preceded by several
years of drought, very poor crops, and much illness.[23]

1630–1633 (tabardillo or tobardillo). For years afterwards,
the major epidemic of 1630–33 served people as a point
of reference. It has commonly been identified as exanthematic typhus.[24] A Jesuit eyewitness stated that it

[18] In June 1618, Crown officials reported that measles was "muy pestilente
y general de que todavía hay residuos" (AGI, Santa Fe 52, no. 132). According to officials the last measles epidemic in Santa Fe had occurred thirty years
previously (AGI, Santa Fe 68, no. 69, Crown officials to the king, June 1618.)
[19] AGI, Santa Fe 19, no. 83, President Borja to the king, June 1619.
[20] Simón ([1626] 1882–92, 3:272) reported that the epidemic of 1617 killed
more than one-fifth of the Indians. Some creoles also caught the disease, but
no *peninsulares.* President Borja reported that the epidemics of 1618 and 1621
killed about one-fifth of the tributary Indians (Lucena 1965:385, Borja to the
king, June 26, 1625). Officials reported that many Indians and slaves died as
a result of the epidemic (AGI, Santa Fe 68, no. 69, Crown officials to the king,
June 1618). It is noted that the president ordered *encomenderos* to care for their
Indians. Borja had gone to Fontibón (an Indian community near Santa Fe),
where he found 700 people sick and many dead. The statement is made that
the Indians lacked the food and resources to care for themselves.
[21] Dobyns (1963:509) notes that measles occurred during 1618–19 in Peru,
Bolivia, and Chile.
[22] No description or place of origin for this outbreak has been found. President Borja estimated that the combination of measles in 1618 and smallpox
in 1621 killed about one-fifth of the tributary Indians (see note 20).
[23] AGI, Santa Fe 61, Cabildo of Santa Fe to the Crown, June 1621. Among
the illnesses noted are smallpox and measles.
[24] A vivid description of the disease in 1630–33 was written by a contemporary priest, one Padre Hazañero. It may be consulted in Pacheco (1959–62,
1:485–86), where it reads as follows:

El principio era lo común de fríos y calenturas, y a dos días la enfermedad hacía rapto a
cabeza, privando totalmente el juicio a las personas. Dejó el postrarse, de suerte que se
hacían ineptos para ayudarse, las desganas de comer, ciertos hastíos, horribles vó-

lasted for two years, beginning in Santa Fe and spreading to other areas of New Granada from the original site of infection.[25] The disease was reported at the time to have produced a heavy toll among the Indians and all other sectors of the population.[26] Zamora exaggerated his account of this epidemic, as he did with earlier ones, writing that it destroyed most of the communities of the Sabana, killing "millions" of Indians and ravaging entire settlements. Referring in general to epidemics since 1565, he wrote: "Adelantado Quesada [Gonzalo Jiménez de Quesada] says of the pueblo of Turmequé that it used to have 2,000,000 Indians. Today it has fewer than 2,000 people."[27]

---

mitos y ansias, el cuerpo estropeado, la cabeza condolida, sin poderse ni aún volver en la cama, decaimientos del corazón, molidos los huesos, la garganta llagada, y los dientes y las muelas danzando, y todo el hombre ardiendo con la fiebre y loqueando con notable frenesíes. . . . Si alguno escapaba de estos rigores, quedaba por mucho tiempo lisiado de los sentidos, sin poder hallar convalescencia, algunos tullidos, otros contrahechos, muchos sordos y los más sin memoria alguna . . . no había contagio como este. Pegaba de solo llegar al enfermo, de tocarle, de respirar el aire de la sala y aún de la cuadra en que estaba. Los vestidos, las camisas, las camas, la ropa y platos de su comida, todo quedaba infectado.

[25] Pacheco (1959–62, 1:485).

[26] President Sancho Girón said that many Indians had died of *tobardillo* in New Granada (AHNC, Miscelánea 3:1033r, 1033r–1042v, 1633). The Archbishop stated that the "peste" that had gone on for six months was not ending, but rather "con mayor rigor se va estendiendo . . . muchos yndios han muerto y pueblos despoblados . . . que en Santa Fe certifican haver muerto más de cinco mil personas" (AGI, Santa Fe 227, archbishop to the king, August 1633). Members of the city council wrote that the epidemic had killed a third of the Indians of Santa Fe, Tunja, and their districts. They stated:

Creían que la peste se daba en los yndios y no los negros, que han muerto una gran suma con daño irreparable, y que luego cuando que había alguna declinación pasó a los mestizos y mulatos y habiéndose detenido entre ellos algunos días con muertes de muchos se ha ido entrometiendo con los españoles nacidos en esos y estos reynos con la misma malignidad que dio a los demás, que han muerto personas de quenta como miembros del ayuntamiento, [y] el arzobispo [AGI, Santa Fe 61, Cabildo de Santa Fe to the Crown, October 1633].

[27] Zamora ([1701] 1930, 394–95). That Zamora's use of numbers and proportions was only impressionistic is indicated by population figures arrived at by modern investigators. Ruiz Rivera's figure for total Indian population in the province of Santa Fe in 1595 is 64,961, and in 1639–40, 46,830. His total Indian population for Tunja in 1600–1602 is 62,473, and in 1635–36, 52,249 (Ruiz Rivera 1975:99). Colmenares's figure for the total population of the province of Tunja in 1602 is 52,313, and in 1635–36, 41,328. For Turmeque he

Groot, a nineteenth-century historian, claimed that four-fifths of the Indian population in the Sabana died as a result of the *tabardillo* outbreak. Some subsequent researchers have accepted Groot's figures.[28] Given the results of recent research, it appears more likely that somewhat less than one-fifth would be a more accurate figure.[29] The epidemic appears to have been limited to New Granada and to have affected agricultural productivity, since people were too ill to work. Scarcity of staples and of wood for cooking was reported.[30]

1651 (smallpox). There was an epidemic of smallpox in the Sabana in 1651.[31] It appears to have been unusually virulent, to have stricken Indians primarily, and to have spread to other areas of New Granada.[32]

---

says that the total number of tributaries in 1562 was 1,500; in 1572, 872; in 1602–3, 580; and in 1635–36, 357 (Colmenares 1970:68, 98).

[28] Groot (1889–93, 1:286–88); Soriano (1966:67–70).

[29] AGI, Santa Fe 164 and Villamarín (1972). On the basis of Ruiz Rivera's figures (1975:99) we have calculated a drop in total Indian population in the province of Santa Fe between 1595 and 1636–40 of about 28 percent, and in Tunja between 1600–1602 and 1635–36 of about 16 percent. On the basis of Colmenares's (1970:68) figures, we have calculated a drop of 21 percent for Tunja during the same period (see note 27).

[30] Pacheco (1959–62, 1:486–87). Padre Hazañero's account runs as follows: "Faltaba la leña, el pan, la carne, las aves y los comunes y ordinarios bastimientos de los vivos, y como duró este contagio por más de dos años, no había quien sembrase ni quien cojiese. Los hombres flacos, macilentos, descoloridos, hechos una estampa de la muerte, que no parecía sino que se sentían ya las vecindades del día último de los tiempos."

[31] The source refers to *viruelas* and *viruelas alfombrilla*. The priest of Pasca used the second term and mentioned that severe *dolor de costado* was associated with it. He stated that many Indians died and that in the pueblo of Pasca (outside of the Sabana) two or three complete households had been wiped out (AHNC, Caciques e Indios 72:f. 919r). Not referring to this epidemic in particular, but to smallpox and *alfombrilla* in general, Zamora [1701] 1930:232) wrote: "El riguroso contagio de las viruelas se ha hecho formidable en este Reyno; porque en los años que lo ha padecido, han muerto innumerables Indios, a quienes se les convierte en alfombrilla, achaque tan venenoso que se les caen a pedazos las carnes."

[32] AHNC, Caciques e Indios 72:f. 916r–924v. In October 1651, Indians held in *encomienda* by the Crown (Fontibón and Cajicá) and some outside the Sabana (Chiasaque, Chivata, and Pasca) asked for doctors and medicines to help during the epidemic. The epidemic also struck the Coyaima Indians (AHNC, Caciques e Indios 72:f. 917v).

1667–1668 (smallpox). There was an epidemic of smallpox among the Indians in the Sabana in 1667–68. The generic term, *peste,* is used in some documents, but the timing and description suggests that the writers were referring specifically to smallpox.[33] Some communities reported a heavy death toll.[34]

1692–1693 (measles and smallpox). There were two epidemics of consequence in the Sabana in the 1690s, one of measles in 1692 and another of smallpox in 1693.[35] The epidemics may have begun before 1692 in certain communities, where death tolls were higher in previous years. There was a marked decline in Indian population at the time. In a sample of thirty-four Sabana communities, the tributary count (males between the ages of seventeen and fifty-four) declined by 30 percent between 1687 and 1692.[36] It is possible that communities with an earlier increase in mortality figures were affected by another disease also. Vargas Jurado wrote: "The great plague [*la peste grande*] was in 1633. There was another of *evacuaciones* [dysentery; influenza?] in 1688."[37] He did not clarify the nature of the disease, and so far we have no other references to it. The epidemics

---

[33]Mention of *peste* in the 1660s is made in AHNC, Visitas de Cundinamarca 11:f. 496r. Reference is made to *viruelas* in 1668 (AHNC, Caciques e Indios 57:f. 641r).

[34]During a tour of inspection of Gachancipá in 1670, the priest reported that a large number of Indians had died during the *peste* (AHNC, Visitas de Cundinamarca 11:f. 496r). Indians in Serrezuela were reported to be sick with smallpox in 1667 (AHNC, Miscelánea 112:f. 188r). In Sopó in January of 1668 many Indians were said to be dying of smallpox (AHNC, Caciques e Indios 57:f. 641r).

[35]Measles (*sarampión*) are referred to in 1692 and smallpox (*viruelas*) in 1693 (Pacheco 1959–62, 2:125, based on "Letras Annuas" of 1691–93). It was reported that almost every house in Santa Fe had someone ill with measles in 1692. In 1693 five Jesuits died of smallpox in a twenty-two-day period.

[36]Villamarín and Villamarín (1981:80, 66–78).

[37]Vargas Jurado ([1780?] 1902:7). Ibáñez (1913–23, 1:216) mentions *peste* during the time, but gives no reference. Soriano (1966:73, 79) stated that there was a serious epidemic of exanthematic typhus in New Granada in 1688. He also thinks that there was another epidemic in New Granada in 1639. No references are given, and no other sources have been found to confirm a 1639 epidemic.

of 1692–93 may have been part of a more widespread one in the Americas.[38]

Other epidemics. Other illnesses appeared in Santa Fe and the Sabana, but their impact on the population is difficult to assess. Typhus (*tabardillo*) was recorded in Santa Fe in 1656.[39] Measles and/or smallpox were reported in 1659. The Indian governor of the community of Chía wrote in February of that year that Santa Fe was experiencing measles (*sarampión*), which had broken out in Chía. The disease was severe, causing many deaths.[40]

In the community of Guasca, to the east of Santa Fe, it was reported in March 1659 that the Indians had smallpox (*viruelas*). Either measles and smallpox were present in the Sabana at the same time, or one was reported as the other.[41] In 1667–68 smallpox was recorded as striking two Sabana communities and causing a large number of deaths in one.[42]

Eighteenth-Century and Early Nineteenth-Century Epidemics (1700–1810)

There were at least four major epidemics during the period, three of smallpox and one of measles.

1729 (measles). An epidemic of measles struck the Sabana and Santa Fe in 1729.[43] It broke out among all populations, urban and rural, in the provinces of Santa Fe and Tunja from February to June 1729. Most Indian

---

[38]Dobyns (1963:510–11). There was an epidemic of measles in Quito in 1692 that spread through the territories of modern Ecuador, Peru, and Bolivia in 1692–94. MacLeod (1973:98) reports *sarampión, viruela,* and *tabardillo* in 1693–94 in Guatemala; Newson (1987:248) identifies measles and smallpox in Nicaragua in 1693–94.

[39]Flórez de Ocáriz ([1674] 1943, 1955, 1:271). Oidor Prado Beltrán was reported to have died of the disease in October of 1656.

[40]AHNC, Caciques e Indios 5:f. 763r–766v.

[41]AHNC, Caciques e Indios 56:f. 864r–865r.

[42]AHNC, Miscelánea 112:f. 188r (Serrezuela); AHNC, Caciques e Indios 57:f. 641r (Sopó).

[43]Vargas Jurado ([1780?] 1902:13) recorded getting measles in March of 1729, "y hacía 30 y 40 años que no venía y murió mucha gente."

communities were affected, some experiencing the epidemic for months. The death toll is not known.[44]

1756 (smallpox). Santa Fe and the Sabana suffered an epidemic of smallpox in 1756.[45] Probably other parts of New Granada were affected as well. Viceroy Solís stated that during epidemics he aided the Indians by allocating small sums of money to them and suspending payment of tribute for short periods.[46]

1781–1783 (smallpox). The smallpox epidemic of the 1780s was a major one, affecting all sectors of the population.[47] According to Archbishop-Viceroy Caballero y Góngora, the epidemic came from Spain via Cartagena and Santa Marta.[48] It was accompanied by loss of crops and scarcity of food in 1782 and 1783.[49] The epidemic was widespread in New Granada and exacted a heavy death toll.[50] It was estimated at the time that between 5,000 and 7,000 people died in Santa Fe alone.[51] In the Indian community of Bogotá (modern Funza), where population in 1778 was 680, recorded deaths rose from

[44] AHNC, Miscelánea 22:f. 443r, 390r–451v.

[45] Vargas Jurado ([1780?] 1902:45) wrote: "En este mes de noviembre [1756] dentraron en esta ciudad las viruelas." Viceroy Solís spoke of *viruelas* in his "Report on the Government and State of New Granada" in December 1760 (AGI, Santa Fe 575).

[46] AGI, Santa Fe 575, Viceroy Solís's "Report on the Government and State of New Granada," December 1760.

[47] Indication of the presence of smallpox in some communities in 1781 is given in AHNC, unclassified no. 18:f. 342r. "Viruelas" is mentioned in AHNC, Tributos 20:f. 571r–575r (1782–83). "Viruela . . . peste" is mentioned in AHNC, Caciques e Indios 25:f. 879r–888v. "Peste de viruelas seguida de otras enfermedades" is mentioned in AHNC, Resguardos de Cundinamarca 2:f. 884r.

[48] AHNC, Miscelánea 2:f. 809v–810r (November 1782).

[49] AHNC, Tributos 20:f. 571r–572r.

[50] AHNC, Miscelánea 2:f. 808r, 811v (November 1782).

[51] Viceroy Mendinueta, "Relación de Mando 1803" (Posada and Ibáñez 1910:464, 469). The viceroy wrote that Santa Fe "sufrió un cruel estrago" with the smallpox epidemic in 1782 and 1783. The *cabildo* of Santa Fe reported to him that more than 7,000 people died in the city: "No he oido hablar de aquel tiempo desgraciado a alguno que no confirme esta mortandad." Caballero ([1813] 1902:93) wrote: "1783. . . . Este año fue la peste grande de viruelas, donde [in Santa Fe] murieron sobre 5,000 personas." In 1778 the adult population of Santa Fe was 15,326 (Villamarín and Villamarín 1979:76).

36 in 1782, to 137 in 1783.[52] In Chía some deaths caused by smallpox were reported by the priest in 1782. In 1783, 351 of 382 deaths there were reported to be caused by the disease.[53] Other communities appear to have been similarly affected.[54] Caballero y Góngora stated:

In America [the epidemics] wreak havoc more than anywhere else because of lack of supplies, help, and doctors. The first and worst of these epidemics is certainly smallpox, which by the lowest estimates kills a tenth of those infected with it. . . . [In 1782] it broke out in the coastal provinces, and the following year it spread throughout [New Granada], bringing the most horrible devastation.

The archbishop-viceroy added that smallpox was "an affliction that greatly deforms and diminishes the population."[55] His attack on the epidemic was two-pronged. The first approach was prayer. On November 20, 1782, Caballero y Góngora wrote:

Humanity is greatly afflicted by the punishments that Divine Providence is accustomed to send from time to time to wake mortals and shake them out of the profound lethargy in which continual prosperity tends to submerge them. Wars, famine, and pestilence are the visitors of the Lord, in keeping with holy scripture, that make his anger manifest to the people. . . . Sins are the true causes of our disasters. . . . If the Lord does not watch over the city, he who guards it does so in vain. . . . With greater activity and more confidence in human aid we must beseech through Divine mercy a lightening of the scourge, a milder form of the disease.[56]

[52] Bogotá (Funza) Parish Records, Libro 2 de Bautismos, Casamientos, Velaciones y Entierros; AGI, Santa Fe 595.

[53] Chía Parish Records, Libro 1 de Entierros (1757–95). In 1758 Chía was reported to have 1,405 Indians (AHNC, Visitas de Cundinamarca 8:f. 817r).

[54] The Indians of Fontibón, Bogotá, Bojacá, Facatativá, and Tenjo were stricken during 1782 and 1783 (AHNC, Tributos 20:f. 571r–575r). In Cucunubá in 1783 there were many sick and dying. In addition, lack of rain caused crop loss (AHNC, Caciques e Indios 25:f. 879r). Lenguazaque was stricken with smallpox from January to October, 1783. Food was scarce because of the lack of rain (AHNC, Resguardos de Cundinamarca 2:f. 884r).

[55] Archbishop-Viceroy Caballero y Góngora, "Relación de Mando 1789," (Posada and Ibáñez 1910:243–44).

[56] AHNC, Miscelánea 2:f. 809v–810r.

Second, Caballero y Góngora ordered that his doctor, José Celestino Mutis, head of the Botanical Expedition, set guidelines to treat the sick because he felt that those who cared for them (whom he referred to as *curanderos*) had little knowledge of how to treat the disease. Mutis recommended inoculation because it had the best effects, and those who took it rarely died. He also recommended that action be taken to isolate smallpox cases to restrict the spread of disease. Caballero y Góngora, probably following the counsel of Mutis, wrote that hospitals for smallpox victims should be set up outside the cities, especially in ports, because diseases were usually brought there by slaves and other passengers. Furthermore, he advised that a sanitation inspection should be carried out on ships to check the health of those who entered ports. Caballero y Góngora stated that smallpox was endemic in Spain.[57]

The recommendations of Mutis and Caballero y Góngora appear to have been followed in subsequent years. Viceroy Ezpeleta wrote in 1796 that inoculation was effective, as were controls that prevented infected individuals from entering the region. He ordered that no one with smallpox be allowed to come to the highland areas because of the heavy death toll and desolation that the disease created there. He also spoke of the horror that people had of the epidemic. He ruled that officials stand on guard in the port of Honda and along the road to the bridge near the entrance to Santa Fe to stop those with smallpox or with "signs of recently having had it." Ezpeleta stated that these measures had previously proven effective in preventing smallpox from coming into the region from the coast, where it had broken out once or twice before. He pointed out that quarantine could work, citing the experience of Vélez, where people, having been informed of an epidemic of small-

[57] Archbishop-Viceroy Caballero y Góngora, "Relación de Mando 1789," (Posada and Ibáñez 1910:243–44).

pox, withdrew to their *haciendas*, where they remained unharmed. Ezpeleta thought that the idea of setting up hospitals outside the city was a good one, but impractical because of the lack of financial resources.[58]

1801–1803 (smallpox). Problems of resources were important in dealing with the smallpox epidemic of 1801–1803 in the colonial capital and the surrounding Sabana.[59] Smallpox appeared in Popayán in 1801 and moved northward to Ibagué, Melgar, and Honda.[60] When Viceroy Mendinueta was informed of the existence of smallpox in Popayán, he set up posts to stop infected people from coming into the Sabana and especially into the capital. Nonetheless, some cases were reported in Santa Fe.[61] In June 1801, the viceroy asked the city council of Santa Fe to take measures in light of the possible epidemic, including setting up a hospital outside the capital to care for individuals afflicted by the sickness. The city council responded with plans to form a commission of thirty or more people and to set up five or six provisional hospitals in the capital to accept the poor because there was no room in the existing hospital, San Juan de Dios. The council members also responded that the city did not have money to pay for the costs of prevention and cure of the epidemic. The viceroy wrote again to point out the city council's duties and advise members that the measures they took were not what he had in mind. The

[58] Viceroy Ezpeleta, "Relación de Mando 1796," (Posada and Ibáñez 1910: 326–27).
[59] Caballero ([1813] 1902:99, 102). One source reads: "Septiembre a 5 [1801]. Se echó bando declarando ya las viruelas, y se dieron órdenes para evitar su propagación, haciendo hospitales en Las Aguas y en el Llano de Mesa; pero con todo esto murió mucha gente. . . . [May 1802] En este mes comenzó a haber viruelas y declaradas. . . . [August 1803] En este mes se acabaron de concluir las viruelas."
[60] AHNC, Miscelánea 33:f. 380r, 391r.
[61] AHNC, Miscelánea 3:f. 1044r–1045v; AHNC, Miscelánea 33:f. 379r–398v; AHNC, Miscelánea 44:f. 495r–524v. In August of 1801 the viceroy ordered that all smallpox cases be reported to the *alcaldes ordinarios* under penalty of fines of 200 pesos (Viceroy Mendinueta, "Relación de Mando 1803," Posada and Ibáñez 1910:463). Also see Caballero ([1813] 1902:99, September 5, 1801).

commission was too large to be effective, and one small hospital would be sufficient.[62] On September 12, 1801, when there were already some cases in Santa Fe, the viceroy ordered that the city council calculate the number of poor who might become ill and how much it would cost to care for and cure them. He ordered that with the aid of two doctors and a committee, the council determine places where hospitals could be established in each neighborhood of the city. Together with the director of the hospital of San Juan de Dios, the council members were to determine how much money would come from the hospital to help the sick outside of it. Other funds were to come from the city resources and from a public subscription. The council was to tell the viceroy how much additional support would be needed.

A census of neighborhoods was carried out as ordered.[63] Infected individuals were removed to the hospital, set up outside of town, a measure (according to the viceroy) that spared Santa Fe the first onslaught of the epidemic in 1801. In June of 1802 there were again reports from one neighborhood that people were ill with smallpox, and a few suffering the disease were in the city's hospital. The council saw this as a sign of an oncoming epidemic, according to the viceroy, and asked that hospitals be set up in the city at the expense of the Crown. Members of the council (*regidores*) stated that from the point of view of the doctors, the hospital outside city limits was not of any use. This was an argument made by the *regidores* to cover the fact that they had dismantled that hospital without informing the viceroy, when they incorrectly thought that the epidemic had ended. The viceroy responded that eight sick

[62]Viceroy Mendinueta, "Relación de Mando 1803" (Posada and Ibáñez 1910:463–64).
[63]Viceroy Mendinueta, "Relación de Mando 1803" (Posada and Ibáñez 1910:465); AHNC, Miscelánea 22:f. 266r–389v; Caballero ([1813] 1902:99).

people were not signs of imminent, universal contagion. Not knowing that the hospital had been taken down, he ordered that the sick be removed from the city. Infected individuals with means could remain in their homes under the care of a doctor, isolated under penalty of fines. *Alcaldes, regidores,* and *oidores* were to search the streets for the sick.[64]

As the confrontation between the viceroy and city council grew, the former took over the latter's functions by suspending all payments except salaries and a few other expenses of the city treasury. The viceroy appropriated the city council's funds, including 500 pesos that it had collected in a lottery to benefit destitute single women, and used the money to set up three hospitals.[65]

The *audiencia* supported the measures adopted by the viceroy, including an inoculation program. Reporting on the benefits of inoculation, the *oidores* wrote that only one of those inoculated died, and the cause of death was not smallpox but typhus. Of those in all three city hospitals and surrounding area, 112 people died (Table 4.2). Another 217 nonhospitalized people died, raising the death toll to 329. The *oidores* noted that in the previous epidemic of 1782–83, more than 7,000 people had died.[66] The inoculation program appears to have been carried out mainly in the city.[67] To help the Sabana Indians, priests were ordered to carry out censuses to determine the number of people who might become ill. Apparently no other measures to stop the spread of smallpox were taken.[68]

[64] Viceroy Mendinueta, "Relación de Mando 1803" (Posada and Ibáñez 1910:465–67). The diarist Caballero ([1813] 1902:99) says that the early cases began a month before, in May of 1802: "En este mes comenzó a haber viruelas ya declaradas."

[65] Viceroy Mendinueta, "Relación de Mando 1803" (Posada and Ibáñez 1910:467–78).

[66] AHNC, Miscelánea 2:f. 932r–934r.

[67] AHNC, Miscelánea 2:f. 946r–949r.

[68] AHNC, Miscelánea 2:f. 930r–931r, 946r–947r.

Table 4.2. Smallpox victims treated in the hospitals of Santa Fe, 1802–1803

Hospital	Patients	Number of Patients Cured	Deaths	Still in Hospital
For both sexes	463	397	65	1
For women only	255	209	46	—
For both sexes (people who had been inoculated)	96	95	1	—
Total	814	701	112	1

Source: AHNC, Miscelánea 2:932r–934r ff.

Attempts were apparently made to develop a vaccine locally. *Haciendas* close to Santa Fe were checked to find cows infected with *viruelas*. These cows were to be brought to the city, to obtain vaccine.[69] Viceroy Mendinueta was knowledgeable about Edward Jenner's successful development of a vaccine. He wrote that the livestock in the Sabana area did not have cowpox, and some people had tried unsuccessfully to infect cows to obtain the vaccine or to "improve the quality of the pus." Mendinueta wrote that he had tried without any success to obtain or produce the vaccine when he knew that the epidemic was threatening the city. He brought some from Spain and Philadelphia, but both batches were inactive by the time they arrived in Santa Fe. Mendinueta spoke of the possibility of using vaccine from Jamaica, taking some young boys to Kingston and having them vaccinated to be the carriers of the vaccine to the coast and the interior.[70] The vaccine finally was brought to the city in 1805, although whether by the Balmis-Salvany expedition or the viceroy is not

[69] AHNC, Miscelánea 2:f. 951v–966r.
[70] Viceroy Mendinueta, "Relación de Mando 1803" (Posada and Ibáñez 1910:462).

yet clear. Vaccination was carried out between 1805 and 1807.[71] The smallpox epidemic lasted until August 1803. In addition to what appear to have been up-to-date public health measures, the archbishop offered special prayers to bring an end to the illness.[72] Viceroy Mendinueta stated that although he had taken precautions to protect other areas of New Granada, he had concentrated his efforts on Santa Fe because in addition to political considerations, the city had a large population, believed to be about 30,000. He argued further that once the epidemic took hold in the capital, the city would serve as a focus, spreading the disease to nearby areas as a consequence of the constant movement of people between it and its environs. The viceroy also noted that it was a just thing to help the poor, who made up most of the city and had suffered such a heavy toll in the smallpox epidemic of 1782–83. In addition, if many individuals became sick at the same time, the *peste* might turn more malignant and destructive, as had happened twenty years previously.[73] As well as being instrumental in establishing hospitals and promoting inoculation, he also ordered that the city be kept clean, prohibited the burial in churches of individuals who died of smallpox, and set up cemeteries. Mendinueta also placed controls on food prices to avoid speculation.[74]

[71] AHNC, Miscelánea 28:f. 74r–121v; Caballero ([1813] 1902:104). Hopkins (1983:224–25) notes that vaccine had been brought successfully to several areas of Spanish and Portuguese America at the time, independent of the royal expedition led by Balmis (M. M. Smith 1974).

[72] Caballero ([1813] 1902:102); AHNC, Miscelánea 2:f. 817r.

[73] Viceroy Mendinueta, "Relación de Mando 1803" (Posada and Ibáñez 1910:463); AHNC, Miscelánea 33:f. 379r–398v; AHNC, Miscelánea 2:f. 817r–868v; AHNC, Miscelánea 2:909r–919v; AHNC Miscelánea 46:f. 724r–749v; AHNC, Miscelánea 3:f. 269r–280v. Most of New Granada was affected by the epidemic.

[74] Viceroy Mendinueta, "Relación de Mando 1803" (Posada and Ibáñez 1910:468). Mendinueta also regulated doctors' services and those of *sangradores*, who bled people in what appears to have been a common treatment for illness. On measures taken see AHNC, Miscelánea 2:f. 818r–868v, 909r–919v; AHNC, Miscelánea 3:f. 316r–326v. In some areas of the Sabana

The steps taken in this epidemic seem to have been unusually systematic. It had been clear to contemporaries since at least the end of the sixteenth century that epidemics were spread by contact, but nothing was effective in stopping the traffic from different areas into the Sabana and Santa Fe. Once in the capital city, the illness found a large population, many sectors of which, as Mendinueta reported, did not have the means to take care of themselves. Disease took heavy tolls there, the population serving as a reservoir for infection. The city council had no funds most of the time, and the Crown did not establish any means to aid people in times of disaster.

Indians outside the capital received token financial aid (usually under 100 pesos per community). Communities held in *encomienda* by the Crown were assisted, if at all, to a lesser degree than ones held privately. The Indians themselves had to petition to be exempted from their tributes after epidemics, rather than Crown officials coming to their aid and offering help.[75]

OTHER EPIDEMICS

The brief accounts below record diseases for which documentation is so fragmentary that it is difficult in certain cases to know the exact nature of the illness. It is also difficult to tell whether or not disease occurred throughout the Sabana or in parts of it. Documentation on Indians indicates substantial negative effects in terms of mortality and subsistence where the disease was widespread and when only one or a few communities were infected.

---

there was scarcity of food because of the insufficiency of rain in 1801–4. See, for example, AHNC, Caciques e Indios 58:f. 94r–96v (Fúquene).
[75]Villamarín and Villamarín 1981:91, note 55; AHNC, Caciques e Indios 25:f. 607r–631v. All the *pueblos* of the *corregimiento* of Bogotá petitioned for exemption from tributes because of past illness [1794].

1739–1740 (peste). Vargas Jurado reported that in July 1739, the nuns of Santa Inés cut off their hair because of a contagious *peste* that later ended. At the end of November 1740, however, Vargas Jurado and his family (nine members in all) caught *peste* and were ill with it throughout the following December and January.[76] There is no more information on what the disease actually was, but typhus is a possibility.

1760 (undetermined illness). An unknown epidemic struck in 1760. Vargas Jurado described it as follows:

On May 19, 1760, at one in the morning, the Precentor D. Antonio de Salazar died. It was he who led the way for the many who numbered among the dead as a result of the epidemic, which came from Japan and ravaged Lima, Quito, and other places in America. It struck here with some mercy and with warnings from those places [where it had already been] regarding methods of curing it, which have been cold sweats, enemas [*ayudas*], and not staying in bed, with blood-letting and cold water being totally noxious, for one has to drink hot water for forty days, since relapses are extremely dangerous, and it continues carrying away the old.[77]

1770s (measles). One community in the Sabana, Usaquén, was reported to have been stricken by measles. All the young men and women had it, and it put the community in great need. It is not known how widespread the disease was elsewhere in the region.[78]

1793–1794 (peste). Indian communities in the *corregimiento* of Bogotá reported that many of their number had *peste*, which was more common among them than in other communities, and that a number of people had died from it. Unfortunately no description of the illness is given. The Bogotá communities were also affected by

---

[76] Vargas Jurado ([1780?] 1902:19, 21).
[77] Vargas Jurado ([1780?] 1902:52).
[78] AHNC, Archivos 1:f. 221r–222r.

insufficient rain, poor crops, and scarcity of food, to the point where Indian were forced to eat their seed crop.[79]

1808 (pasa-diez). In March 1808 there was an epidemic of unknown nature in the city. It was described as ". . . a raging illness of cough and fevers, and novenas were made to several saints. It was named *pasa-diez*, and some people died during this outbreak."[80]

1802, 1809 (tabardillo). The only person reported to have died after being inoculated with smallpox in 1802 was noted by Crown officials to have died of *tabardillo*. The extent of the disease is not known because the officials gave no statistics related to it.[81] The diarist José María Caballero reported that his wife had *tabardillo* on December 18, 1809, even noting that she was stricken at ten in the morning. On December 28, she was administered the last rites. Caballero wrote that a Franciscan, Fray Fierro, took care of her. She must have recovered, because the following April, Caballero registered the birth of a daughter.[82]

THE CASE OF CHÍA

Other epidemics that most likely affected communities in the Sabana are revealed by parish registers. In these cases, identification of the illness in question is difficult, for so little information was recorded by the local parish priest. In Chía, for example, which in 1758 had a population of 1,405, 42 deaths were reported in 1761; 54 in 1762; and 37 in 1763. In 1764 the number of deaths jumped to 109, with no comment about what caused this significant increase in the priest's records. Throughout 1764, deaths were registered as follows: 2 each in January and February, 5 in March, 2 in April, 3 in May,

---

[79] AHNC, Caciques e Indios 25:f. 607r–631v.
[80] Caballero ([1813] 1902:108).
[81] AHNC, Miscelánea 2:f. 932r–934r. Viceroy Mendinueta, "Relación de Mando 1803" (Posada and Ibáñez 1910:469).
[82] Caballero ([1813] 1902:118, 121).

2 in June, 4 in July, 8 in August, 19 in September, 29 in October, 28 in November, and 5 in December. For 1765, a total of 37 deaths was registered; in 1766, 18; in 1767, 25; and in 1768, 15. The figures then climb again. In 1769, 61 deaths were registered, and in 1770, 81. The next three years see a fall: in 1771 to 31, in 1772 to 18, and in 1773 to 37. Figures then rose again, to 130 in 1774, dropping the following year to 44, and to 40 in 1776.

During the smallpox epidemic of the early 1780s, Chía had 64 recorded deaths in 1782 and 382 in 1783, of which 351 were reported by the priest to be a result of the epidemic. In 1784, 50 deaths were registered; in 1785, 72. Then followed four years with yearly death figures between 40 and 50. In 1790 some 29 were reported. In 1791 records showed an upturn to 65. There were 64 deaths in 1792, 78 in 1793, and 77 in 1796. During this last year, an epidemic hit children in particular, reports indicating that several boys and girls were buried each day. On April 9, for example, 3 children were interred; on April 10, 2; on April 13, 2; on April 16, 4; and on April 18, 6. Again the priest did not register the cause of death.

Between 1797 and 1801 registered deaths varied between 8 and 35, with an average of 21 each year. During 1802 and 1803, when smallpox prevailed, deaths numbered about 40 each year, a figure that dropped in 1804 to 18, in 1805 to 20, in 1806 to 21, and in 1807 to 22. There was an upward turn to 41 in 1808. From then until 1815 the highest number of deaths registered in any one year was 26, which occurred in 1809. Deaths registered between 1809 and 1815 fluctuated between 8 and 26, with an average of 16 each year.

In Chía, therefore, upward swings in mortality for the years 1764, 1769–70, 1774, 1793, and 1796 suggest the presence in the community of an epidemic, starvation as a result of crop failure, or both. No parish registers found to date provide descriptive data to indicate the causes of death, but their examination reveals disease and/or famine at a community level that is not always reflected in a general regional panorama.[83]

Conclusion

Smallpox, measles, and typhus were the major epidemic diseases in the Sabana de Bogotá during the colonial period. Smallpox in particular is documented as having broken out repeatedly, causing great personal, social, and economic upheaval among all sectors of the population. The first recorded epidemic was one of smallpox. It struck in 1558, two decades after the arrival of the Spaniards, and affected the Indians primarily. Thirty years later, in 1588, an outbreak of sickness occurred that had a major impact on the entire population, Spaniards as well as Indians. Serious attempts to control the spread of smallpox were not put into effect until the outbreak of 1801–1803, even though some aspects of prevention were partially understood earlier.

Many of the epidemics were noted to have been accompanied by crop failure and scarcity of food. In some cases (measles in 1618, smallpox in 1621) it is clear that crop failure preceded major outbreaks. In Indian communities, scarcity of food probably always followed major diseases because, given the institutionalized demands on the natives, there was no margin for loss of laborers.

In addition to the epidemics that affected most, if not all, Sabana communities, there were also micro-epidemics or food crises that usually went without major notice. Information on these episodes, as in the case of Chía, comes from parish registers, sources that present many difficulties for the researcher. Local priests seldom wrote observations about the cause of death in these registers. Neither is comment made on very pro-

---

[83]Chía Parish Records, Libro 1 de Entierros, 1757–95; Chía Parish Records Libro 2 de Entierros, 1795–1829. AHNC, Visitas de Cundinamarca 8:f. 817r.

nounced changes in mortality. In Chía, records relating to the sixteenth, seventeenth, and part of the eighteenth centuries are missing. Incomplete or badly kept records are the rule for many communities in the Sabana and so hamper our knowledge of local variations within the region. Parish registers nonetheless complement information about regional historical demography and should continue to be sought out for the unique insight they afford into population dynamics at the community level.

Death in Aymaya
of Upper Peru, 1580—1623

Brian M. Evans

Abscesses of the Neck
(*Florentine Codex*)

This chapter traces, in general terms, the population history of one Andean village from 1573 to 1692. After establishing that framework, attention is focused on a detailed examination of patterns of births and deaths from 1580 to 1623. While there is now agreement as to broad demographic trends in the southern Andes during the colonial period, we still lack local, community-level investigations. As the Villamaríns have pointed out, most parish registers of the sixteenth and seventeenth centuries are either no longer extant or are as yet undiscovered, so it is rare to be able to provide specific year-by-year birth and death profiles for so early a date. Similarly, it is not often that one can trace the age-specific mortality of an Andean Indian group before the eighteenth century or show how general mortality differed from that of a disease-specific epidemic.

Historical and Geographical Setting

Aymaya, thanks to remarkably well-preserved records, serves as a case study that enables us to see how regional demographic trends of the late sixteenth and seventeenth centuries actually were manifest in one particular village. Today, Aymaya has a population of a little under 4,000 (*Censo Nacional de Población, Resultados Provisionales 1977*, Bolivia). The community is situated at an elevation of some 3,600 meters, and lies close to the provincial capital of Uncía in the Department of Potosí (Figure 5.1).

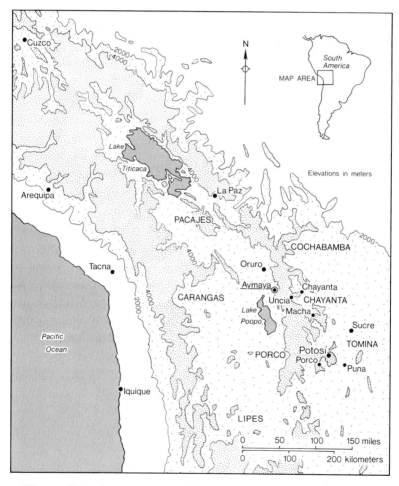

Figure 5.1. AYMAYA AND UPPER PERU

The local economy in Inca times was based primarily
on the growing of tubers, especially potatoes, and, at
slightly lower altitudes, the production of quinoa and
some maize. Llamas and alpacas were both numerous
and important, and most households no doubt kept
Muscovy ducks and guinea pigs to supplement the diet.
The province of Chayanta, to which Aymaya belonged
in colonial times, was an area where altitudinal zona-
tion, or "verticality," to quote Murra's (1975) term, was
well developed. There was much short- and medium-
distance exchange. After the Spanish conquest, Aymaya, together with neighboring areas, was grouped
within the *repartimiento* of "Macha Chaqui y sus añe-
jos." By 1575, tribute in the area had passed from private *encomenderos* to the Crown.

Chayanta as a whole has well-preserved demographic
records. It was an area wholly subject to the full rigor of
the *mita* or forced labor draft of Potosí, but one, unlike
most of the other provinces also so subjected, that did
not suffer drastic depopulation in the seventeenth century (Sánchez-Albornoz 1983; Evans 1985, 31–37). In
1575 the results of the tribute assessment of Viceroy Toledo (N. D. Cook 1975:17–22) indicate that Chayanta
had a total of 5,759 tributaries (adult Indian males, 18 to
50 years of age) and a total population of some 30,400.
This indicates a "tributary index," the proportion of
tributaries to the overall population, of 18.94 percent,
roughly one to five. We do not, alas, have a Toledan
figure specifically for Aymaya because the village was
included in the overall figure for the *repartimiento* of Macha. If, however, we assume that the percentage of the
population between the various pueblos of that *repartimiento* was similar to that recorded in the various seventeenth-century counts, then Aymaya's population in
the 1570s must have been around 1,600 to 1,700 souls.
Although this method is open to many dangers, evidence available in parish registers indicates this estimate to be reasonable.

In 1683, the *Numeración General* recorded Aymaya's population as 367 tributaries, of whom 296 were *originarios* (native residents) and the remaining 71 *forasteros* (newcomers to the village). *Forasteros* thus composed 24 percent of the tributary population. Full details on age, marital status, and family structure were recorded for most of the *originario* population, a total of 1,062 individuals. Figure 5.2 shows the age distribution of this sample. The *Numeración General* for Chayanta, however,

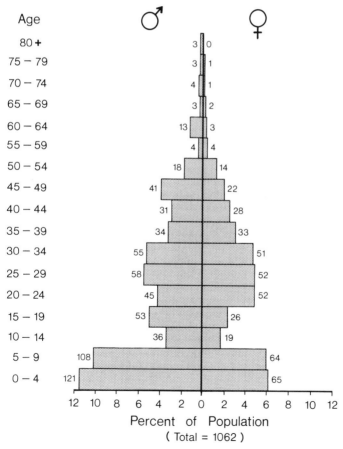

Figure 5.2. AGE DISTRIBUTION OF AYMAYA, 1683

Table 5.1 Male Baptisms and Burials in Aymaya,
1574–1623

Year	Baptisms	Burials	Difference
1574	24	—	—
75	57	—	—
76	30	—	—
77	32	—	—
78	34	—	—
79	42	—	—
1580	49	23	+ 16
81	38	27	+ 11
82	51	24	+ 27
83	37	35	+ 2
84	29	26	+ 3
85	41	28	+ 13
86	38	27	+ 11
87	53	15	+ 28
88	47	11	+ 36
89	52	9	+ 41
1590	35	194	− 159
91	57	18	+ 39
92	37	18	+ 19
93	25	20	+ 19
94	33	19	+ 14
95	21	13	+ 7
96	13	15	− 2
97	21	20	+ 1
98	19	33	− 14
99	26	25	+ 1
1600	22	24	− 2
01	36	40	− 4
02	34	23	+ 11
03	3	38	+ 6

was not carried out efficiently. The returns are orderly, but they are far less detailed than those for many other provinces. There is gross undercounting of females, and following the census the Chayanta returns were the subject of intense debate. A new recount was made in 1695. The female *originario* population was clearly undercounted, especially the infants and children, and the information on *forasteros* is also suspect. Allowing for all the uncertainties, in 1683–84 Aymaya's population was probably in excess of 1,600 souls, or roughly similar to

Table 5.1 continued

Year	Baptisms	Burials	Difference
04	46	32	+ 14
05	30	26	+ 4
06	45	21	+ 24
07	51	32	+ 19
08	47	37	+ 10
09	42	61	− 19
1610	37	55	− 18
11	35	30	+ 5
12	29	42	− 13
13	15	17	− 2
14	48	24	+ 24
15	54	28	+ 26
16	32	5	+ 27
17	40	24	+ 16
18	46	21	+ 25
19	30	47	− 17
1620	41	51	− 10
21	42	31	+ 11
22	39	59	− 20
23	51	35	+ 16
Total 1573–1623	1877		
Total 1580–1623	1658	1403	+255
Average Annual Total 1580–1623	38.56	32.62	

that of Toledan times. Structurally, however, the intervening period had witnessed several interesting and significant changes, and it is upon these that the extracts from parish registers shed light.

Included among the Chayanta returns for the *Numeración General*, conserved in archives in Buenos Aires (Archivo de la Nación, sala 13, legajo 17.7.3) are some intriguing documents. They were compiled in 1623. Why they were prepared, however, is not clear because they are not attached to any legal case involving tribute, nor to any census. Who prepared the documents and under whose authority is also unclear. They comprise all the male baptisms recorded in the pueblo from 1574 to 1623. The returns are arranged by *ayllus* (the basic kin unit of Andean society), first those of the *originarios*, Hanansaya and Hurinsaya, the latter of which includes the migrants known as *mitimaes*, and then those of the *forasteros*. *Saya* designation in the southern Andes was particularly important and continues in the terminology into the republican era. Population units were traditionally split into separate residential halves or *sayas*, designated as "upper" and "lower." The age at baptism is also recorded. Furthermore, there is a list of all male burials from 1579 to 1620, again arranged by *ayllus*. The age of death is provided and, in some years, information as to the cause of death, especially in time of epidemics. One can thus make a detailed reconstruction of demographic patterns in the male population for a forty-year period. By extrapolation one can also draw some conclusions on birth and death rates, expectation of life at birth, and the changing structure of the population. Table 5.1 and Figure 5.3 present the annual totals of male baptisms and burials, and the annual positive

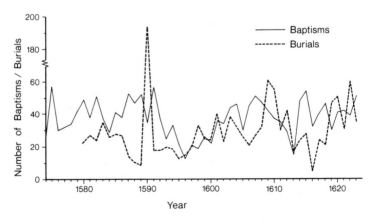

Figure 5.3. Baptisms and burials in Aymaya, 1574–1623

Table 5.2 Male baptisms and burials by intervals,
1574–1623

Dates	Baptisms	Burials	Difference
1574–79	219	—	
1580–89	435	225	+ 210
1590–99	287	375	− 88
1600–1609	397	334	+ 63
1610–19	366	293	+ 73
1620–23	173	176	− 3

or negative balance, together with totals for various
periods: 1574–79 (baptisms only), 1580–89, 1590–99,
1600–1609, 1610–19, and 1620–23.

Patterns of Epidemic Mortality

If the total population of Aymaya was approximately
1,700 in the 1570s, then clearly the period up to 1590
was one of considerable if irregular growth in population. All years in the 1580s showed a positive balance of
births, which amounted over the decade to 210. Then
disaster struck. In 1590, 194 burials were recorded, 147
of which were specifically attributed to *viruelas* (smallpox). The majority of these deaths were of children less
than two years, but there were also over 60 deaths of
young adults in the age category 18–40. One can safely
assume that female mortality from smallpox would be
equal to male mortality, so in 1590 Aymaya must have

Table 5.3 Average yearly male baptisms and
burials in Aymaya, 1574–1623

Dates	Baptisms	Burials
1574–79	36.5	—
1580–89	43.5	22.5
1590–99	28.7	37.5
1600–1609	39.7	33.4
1610–19	36.6	29.3
1620–23	43.3	44.0

lost over 400 people, or 20–25 percent of the total population.

At first sight, rebound seems rapid, for both 1591 and 1592 show positive balances. Then things falter, and the annual total of births throughout the 1590s remains low. Population began to stagnate. In 1600 Aymaya must have had fewer people than in 1580. When recovery commenced (1602–8), there is some evidence that it derived from an influx of *forastero* families. The improvement, however, was shortlived. The years 1609–13 were unfavorable, and although these were followed by high rates of natural increase (1614–18), the cycle was again reversed by the high mortality of the early 1620s. One suspects that, in 1623, population had still not recovered its pre-1590 level.

The age at baptism, as one might expect, was usually only a few days, or at most a month. One might assume therefore that the number of baptisms is fairly close to the number of actual live births, an assumption that is not valid for all Andean parochial records. The actual number of baptisms, however, fluctuated widely (and wildly) from one year to the next (Figure 5.3). While such considerable annual variation is not unusual in pre-industrial societies, the degree of variation is more marked in Aymaya, for example, than in seventeenth-century Europe. To quote but one example, however, N. D. Cook (1982:68) found a similar pattern of wide annual variation in the village of Yanque, in the Andes of southern Peru, so we need not automatically assume that such annual variations are a sign of capricious registration. The ten-year average shows a more even pattern, except for the disastrous 1590s.

The annual pattern of death shows, as we might anticipate, enormous variations. The healthiest year (1589) showed only nine burials, but the good year was immediately followed by the 194 interments of 1590. This year was exceptional because it was marked by the great smallpox epidemic. Apart from 1590, the other years of recorded high mortality (over fifty entries) were 1609 and 1610 (when again there are references to smallpox), 1620, and 1622.

Table 5.4 and Figure 5.4 show the overall picture of the recorded ages at death of the male population. First examination of the figures shows some of the shocking realities of existence in Aymaya. Fully 40 percent of all deaths occurred at age 15 or less, and, if we allow for possible under-registration of burials of the newborn and stillbirths, we are probably correct in assuming that half those born were dead before the age of 15. This extremely high childhood mortality is again character- istic of all preindustrial societies, although worse in Ay- maya, say, than was typical of seventeenth-century Eu- rope. The second peak of deaths of young male adults 20 to 45 years of age, however, is more unusual. This peak at Aymaya must be connected with the hardship and consequent mortality directly or indirectly attribut- able to the *mita* of Potosí, and one suspects that tuber- culosis must have been rampant.

The recorded age at death seems to be fairly accurate up to 50 years, beyond which the evidence shows that ages were estimated very roughly, with extreme bunch- ing at 60, 70, and especially 80 years. Beyond 50, men were no longer liable for tribute and *mita,* and these el- derly were no longer of such economic use and interest to their exploiters.

The deaths from the 1590 smallpox epidemic indi- cate the characteristics of mortality from that disease to perfection. Above all it was fatal to children and, sec- ondly, to young adults. These features, of course, en- sured that demographic recovery after a devastating outbreak would be slow.

A comparison of mortality before and after the 1590 epidemic seems to indicate some changes in the ages of death. All told, 202 deaths were recorded from 1580 to 1589, and 883 deaths from 1591 to 1623. Thus, overall percentage of deaths in 1580-89 was 22.9 percent of the

Table 5.4 Male age at death in Aymaya

Age at Death	Total	Percentage	Number Killed by 1590 Smallpox
Under 5	294	23.88	36
5–9	147	11.94	30
10–14	45	3.66	5
15–19	38	3.09	7
20–24	78	6.34	24
25–29	81	6.58	23
30–34	117	9.50	12
35–39	84	6.82	6
40–44	104	8.45	—
45–49	37	3.00	1
50–54	63	5.12	—
55–59	6	0.49	—
60–64	46	3.74	—
65–69	2	0.16	—
70–79	39	3.17	—
80 and older	50	4.06	3
Total	1231		147

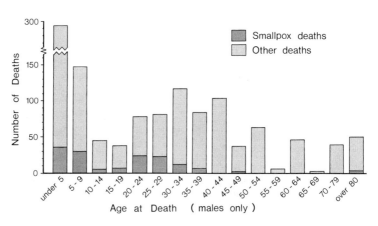

Figure 5.4. AGES OF DEATH IN AYMAYA

total in the later period. Now, if in a specific age bracket the proportion of deaths is much greater than 22.9 percent, it suggests tentatively that the mortality for that group was higher in the 1580s than it later became. It is of course speculative, but in Aymaya it would seem to show that the mortality in early manhood was higher in the 1580s than it became in the seventeenth century. Thus in the age cohort 25–29, the ratio between the deaths in 1580–89 to that in 1591–1629 is 70.6 percent, for the 30–34 cohort 34.6 percent, and for the 35–39 group 41.8 percent. One possible explanation for the lower mortality of these groups in the early seventeenth century is that the enforcing of the *mita* directly on Aymaya tributaries was becoming less effective as more and more Indians began claiming exempt status or sought relief through cash payments (Cole 1985).

Important changes in *ayllus* and status can also be discerned from the documentary evidence on Aymaya. As most other Andean communities, Aymaya had its *ayllus* divided into two *parcialidades*, or districts: Hanansaya and Hurinsaya. The Hanansaya, or "upper" *parcialidad*, seems in most areas to have had a certain ritual priority. In Aymaya it contained in the late sixteenth century five *ayllus*: Carache, Yanaque, Collana, Chiaco, and Yaira. The Hurinsaya contained three *ayllus*: Coyco, Sazacara, and Tucari, plus one *ayllu* of *mitimaes* of unknown provenance, but which had been present since Inca times. *Forasteros*, usually outsiders without land, were present, most of them settled in the *anexo* or outlying settlement of Micari and not forming part of the *ayllu* structure.

If we divide, by *parcialidad*, the *ayllu* affiliation recorded in the lists of baptisms over our period of study, several patterns emerge. In the first place, even allowing for the difficulties of interpretation of some of the material, the figures indicate important changes in the makeup of Aymaya's population over fifty years. The rapid decline of Hanansaya after the epidemic of 1590 calls for comment. The *ayllu* Collana, for example, which had averaged about fifteen baptisms annually, declined precipitously: after 1591 the annual totals were only three or four. Although no other *ayllu* suffered proportionately as severely, the trend for all others of the Hanansaya was also downward. In contrast, all the *ayllus* of the Hurinsaya remained fairly stable. Lastly, the proportion of *forastero* baptisms increased rapidly after 1600, and by 1620 accounted for over 40 percent of the total. *Forasteros*, of course, were not liable for the *mita*, nor did they meet full tribute obligations.

Because the proportion of *forasteros* in the total population in 1683–84 was less than 25 percent, one may conclude that the period of mass immigration of outsiders into Aymaya was essentially an early seventeenth-century phenomenon. By the 1680s, the declining proportion might either be a sign of possible assimilation with *originarios* or the result of out-migration after 1623, for we know (Sánchez-Albornoz 1983; Evans 1983) that the seventeenth century *forastero* population of Alto Peru in general, and Chayanta in particular, was highly mobile.

We can tentatively estimate the crude birth and death rates and the expectation of life if we make the following assumptions: (1) the record of baptisms in Aymaya is a reasonable record of the total of live births; (2) the number of female births was about 7 percent less than that of the males; (3) the crude female death rate was about the same as the male death rate, although the age-specific mortality was undoubtedly quite different; and

Table 5.5 Baptisms by *parcialidad* in Aymaya, 1573–1623

Period	Hanansaya (percent)	Hurinsaya (percent)	Forastero (percent)	Baptisms
1573–90	53.40	29.17	17.24	689
1591–1605	32.76	50.86	16.38	464
1606–23	22.65	38.81	38.54	724

Table 5.6 Estimated crude birth rates for Aymaya, 1573–1623

Period	Population of Pueblo	Assumed Birth Rate per 1,000	Crude Death Rate per 1,000	Crude Natural Increase per 1,000
1573–80	1,700	42	No information	No information
1580–89	1,800	46	25	+ 19
1590–99	1,300	42	58	− 16
1600–1609	1,400	54	47	+ 7
1610–19	1,500	47	39	+ 8
1620–23	1,600	51	55	− 4

(4) Aymaya's total population in 1573 was about 1,700 souls. The most unreliable assumption in this exercise is, as we have seen, the fourth. For the purposes of this reconstruction, let us assume an average gross total population of 1,700 before 1580; 1,800 for 1580–89; 1,300 after the epidemic of 1590, a figure that remained constant to 1600; then an average growth of 100 per decade thereafter.

We cannot, of course, estimate immigration or emigration. If, however, we allow these figures, we obtain the results shown in Table 5.6. Despite all uncertainties, one can draw a number of conclusions. First, the birth rates were high, almost certainly over 40 per thousand. Death rates, however, were equally high, although subject to much wider fluctuation on an annual and decade basis. Natural increase was therefore subject to violent fluctuations and was frequently negative. Given the high death rates, expectation of life at birth was less than twenty years. In fact, all the statistics show a grim situation in relation to life expectancy.

Conclusion

I conclude this examination by looking, first, at Aymaya's population as recorded sixty years after the end of the parish registers and, second, by comparing the Aymaya records with documentary extracts from other parts of seventeenth-century Alto Peru. We have already reviewed some of the deficiencies in the figures for the *Numeración General* in Aymaya. In addition to those already mentioned, one might also draw attention to the peculiarly severe under-registration of teenagers. Other details, however, shed light on several seventeenth-century developments. The *ayllu* names and structures had not changed since the early 1600s, nor had Hurinsaya lost its numerical superiority. The percentages of the recorded population were 28 percent for Hanansaya, 48 percent for Hurinsaya, and 24 percent for *forasteros*. The provinces of origin were given for

seventy-one of the *forasteros*. Most were from the alti-
plano provinces of Pacajes, Paria, Carangas, and Chu-
cuito, but fully a third were from the region between
Lake Titicaca and Cuzco, proportions similar to those of
Chayanta as a whole (Evans 1981:39). A feature of Aymaya's population in 1683, however, was a high number
of absentees, amounting to some 26 percent of the total
male *originarios*. Details were not supplied about their
whereabouts, although one suspects that many were
mitayos and *mingayos* (free wage laborers) at Potosí.

The period immediately following the *Numeración General* saw much turmoil about the proposed new tribute
levels (AGI, Charcas 270; Cole 1981:381–461) and the
alleged and real inaccuracies in the census. There are
many references to widespread epidemics from 1684 to
1692, as noted by N. D. Cook (1981:243) for Yanque. In
Chayanta, complaints eventually led to a new census
in 1695. Most of the allegations concerned the over-
counting and double-counting of tributaries, but Aymaya does not feature among the communities specifically mentioned.

Other seventeenth-century parish records of Alto Perú
provide useful comparative data, some in the form of registers, some as actual *padrones*. In light of N. D. Cook's
(1981:243) remark that surviving sixteenth-century and
seventeenth-century parish registers are rare for South
America, it is appropriate to comment briefly on their
nature and the way they compare to the Aymaya material. For Tomahave (Porco) there are extracts listing
the burials for males and females from 1685 to 1709
(AGN, legajo 18.7.4). Age at death is provided. As the
Numeración General records for Tomahave are complete
and detailed, the extracts can be "tied" and thus we can
trace developments in the pueblo. There is identical information available for Puna (Porco) from 1684 to 1712,
which is of equal value (AGN, legajo 18.7.3). Lastly, for
Calcha (AGN, legajo 17.7.4, Chicas) we have at our disposal a list of all baptisms from 1628 to 1660 plus some

summary information from 1660 to 1670. Burials are listed for the period 1628 to 1670, and there are population counts for 1670 and 1684. The Calcha material presents some interesting problems, among them age at baptism. In this example, the figures are high, usually between six weeks and three months. Why this should be is not explained, though with infant mortality as high as it was, many infants must have died before they were brought to the font, and hence the number of baptisms is not a good guide to the total number of births.

The fact that these extracts exist suggests that at least some of the originals may still be extant. It further suggests that there is a rich field of demographic information awaiting the researcher prepared for the hardship of transcribing the actual registers in local archives or in the parish churches themselves. Future painstaking research of this nature is imperative before we will be able to answer adequately many of the questions touched on here.

DISEASE, POPULATION, AND PUBLIC HEALTH IN EIGHTEENTH-CENTURY QUITO

Suzanne Austin Alchon

A Bloody Flux (*Florentine Codex*)

In many respects, the history of disease and epidemics among the native peoples of the Audiencia of Quito resembles that of other regions in colonial Spanish America. During the sixteenth century, epidemics of smallpox, measles, and typhus occurred every ten to twenty years, claiming the lives of large numbers of infants, children, and young adults, as well as the elderly and infirm. The demographic impact of these epidemics reverberated long after the outbreaks subsided. As the deaths of thousands of children and young adults left few to reproduce, birth rates remained low for many years. Consequently, by the end of the sixteenth century the number of Indians residing in the Quito area had been reduced by approximately 85 to 90 percent, from between 750,000 and 1,000,000 in 1534 to approximately 95,000 in 1590.

Patterns of disease in Quito during the seventeenth and eighteenth centuries continued to resemble those of other parts of the empire. As the number and size of urban centers grew, the disease environment became

more complex. Numerous endemic infections posed
a constant threat to the health of local residents and
claimed many lives. While records of the *cabildo* or city
council often refer to these illnesses simply as *pestes* or
achaques (epidemics or illnesses), other more specific
descriptions include references to *calenturas, catarros,
fuertes fluxiones,* and *disentería de sangre* (fevers, coughs,
diarrhea, and bloody dysentery). According to Jorge
Juan and Antonio de Ulloa (1758, 1:294–95), Spanish
naval officers who visited Quito during the late 1730s,
syphilis was so common "that few persons are free of
it, though its effects are much more violent in some than
in others." They also noted the presence of "a dis-
temper unknown in Europe . . . called *peste;* its symptoms are convulsions in every part of the body, a continual endeavor to bite, delirium, [and the] vomiting
[of] blood." Juan and Ulloa added that *peste* was common throughout South America and that most individuals contracted it at some time in their lives. Having survived an attack, the victim acquired lifetime immunity.
The disease may have been a form of hemorrhagic fever.
In addition, epidemics of smallpox, measles, and typhus continued to sweep through the area every few
years. When they did, the death toll was staggering.
In spite of these depredations, however, the tributary
population of the central highlands of Ecuador more
than doubled between 1590 and 1670, from 21,250 in
1590 to 56,924 in 1670 (Browne 1984:69–91). Natural increase and immigration from other regions within the
viceroyalty of Peru accounted for this remarkable demographic recovery, which occurred when the number of
Native Americans in most other parts continued to decline, or at best to stagnate. Demographic recovery was
short-lived, however, because between 1691 and 1695,
epidemics of *sarampión, viruelas, tabardillo,* and *garrotillo*
(measles, smallpox, typhus, and diphtheria) claimed
the lives of 25 to 50 percent of all natives. Once again,

mortality rates among children and young adults were especially high (Browne 1984:105–10).

Throughout the eighteenth century, endemic infections and epidemic outbreaks continued to bring suffering and death to local residents. While the disease environment remained largely unchanged, ideas and attitudes inspired by Enlightenment thinking prompted physicians and officials to alter their perception of the relationship between disease, sanitation, and public health. Enlightenment thinking involved a shift away from the ecclesiastical assumption that the Christian God brought on sickness as punishment for human sins, to a growing awareness that certain diseases, at least, had noncosmological causes, which human beings could influence if not control. A rise in the number of licensed doctors, surgeons, and apothecaries, the regular funding of hospitals, and the growing involvement of local officials dealing with epidemics and problems of public health and sanitation indicate an increasing awareness on the part of Quito's educated elite that more could be done to improve the health of the local population.

This chapter, then, addresses three interrelated issues: (1) accurate identification of the epidemics that occurred in the city of Quito during the eighteenth century; (2) assessment of the demographic impact of these outbreaks; and (3) analysis of the attitudes and responses of local officials and medical practitioners to epidemic disease and other matters concerning public health and sanitation.

Epidemics

Of the many social problems confronting Spanish officials throughout the colonial period, epidemics remained the most serious and frustrating. The economy of the Quito area, based on agriculture and textile production, depended upon large numbers of native labor-

ers. In such a labor-intensive economic system, the illness or death of hundreds or thousands of workers
produced dire consequences: *obrajes* (textile mills) closed
down, and crops were neither planted nor harvested.
During these difficult periods, administrators and owners could do little except pray and wait.

Sebastián de Benalcázar founded the city of San Francisco de Quito on a long, narrow shelf of land, rising
some 500 meters above the surrounding countryside.
Capital of both the *audiencia* and the *corregimiento* of
Quito, the city was the largest and wealthiest in the region, but small and poor in comparison to the viceregal
capitals of Lima and Mexico City. The Quito area was
long regarded as a backwater because of its failure to
develop a productive mining economy. Consequently,
relatively few Spaniards chose to settle in the region.
Even Benalcázar relinquished his claim on the Quito
area to continue north in search of still greater wealth.

By the beginning of the seventeenth century, most
highland *encomiendas* were held by Spaniards who would
never set foot in the New World. In their place, *audiencia*
and *cabildo* officials, along with the owners of *obrajes* and
haciendas, comprised the new elite. The demographic recovery of the native population triggered an economic
boom in textile production. As a result, throughout
most of the seventeenth century, members of the ruling
class, the majority of whom resided in the city of Quito,
enjoyed a modest prosperity.

Just as the demographic and economic patterns of the
audiencia changed over time, so too did the racial com-
position of the city. A description written in 1577 (Cabildo de Quito 1978:45–70) estimated that some 1,000
Spaniards, many with families, had taken up residence
in the city. The author of this document also included
2,000 *mestizos* and "many *mulatos*" among the population of the *audiencia* as a whole. Even if the description
of 1577 underestimated the number of *castas* and Europeans, both of these groups were tiny in comparison to

the native population. During the sixteenth century, the indigenous elite often maintained homes in the city, while native workers lived on the outskirts. By the seventeenth century, the Spanish population remained small, while the number of *mestizos* and *mulatos* had increased rapidly. Nevertheless, natives continued to comprise at least one-half of all urban residents.

In the Audiencia of Quito, disaster ushered in the eighteenth century. The deaths of a quarter to a half of the native population during the epidemics of 1691–95 resulted in the collapse of the regional economy. Owners of *haciendas* and *obrajes* were so desperate for workers that they frequently resorted to kidnappings. In January 1700, the *cabildo* of Quito reported that the highlands continued in the grip of a drought that had begun nine years earlier. Food had been in short supply for several years, and now an epidemic of fevers afflicted the hungry. As often happened, unscrupulous individuals were ready to take advantage of desperate people: the number of unlicensed medical practitioners increased as the epidemic worsened. *Cabildo* members published the names of two men who were suspected of practicing without licenses. They ordered Jacinto Rondón and Fulano Estupinán to present their *títulos* (medical diplomas) within two days or pay a fine of 200 pesos (AMQLC 00117:43). Because of a chronic shortage of licensed physicians and surgeons, preventing individuals with little or no training from practicing medicine proved to be a constant struggle for local officials, although a patient's chances of recovery were not much better with a university-trained doctor than with a local *curandero* (healer).

Following the epidemic of fevers in 1700, another outbreak of disease serious enough to warrant inclusion in *cabildo* minutes did not occur for eight years. In May 1708, an epidemic of *catarros* attacked men, women, and children, affecting Spaniards as well as Indians. Some people contracted the disease more than once, and many died as a result (AMQLC 00119:45–46). That this respiratory illness attacked everyone regardless of age, class, race, or gender suggests that it may have been an outbreak of influenza.

A year later, the *cabildo* (AMQLC 00119:128–29) reported drought as well as an epidemic of smallpox. As urban mortality climbed, the epidemic spread throughout the surrounding region. Council members noted in addition that, because of the drought, "other infections" were also appearing, although they failed to describe the symptoms.

According to the *cabildo* records, no significant incidents of disease occurred during the next fifteen years (AMQLC 00122:117–28), although endemic infections continued to exact their toll. The 1720s proved, on the other hand, to be particularly difficult years for residents of Quito. Wheat rust, introduced into the region during the 1690s, afflicted the surrounding countryside. As food supplies dwindled, famine threatened. To make matters worse, in certain areas years of constant use had lowered soil fertility, and many wheat farmers close to Quito and provincial capitals (see Figure 3.1) were forced out of business because of declining production and profits. *Haciendas* rented for one-half of their seventeenth-century rates and *novenos* (church tax on agricultural production) yielded only half of their previous amount (Herrera and Enríquez 1916, 1:311).

Between 1724 and 1726, one or more unnamed diseases that may have been smallpox, or complications arising from it, afflicted highland residents. In August 1724, the *cabildo* reported (AMQLC 00122:164) that "many people had died as a result of the pestilence that has been introduced." A year later, the epidemic still lingered. By February 1726, the council (AMQLC 00123: 30, 100) noted the presence of *achaques*. Whether or not all three descriptions refer to the same infection is not clear.

Measles appeared in the city during the spring of

1728. Although the disease continued to spread throughout the highlands during 1729, it caused few deaths, at least according to the president of the *audiencia* (AGI, Quito 172). If measles was by then endemic to the region, reaching epidemic proportions only occasionally, many people, especially in the city of Quito and provincial capitals, would have already been exposed to the virus, thus explaining the low rate of mortality. Although scattered outbreaks of disease occurred between 1733 and 1736, it was not until 1746 that another epidemic struck. This episode can be traced to an outbreak of smallpox that appeared in Lima late in 1744 (*Gazeta de Lima*, November-December 1744). A few cases were reported in the Audiencia of Quito that same year, but the disease did not reach epidemic levels until two years later, in July 1746 (Herrera and Enríquez 1916, 2:143). This epidemic eventually made its way eastward into Amazonia, where it claimed many lives (Polo 1913: 80). Five years later, in 1751, an outbreak of smallpox occurred in Quito, but according to Dr. Eugenio Espejo "it appeared not to be especially malignant" (AJC 01229, "Sobre viruelas," Quito, 1784:39).

In November 1758, another epidemic of smallpox broke out in Lima, arriving in Quito in October 1759. By the spring of 1760, the epidemic had moved northwards to attack the population of Popayán. As smallpox continued to spread north, another disease, *peste de Japón* (possibly influenza), flared up in Bogotá, moving south to Quito and then on to Lima. Although many Spaniards and natives became seriously ill, few died, probably because of previous exposure in 1746–47 and again in 1751 (Polo 1913:81; *Gazeta de Lima*, January–March 1759, June–August 1759, November 1759–January 1760, March–May 1760).

A far more lethal disease spread throughout the Audiencia of Quito in 1763. Between February and April, many natives became ill. By October 1764, many had died. In Quito, *cabildo* members expressed concern that the price of sugar, an important ingredient in many medicines, was too high, fetching twenty-four *reales* per *arroba*. The *cabildo* ordered the price to be lowered to 18 to 20 *reales*. But the Jesuits, who controlled the local sugar supply, opposed the *cabildo* ruling. A month later, the Jesuit fathers persuaded officials to restore the price to its previous level (AMQLC 00129:42–43).

As mortality rates increased during 1764, the city council did what little it could to mitigate the disaster. Their first step was to inspect the licenses of all doctors and surgeons to protect the public from untrained individuals. The *audiencia* initiated the second step when it ordered all medical practitioners in the city to report to the hospital, there to perform an autopsy on a victim of the epidemic in hopes of determining the cause of the outbreak responsible for the deaths of so many of "all classes." The *audiencia* further instructed all doctors and surgeons to continue performing autopsies until they discovered the nature of the disease and how best to treat it (AMQLC 00129:34–35).[1] Four days later, Don Francisco de Borja y Larraspuro, the official in charge of conducting the operations, returned to request that the *cabildo* appoint a *protomédico* (medical examiner) because the doctors did not want to perform the surgeries and they needed one doctor to take charge. In response, the council appointed Dr. Don Joseph Gaude, "profesor de medicina," to preside over the proceedings. Within a few days, several autopsies (AMQLC 00129:117) had been performed, but the doctors claimed they had learned nothing new, and the epidemic continued.

Between 1769 and 1783, the city council noted several serious outbreaks of disease. In March 1769 an epidemic of *esquilencia* (scarlet fever) and dysentery ravaged the city (AMQLC 00130:23). In February and March 1777, the council reported that the city was infested with

[1]According to Dr. Eugenio de Espejo, *viruelas* was the disease at large in 1764. If this were the case, however, it seems unlikely that officials would have ordered autopsies to determine the cause of death (AJC 01229, 1784, 40).

"various diseases" (AMQLC 00131:15). Two years later, in October 1779 (AMQLC 00132:132–33), many residents died of *mal de pujos*, yet another description of dysentery. During the next three years, *disentería de sangre* and other illnesses spread throughout the highlands (AMQLC 00132:177, 186, 232), claiming many lives. According to Dr. Eugenio Espejo, in 1783 smallpox was responsible for the deaths of "many children" and had become "almost endemic" in urban neighborhoods (AJC 01229, Quito 1784:40).

The most devastating epidemic of the eighteenth century arrived in August of 1785. As measles began to spread throughout the city, complaints reached the *cabildo* that *boticas* or pharmacies, even that of the hospital, were only open from 11 A.M. until 3 P.M. The public also complained that the price of medicines was too high. In response, *cabildo* members met with druggists and hospital administrators, ordering them to stay open around the clock and lower their prices or face severe penalties (AMQLC 00133:180).

When it became clear that this outbreak was particularly virulent, the city council convened an extraordinary session to address the problem of providing medical assistance to poor neighborhoods. Complaints had reached the *cabildo* that doctors treated only those who could pay them. Furthermore, during the emergency doctors allegedly were overcharging for their services. After serious deliberation, the city council ordered all four licensed doctors in the capital to spend three hours each day, without pay, visiting patients in the neighborhoods to which they would be assigned. To ensure compliance, four council members would also visit these districts daily. The *cabildo* went on to establish four *reales* as the maximum fee doctors could charge their paying customers (AMQLC 00133:181–82). Finally, two druggists agreed to supply medicine free upon receipt of a doctor's prescription. In return, the *cabildo* promised to reimburse the apothecaries for one-half of their expenses at the end of the emergency. Several days later, the city council decided to meet each Friday with the four doctors to discuss the course of the epidemic and the measures they could take to mitigate its effects (AMQLC 00133:184). During one of these Friday meetings (AMQLC 00133:184–85) they agreed to distribute 500 pesos of city funds among poor residents.

Throughout Quito, however, residents continued to fall ill. In September and October, the two worst months of the epidemic, at least 2,400 people died, adults as well as children (Arcos 1933:142). In the parishes of Santa Bárbara, San Roque, and La Catedral, priests recorded 362 deaths between August 23 and October 4. According to local clergymen, these totals did not accurately reflect mortality rates because many victims were buried in other cemeteries throughout the city and in outlying areas (AJC 00029, September 30 and October 4, 1785). To the south, in Latacunga, at least 417 Spaniards and 2,333 natives died between September 1785 and March 1786 (Tyrer 1976:61).[2]

The population of neighboring Ambato was also hit hard. Ramón Puente, administrator of the *obraje* and *hacienda* of San Ildefonso, testified that so many natives fell ill that he was forced to close the operation from October 15, 1785, until March 30, 1786. *Obraje* closings for that length of time had not occurred since the disruptive epidemics of the 1690s. Puente also stated that when workers finally began to return to their jobs they became even sicker than before, and production shut down once again. In the town of Pelileo, 90 adult males—approximately 8 percent of the tributary population—and 225 women and children had died by April 1786. According to Puente, many continued to perish.

The situation resembled that of the 1690s disaster complex in at least two ways. First, in addition to the

---

[2] Among Spaniards, 125 adults and 292 children perished, while 710 adult natives and 1,623 children died. According to Tyrer (1976:61), 6 percent of Latacunga's native population died during this epidemic.

epidemic, natural disasters (in this case heavy rains and freezing temperatures) were destroying crops and killing livestock. During the 1690s, a severe drought eventually led to food shortages and famine. Second, so many workers were sick or dying that a serious labor shortage developed. Few people were available to harvest the crops that had managed to survive the rains. Puente predicted that the labor shortage would continue for a long time because many young boys had died during the epidemic (ANHQ, caja 20, folder 119:60–67). The epidemic of measles spread north into New Granada, reaching Bogotá by 1788. The following year, this epidemic, or possibly another unrelated outbreak of measles, moved south from Bogotá throughout the Audiencia of Quito and on into Peru.

Epidemic Disease and Demographic Trends in the Eighteenth Century

Any attempt to assess the impact of disease on demographic trends in the city of Quito during the eighteenth century must begin with the epidemics and natural disasters of the 1690s. Throughout the highlands, the number of natives had been reduced by 25–50 percent, and the region was entering a period of demographic stagnation and economic depression from which it would not fully recover until the present century.

During the mid-seventeenth century, approximately 50,000 persons resided in the city of Quito and its immediate vicinity. Of that number, only 5 percent were whites; natives, *mestizos*, and *mulatos* comprised the remainder (Phelan 1967:49). Although no data exist on the population of the city for the years immediately following the 1690s, the deaths of one-quarter to one-half of the population would have reduced the number of inhabitants to approximately 25,000–37,000. Moreover, the collapse of the regional economy, particularly the closing of numerous urban *obrajes*, pushed many survivors out of the city to find work in rural areas. Data from the second half of the century also indicate that demographic decline was especially severe in urban areas. Therefore an estimate for Quito of 20,000–25,000 inhabitants in 1700 may be more accurate. Constant complaints from both *hacendados* and *obraje* owners regarding severe labor shortages support this low estimate. Between deaths and absenteeism, the number of tributaries in most highland jurisdictions had declined 30 to 50 percent or more. Officials in the village of Lican, Riobamba, reported that 38 percent of the adult male population was gone. Tribute rolls in the neighboring towns of Cubijíes, San Andrés, and Puni showed declines of 72, 42, and 27 percent, respectively. These figures included both dead and absent males (ANHQ, Presidencia de Quito, tomos 16–17, November 13, 1706, October 21, 1707). In Pillaro, Ambato, one *cacique* reported that only nine tributaries and five boys remained in his *parcialidad* in 1699 (ANHQ, Indígenas, caja 24, 1699). To the north, the labor shortage was just as critical. In 1697, the *corregidor* of Otavalo wrote that "the population used to be 3,000 Indians, resulting in tribute collections of 16,000 pesos. But now it has been reduced to only 100 Indians" (AGI, Quito 15, 1697). Although this report may have exaggerated the degree of demographic decline (a decrease of 97 percent seems too extreme), it indicates nonetheless the severity of the crisis.

Simultaneously, tithe and tribute revenues dropped sharply not only because fewer taxpayers remained, but also because the drought had reduced agricultural production to such a low level that survivors had nothing to give tribute collectors. In 1697, for example, representatives of the princess of Estillano, *encomendera* of Sigchos, claimed that she had not received one *real* from her holdings in several years (AGI, Quito 59, January 28, 1697).

As the full extent of the destruction became apparent, officials confronted the fact that the disasters would

have long-term as well as immediate demographic consequences. Not only was the existing tributary population seriously depleted, but future tributaries would
remain low in number owing to the deaths of approximately one-half of all children and young adults during
the epidemics. While birth rates probably rose quickly
after 1695, the number of persons left to reproduce continued to hamper demographic and economic recovery
for at least a generation.

In response to the labor shortage, *obraje* owners and
hacendados increased pressure on *caciques* to supply
more workers. Because officials had not revised tribute
rolls following the epidemics, Spaniards could legally
demand the same number of workers. Many *caciques* petitioned the *audiencia* for new censuses, which would
more accurately reflect the bleak demographic reality.
Members of the Quito elite did not wish to see the rolls
adjusted downward, however, and opposed the census
on the grounds that it would be too costly. While some
tribute lists were amended between 1708 and 1712,
many were not, and tensions between native communities and local landowners continued.

Confrontations over forced labor in *obrajes* had become such a divisive issue that as early as December 31,
1704, a royal order banned *obraje* labor drafts altogether.
Stiff resistance from owners and administrators delayed
enforcement of the ruling for ten years. By 1714, however, the point was mute, as most community *obrajes*
had permanently closed down, and the private enter-
prises that continued to function still had trouble find-
ing enough workers.

Labor shortages, however, were not the only problem
confronting the textile industry. By the first decade of
the eighteenth century, large quantities of European
cloth arriving in the viceroyalty of Peru had reduced demand for Quito's product (Washburne 1983:3). In addition, the decline of mining production in Upper Peru
during the seventeenth century had prompted many

Peruvian entrepreneurs to turn to textile manufacturing as an alternative form of investment. Beginning in the 1680s, numerous *obrajes* opened in Lima and Upper Peru, further weakening the market for Quito's cloth, an item increasingly unable to compete because of higher transportation costs. Between 1700 and 1750, labor costs and the price of raw materials rose 45 percent, while cloth prices declined 50 percent (Washburne 1983:3). According to President Juan Antonio Mon y Velarde, Quito's *obrajes* in 1700 exported 12,000 bales of cloth per year. By 1754, only 3,000 bales left the *audiencia*, a drop of 75 percent in half a century (Washburne 1983: 8). Throughout this period, urban *obrajes* and *chorillos* (small operations with less than twenty workers) experienced the greatest rate of decline.

Because the economic fortunes of Quito's entire business community depended on revenues generated by the textile industry, in the 1720s wholesale and retail merchants throughout the city suffered severe losses. Herrera and Enríquez (1916, 1:307–8) wrote that "because of the lack of silver the number of businesses in the city has declined from more than 400 to only 70 or 80; and of these, 10 or 12 are unable to sell their cloth and other goods." Real estate prices in the city also plummeted, and buildings sold for a half or a third of their previous value. The rapid decline of Quito's commercial sector illustrated the severity of the economic depression.

Describing the city of Quito as they saw it in 1736, Juan and Ulloa (1758, 1:263–65) later wrote: "Quito . . . was formerly in a much more flourishing condition than at present, the number of its inhabitants being considerably decreased, particularly the Indians, whole streets of whose huts are now forsaken, and in ruins." The two travellers (1:276) then went on to estimate the city's total population at 50,000–60,000. This figure is grossly inflated, however, because by the 1730s the highland population had experienced only moderate demographic recovery. In fact, the epidemics and food shortages of the 1720s had slowed population growth. Moreover, the disastrous state of the city's economy continued to discourage immigration. It seems likely, therefore, that the figure given by Juan and Ulloa was probably double that of the actual number of inhabitants. The two officers, however, were correct in noting that the native population had undergone the steepest decline and now comprised only one-third of all urban residents.

By the 1740s, some 30,000 persons lived in the city of Quito, an increase of 25–33 percent since the beginning of the century (Minchom 1986:12). While this represents a substantial rate of growth, the number of urban dwellers nonetheless remained well below the estimated population of 50,000 in 1650. Owing to the absence of any major disease incidents, the number of city residents continued to expand for the next twenty years.

With the arrival of the epidemic of 1763–64, however, this period of recovery came to an end. To date, the only estimate of mortality comes from the administrative unit of Ambato, where at least 513 tributaries, approximately 15 percent of the adult male population, died during the outbreak (Tyrer 1976:61). While *cabildo* records do not contain estimates of urban mortality, the extraordinary amount of time devoted to discussions of the crisis and the authorization of autopsies indicate the serious threat that the epidemic posed to residents of the city.

Numerous incidents of disease between 1769 and 1779 only accelerated the demographic downturn. Two censuses taken in the late 1770s indicate that the urban population numbered between 21,000 and 25,000, and that 25 to 30 percent of those who died were classified as Indians. Depending upon which figure is used, the number of inhabitants had contracted 16 to 30 percent since the 1740s. The epidemic of 1763–64 probably accounted for much of the loss (Minchom 1986:9).

Five years elapsed between the taking of the censuses and the outbreak of measles in August 1785. Although this epidemic did not have the demographic impact of those of the 1690s, it claimed thousands of lives throughout the *audiencia*. In the city of Quito, the deaths of 2,400 persons meant the loss of approximately 10 percent of the population. In the town of Pelileo, in Ambato, 8 percent of all tributaries perished. Reports from other areas of the highlands suggest that mortality rates averaged between 5 and 10 percent.

Neither demographic trends nor the economic fortunes of the Quito region improved during the remainder of the eighteenth century. The political and social disruption associated with the coming of the wars for independence only led to further loss of population. By 1830, the population of Quito numbered only 21,674 (AMQLC 00064, Padrón 1831).

Public Health and Sanitation

Another way of gaining insight into the impact of epidemics on colonial society is by analyzing the attitudes and responses of local officials and members of the medical profession to issues involving public health and sanitation. While Spanish America remained far from the center of Enlightenment-inspired reforms in education and medicine, many of these new ideas and attitudes did cross the Atlantic. As a result, during the eighteenth century local officials and medical authorities assumed a more active role in dealing with problems affecting the health of Quito's citizens. A survey of *cabildo* records for the city shows that during the 1700s the number of entries concerning health-related issues increased twenty times over the number of entries for the previous two centuries.

Undoubtedly the greatest obstacle to improving the lives and health of Spaniards and natives alike was lack of funds. Quito could never afford to establish its own, permanent *protomedicato*. Throughout the colonial period, *cabildo* members with no medical training assumed many of the responsibilities traditionally associated with that office, including the examination of candidates (and their credentials) for medical, surgical, and apothecary licenses, as well as the inspection and regulation of pharmacies. In addition, the city council also passed ordinances prohibiting untrained, unlicensed individuals from practicing medicine. When such persons were apprehended, it was the *cabildo*'s responsibility to deal with them.

Hospitals and their patients also suffered because of a chronic lack of funds. Even in major cities such as Quito, hospital administrators waged a constant struggle to provide adequate care and medicines to all who needed them. The Bethlemite order ran the city's hospital, as it did in many other areas of Spanish America. According to *cabildo* members, the Bethlemites were dedicated and hardworking and did an excellent job given the limited resources available (AGI, Quito 139, August 24, 1723). The Bethlemites, on the other hand, believed that resources were inadequate. In 1729, brothers requested permission to charge one *tomín* from each native in the *corregimiento* to augment their funds. Two months later, the council denied the request without explanation (AMQLC 00123:154–58).

If financing the hospital in the *audiencia*'s capital was difficult, the situation in provincial capitals was even worse. As late as the last quarter of the eighteenth century, the Riobamba area had no functioning hospital, and the one that was planned was intended to serve over 100,000 people (AGI, Quito 273, Hospitales, Riobamba, 1771–97). Obviously, even the best facilities and staff would be inadequate to serve such a large population. Nonetheless, minor improvements in hospital services did occur. As local governments realized the important responsibilities a hospital could assume, including the control and care of the destitute and chronically ill, they also took seriously the need to provide those institutions with operating expenses. This helps explain the effort made in Riobamba during the 1770s to establish a sizeable endowment for the new hospital. By 1785, at least two hospitals operated in the city of Quito. One served as both a poorhouse and a home for victims of infectious diseases. The other functioned as a hospital for lepers. In an attempt to reduce royal expenditures, in October 1785 the viceroy of New Granada ordered all twenty-two patients in the hospital of San Lázaro transferred to the hospital of Lazarinos in Cartagena. After describing the condition of each patient, the *protomédico* (Dr. Don Bernardo Delgado) concluded that only five patients were capable of making the arduous journey. Not surprisingly, those five were most upset by the prospect of being uprooted and transferred hundreds of miles from their homeland. They told Dr. Delgado that they were terrified of making the trip, especially the voyage from Guayaquil. They warned that if he tried to force them to go, they would flee into the most remote areas of the highlands (ANHQ, Hospitales, caja 4, October 10, 1785). Whether or not the *protomédico* ever complied with the viceregal decree is not clear. In April 1789, however, the *cabildo* met to discuss funding the transfer (AMQLC 00134:103). The most significant aspect about this episode is that for fiscal reasons the viceregal administration attempted to centralize and consolidate the care of "lepers" throughout New Granada.

Perhaps the area in which money could have made the greatest impact on the health of colonial society was sanitation. *Cabildo* members understood that the garbage and human waste fouling local streets provided a breeding ground for disease. In spite of that knowledge, the city was never able to organize services of systematic waste collection. Nor was the city ever able to convince, or force, citizens to accept responsibility for cleaning the street in front of their homes and businesses. Only when threatened by an epidemic did council members take action, and then to little avail. In July 1743, for example, the *audiencia* and Don Joseph Sisiu, a doctor, directed the *cabildo* to publish a ban throughout the city ordering residents and property owners to clean the streets. The ban prohibited shopkeepers from disposing of garbage on the streets where it "rotted and corrupted the air, leading to the epidemic currently claiming many lives." The *audiencia* also directed council members to inspect all mills, bakeries, and shops to discover contaminated wheat and barley flour and to throw all confiscated materials into rivers and ravines (AMQLC 00126:41–42). The *cabildo* also assumed responsibility for such basic services as ensuring a clean and reliable supply of water and repairing public fountains. The city's water originated in mountain streams. In February 1717, *cabildo* members expressed concern that, at some point, contaminated water was entering the delivery system. They requested that an investigation be carried out to determine the source of the problem (AMQLC 00121:72). The same issue arose in January 1787, when the *cabildo* reported that "dirty" water flowed from plaza fountains. Furthermore, the water supply was inadequate, often running for only part of the day. In response, the council delegated two members to inspect the system of channels and pipes that conducted water into the city (AMQLC 00134:10). Without adequate clean water and the maintenance of public fountains, the city would have ceased to function. In spite of the importance of the local water supply, however, the city council never established a permanent office to monitor the system. Only when a crisis arose did the *cabildo* act.

Conclusion

During the eighteenth century, epidemics passed through the city of Quito, on average, every seven years, the actual intervals between outbreaks ranging from four to fourteen years (Table 6.1). Although *cabildo* records present an incomplete history of encounters between the human population and disease, these documents

Table 6.1 Local outbreaks of disease in Quito, 1700–1786

Date	Place	Comments	Source
1700	Quito	"fiebres"	AMQLC 00117
1708	Quito and surrounding area	"catarros"	AMQLC 00119
1709	Quito and surrounding area	"viruelas y diferentes achaques"	AMQLC 00119
1724–26	Quito	"pestilencia y achaques"	AMQLC 00122, 00123
1728–29	Quito and surrounding area	"sarampión"	AGI, Quito, 172
1746	Throughout the *audiencia*	"viruelas"	Herrera and Enríquez 1916, 2:143
1751	Quito	"viruelas"	AJC 01229
1759–60	Quito and surrounding area	"viruelas y peste de Japón"	Polo 1913:81, *Gazeta de Lima*, Nos. 2, 5, 8
1763–64	Quito and surrounding area	"epidemia de peste"	AMQLC 00129
1769	Quito	"esquilencia y disentería"	AMQLC 00130
1777	Quito	"varias enfermedades"	AMQLC 00131
1779	Quito	"mal de pujos"	AMQLC 00132
1780–83	Quito and surrounding area	"disentería y otros enfermedades"	AMQLC 00132
1783	Quito	"viruelas"	AJC 01229
1785–86	Quito and surrounding area	"sarampión"	AMQLC 00133

were much more complete than they had been during the two previous centuries. Certainly council minutes at least made reference to every major epidemic. Similar to most eighteenth-century cities, Quito was an unhealthy place even at the best of times. Poor hygiene and the absence of strict policies of public sanitation encouraged the spread of numerous infections, including tuberculosis, syphilis, and dysentery. Except for the incidence of respiratory illnesses, which increased during the cool, rainy season, from January through May, outbreaks of disease do not appear to be seasonally related, and so could occur during any month of the year.

After 1700, even the most severe outbreaks did not result in the devastating degree of mortality that occurred during the sixteenth century and again during the 1690s. According to Dr. Eugenio Espejo, smallpox was "almost endemic" in the city in 1783. Earlier records describing low rates of mortality during epidemics of both measles and smallpox suggest that these infections may have been an almost constant presence, infecting individuals, especially children, conferring immunity on survivors, and only occasionally flaring to epidemic proportions.

What triggered these major incidents is, in most cases, impossible to say. Perhaps a particularly virulent strain of disease organism was introduced, or perhaps a previously unknown infection appeared, as was the case in 1763–64. But in at least four instances, *cabildo* records clearly attributed the arrival of epidemics to areas outside of the *audiencia*. In 1724, council members described a "peste" as having been introduced. No place of origin, however, was ascribed. On the other hand, entries regarding the smallpox epidemics of 1744–46 and 1758–60 clearly trace the beginnings of those outbreaks to the city of Lima, while the "peste de Japón," which also appeared in 1760, originated in Bogotá and spread south. No available documents indicate that local officials ever attempted to impose quarantines on people or merchandise from any area either within or outside of the *audiencia*. Insofar as *audiencia* officials did impose at least one such quarantine during the seventeenth century, it seems likely that this measure had proven ineffective and had simply been abandoned.

While the history of disease and epidemics in the city of Quito resembles that of other urban centers in Spanish America, the demographic and economic history of the area during the seventeenth and eighteenth centuries does not. As the number of indigenous inhabitants in central Mexico, Peru, and Guatemala continued to decline throughout the first half of the seventeenth century, the native population of Quito entered a period of rapid growth. Then the epidemics and natural disasters of the 1690s dealt the city a blow from which it would never recover. As other parts of the Spanish Empire began to experience significant demographic and economic expansion, food shortages and disease outbreaks hampered recovery in and around Quito. With a population only one-half the size of that of the 1650s, the city sank into an economic depression that only reinforced negative demographic trends. Between 1730 and 1763, the number of urban residents began to increase, but this brief period of recovery ended when an epidemic sent mortality rates climbing. Throughout the remainder of the century, disease and increasing social turmoil again prevented any significant population growth. At the same time, Quito was becoming less a city of Indians and more a city of *castas*.

Epidemiologically, little changed in the city of Quito after 1700. What did change, however, were the attitudes and responses of royal officials who instituted a number of new policies aimed at mitigating the damage caused by epidemics. Although the *cabildo* was the agency ultimately responsible for implementing policies regarding public health, only the *audiencia* possessed the authority to order important policy changes. It was therefore the *audiencia*, not the *cabildo*, that issued the order for all doctors and surgeons to perform autopsies on victims of the epidemic of 1763. Not only did the *audiencia*'s decree force doctors and surgeons to carry out an operation they rarely, if ever, performed; it also forced them to collaborate with each other, an activity they apparently found even more distasteful than conducting autopsies.

During the epidemic of 1785, the *cabildo* again had to force doctors to cooperate in instituting and enforcing emergency measures. For the first time in the city of Quito, the *cabildo* required that each doctor spend three hours per day treating the poor. In addition, the council reached an agreement with local apothecaries to provide free medicine to the public. Finally, the *cabildo* appropriated 500 pesos from the city treasury to distribute among the poor. These unprecedented actions indicate a growing awareness among local officials and physicians that in times of medical crisis they could do much more than simply appeal to God. The spirit of scientific inquiry and experimentation that originated in Europe had arrived in the New World, and with it came a new sense of responsibility, which included taking care of those less fortunate.

Another, less charitable motivation for these changes may also exist. Why, after more than two centuries of allowing or expecting the church to deal with health-related matters, were *cabildo* and *audiencia* members becoming so interested in the operation of hospitals, the care of the chronically ill, and the dispensing of medicines? The answer lies in the intrusive nature of the Bourbon state. The impetus behind the Bourbon Reforms was the need to increase governmental control over the colonies in order to strengthen defenses and increase revenues. One of the most obvious ways for the state to achieve its goals was to curtail the power and influence of the church, the only other institution strong enough to pose a threat to governmental hegemony. Thus the drive for control manifested itself in all arenas, from the implementation of new trade and tax policies to the regulation of hospitals and medical practitioners. Enlightenment notions of charity may account, at least in part, for the increased responsibility shown by local officials. The drive to increase the power and wealth of the state, however, accounted for the rest.

Smallpox and War in Southern Chile in the Late Eighteenth Century

Fernando Casanueva

The Herb Seller (*Florentine Codex*)

In 1791 an epidemic of smallpox broke out in the Reino de Chile, spreading well beyond the limits of imperial control to bring death and disruption to native peoples south of the Bío-Bío River. Here, at the edge of the empire, an outbreak of disease helped make possible effective Spanish penetration of lands that for centuries lay on the other side of the frontier. Drawing on a rich body of documentation (AGI, Chile 197), this chapter pieces together the repercussions of the disease outbreak, showing how smallpox tested the manner in which the various arms of colonial government, as well as Indians themselves, responded to a crisis situation.[1]

The Setting

The most distant of imperial Spain's American possessions, the Reino de Chile was a long strip of land straddled between the Andes and the Pacific Ocean, ex-

[1] Unless indicated otherwise, all quotations in this chapter come from the contents of AGI, Chile 197.

tending uninterrupted from the Atacama Desert in the
north as far south as the Bío-Bío River, the frontier beyond which lived "rebellious" and "heathen" Indians
who resisted Spanish efforts to conquer and convert
them (Figures 7.1, 7.2). Two extensions of the *reino* lay

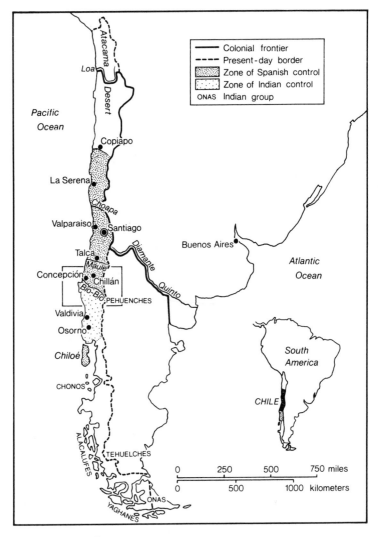

Figure 7.1. CHILE IN THE LATE EIGHTEENTH CENTURY

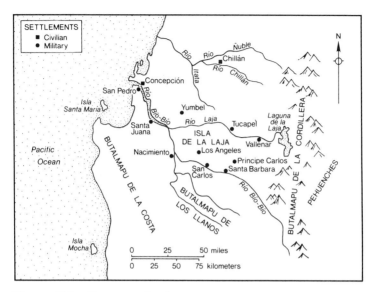

Figure 7.2. Zone of Spanish-Indian conflict in southern Chile

on the far side of the river: the garrison of Valdivia, a Spanish enclave surrounded by unsubjugated terrain, and the Chiloé archipelago, the southernmost Spanish settlement in the New World.

During the second half of the eighteenth century, as elsewhere in the empire, the Reino de Chile experienced profound social, economic, and demographic changes as a result of the Bourbon Reforms (Barbier 1980). In Chile, administrative and financial restructuring enhanced considerably Spanish exploitation of a possession that had long been a burden to the royal treasury, especially in times of war. A striking feature of the way in which the Reino de Chile developed under the Bourbons was the steady growth of the colony's population. The number of people living in the diocese of Santiago doubled twice in the course of the eighteenth century, increasing from 83,750 in 1700 to 182,514 in 1777, and reaching 382,704 by 1813. During this same period, the population of the diocese of Concepción doubled roughly every twenty-five years, growing from 11,419 in 1719 to 200,323 in 1812 (Carmagnani 1967-68: 183–84). The official population of the Reino de Chile during the last years of colonial rule may therefore be estimated at around 600,000, but was likely higher due to statistical error and omission. To this estimate must also be added some 27,000 inhabitants of the Chiloé archipelago; the combined total of 10,000 inhabitants of the enclaves of Valdivia and, after 1796, Osorno; and the "rebel and heathen" Indians, numbering at least 200,000, who lived south of the Bío-Bío (Casanueva 1981:13).

Another manifestation of the Bourbon Reforms in Chile was the state's assertion of authority over colonial space in founding thirty important settlements in the Central Valley between 1740 and 1795. The residents of these towns and cities contributed significantly to the public revenues of the *reino*, which jumped from 100,000 pesos at the beginning of the eighteenth century to over 600,000 pesos by 1806 (Barros Arana 1884–1902, 7:333–34). Most of these revenues were generated by agriculture and cattle raising and, to a lesser extent, the mining economy of the north.

Two completely different societies came face to face at the Bío-Bío River. Firmly established to the north of the river, protected by a chain of sixteen garrisons stretching from the mountains to the sea, stood a colonial society, one characterized by European notions of order and government, class divisions, an army equipped with swords and firearms, and an agricultural economy in which Spanish landowners exploited an indigenous work force. South of the Bío-Bío lived several native groups described by Pierre Clastres (1974) as "societies opposed to the state," among them the Mapuches (known to Spaniards as the Araucanos), the Huilliches, the Cuncos, the Pehuenches, the Puelches, and the Poyas. These peoples lived in ways that differed markedly not only from cultural norms north of the Bío-Bío but that also contrasted with the more advanced native American civilizations the Spaniards encountered in Mexico, Guatemala, and Peru. Mapuche society, about which we know more than any other in the region, was characterized by large, polygenic family units, each of which was composed of 40 to 100 individuals. Many families functioned as independent tribes, or *rehues*, which occupied an autonomous unit of land and which were ruled by chiefs, or *loncos*, whom the Spaniards referred to as *caciques*. The position of *lonco* was a hereditary one. Large *rehues* were made up of between 1,500 and 2,000 people. A group of nine *rehues* formed an *ayllarehue*, in which the highest office was that of *apo-gulmen*. In turn, each group of five *ayllarehues* constituted a *butalmapu*, whose chief was called a *toqui*. He would be the oldest member of the group, the head of a noble lineage and of all five *ayllarehues*. This position was also hereditary. In addition, *butalmapus* were presided over by two other *toquis*, one a warrior chief (*nguentoqui*) and another a peacemaker chief (*nguenvogue*). The pattern into which *butalmapus* were arranged territorially corresponded more or less with the three physiographic divisions of Chile: one *butalmapu* controlled the Cordillera de la Costa (*lobquen-mapu*); a second the plains, or Central Valley (*lelbun-mapu*); and a third the Cordillera de los Andes (*inapire-mapu*). The Pehuenches, nomads who lived on both sides of the Cordillera de los Andes, made up a fourth *butalmapu* (Casanueva 1981).

The final, all-important Spanish settlement of the Bío-Bío region took place during the second half of the eighteenth century, when soldiers and farmers penetrated well beyond the acknowledged frontier that the river represented up to that time. The reasons behind this belated thrust were primarily demographic and economic. During this period, the subsistence economy geared to the production of cereals and cattle for the

garrisons located along the frontier became more export-
oriented, producing cereals not just for an expanding
Chilean population but also for other parts of the viceroyalty of Peru (Carmagnani 1973:249). Labor require-
ments meant an increased need for permanent agricultural workers who would live on Spanish *haciendas*, the
centers of production.

Much of this economic and demographic transformation came about through the initiatives of Ambrosio
O'Higgins, one of Bourbon Spain's most gifted states-
men. O'Higgins, an army officer of Irish extraction, had
come to realize that founding towns artificially in pre-
carious locations was not the best method of defending
the frontier. The answer, he believed, lay in resettling
the region with the aim of expanding agricultural production and increasing the number of cattle raised. In
this way, military garrisons would always be well stocked
with food in case of emergency, but they would have a
support base behind them. Following the Indian uprising of 1766, O'Higgins organized the resettlement of the
Isla de la Laja, a region between the Laja River and the
northern banks of the Bío-Bío. O'Higgins considered
the Isla de la Laja to be "the key part of our frontier with
the heathen *butalmapus*." He granted land to families
who came from various parts of the diocese of Concepción and established two strategic garrisons, Príncipe
Carlos and Vallenar, thus strengthening those already
built at Purén, Santa Bárbara, and Los Angeles—garrisons that stood opposite the *butalmapu* of the Central
Valley and on the mountain passes occupied by the Pehuenches. He also located general army headquarters at
Los Angeles, which lay in the center of the Isla de la
Laja. Henceforth, as O'Higgins himself wrote to the
Marqués de Bajamar, "many of those who come to settle
in the Isla are enticed by land which is today the most
densely populated and the most fruitful in trade and
agriculture in all the province of Concepción" (AGI,
Chile 197).

It was within this particular setting, as an expansionist colonial state moved to assert its hegemony over lands hitherto beyond its control, that smallpox broke out between June and October 1791 among Indians belonging to the four *butalmapus* south of the Bío-Bío River.

Origins and Diffusion of the Epidemic

It is difficult to establish precisely the origin of this outbreak of smallpox. In all likelihood the epidemic was a continuation or a recurrence of the disease that laid to waste the population of Concepción in 1790. According to Capt. Fermín Villagrán, writing in June 1791 to the commander of the garrison at Los Angeles, Pedro Nolasco del Río, the epidemic first appeared south of the Bío-Bío at Boroa, from where it spread to Repocura (AGI, Chile 197). Both Boroa and Repocura are located in the Central Valley, but their inhabitants were in trading contact with the nomadic Pehuenche, whose movements facilitated not just the exchange of goods but also the spread of disease and infection from one *butalmapu* to another.

By August, smallpox had extended as far as the *butalmapu* of the Cordillera de la Costa. In this instance the contagion was spread as a result of another social network of primary importance to native groups: the ritual burial of *loncos*, which were focused around well-attended collective ceremonies. In this particular case, an Indian who had attended the burial of Don Agustín Yaupi-labquen, the *lonco* of Lleu-Lleu on the Araucanian coast whose cause of death is known to be smallpox, inadvertently carried the virus back to his *rehue*. According to a report filed by Manuel de Santa María, commander of the garrison at Arauco, smallpox then spread quickly over a distance of some five or six leagues, about thirty kilometers (AGI, Chile 197).

That the sickness diffused over a considerable area may easily be deduced from the testimonies that Indians passed on to *capitanes de amigos* (friendly captains). The Indians of Quechereguas, for example, informed Captain Villagrán that the disease "is now present among all four *butalmapus*." The *cacique* of Chacaico, Don Pablo Millagueque, likewise declared to Villagrán that his people "no longer try to guess the source of the infection, since it is everywhere." In response to the questions of Lt. Ignacio Cotar, Curilab, a *cacique* of Tub-Tub, stated that smallpox had "engulfed the land," adding that "few of these who were infected have been left alive." Llanquinao, another *cacique*, told Cotar that the land of his people "is now riddled with pestilence."

Spanish military envoys made it clear why they thought smallpox spread among the Indians so virulently. After a tour of inspection of the region affected, Captain Villagrán wrote to the commander of the garrison at Los Angeles on July 20, 1791 (AGI, Chile 197). Villagrán stated: "I find that this occurs after their drinking parties, and at the burial ceremonies held for those who have died after contracting the same infection. That is what happened to the *cacique* Catrirupai who, having attended the burial of the Pehuenche Chibcalabquen, brother of the *cacique* Quintrelb, was infected with the disease, and died from it."

These "drinking parties," which sometimes lasted days on end, were the inevitable postscript to all Mapuche social gatherings, or *cahuines*. *Cahuines* were bonding rituals that united the various families and clans that made up a *rehue*, and also the various *rehues* of which an *ayllarehue* was comprised. On some occasions *cahuines* were held on an even larger scale, at the *butalmapu* level, especially at times when war had been declared or a peace accord had been reached.

Many events could provide the pretext for a *cahuin*: collective work, weddings, burials, the end of trials of strength and of sporting or battle skills. These social gatherings, which expressed the generosity a chief owed his people, were rounded off with a huge meal, during which copious amounts of alcohol were consumed. They were described with obvious contempt as "drinking parties" by contemporary Spaniards, especially missionaries, who saw them as a major obstacle to the process of Christian conversion and who condemned their outward, Dionysiac appearance without understanding the real reasons for the existence and survival of such activities.

The Colonial Response

What most concerned the colonial administration was the possibility that smallpox might spread to the Isla de la Laja or even reach the Spanish enclave in Valdivia and the Chiloé archipelago, causing harm to Spanish inhabitants there. This concern forced the authorities to exploit fully every mechanism of colonial control in an attempt, first, to restrict the spread of disease and, second, to eradicate it. Correspondence from Governor O'Higgins to army officers serving in the frontier zone shows clearly the extent of government preoccupation. The route taken by this correspondence illustrates how different arms of the state apparatus, whether political, military, or religious, responded to the crisis.

QUARANTINE

The first measure adopted by the colonial administration was to impose quarantine regulations in the Bío-Bío region in general, thereby seeking to suspend all lines of communication and contact between Spaniards and Indians. The commanders of the main frontier garrisons at Los Angeles, Nacimiento, Arauco, San Carlos, and Tucapel were to play important roles in executing this order. These officers were expected to gain control of the mountain passes connecting coastal and interior *butalmapus*. With the assistance of *caciques* who chose to cooperate with the Spanish army, known as *caciques gobernadores*, they were also expected to monitor movement along streams and rivers, thus helping to seal hitherto open thoroughfares and remove infected Indians from areas considered to lie within colonial jurisdiction. Reality, however, was quite different from intent. First, in certain rural districts, Spaniards and Indians lived side by side, sharing the same area of land. Around Arauco, for instance, the commander of the garrison wrote in a letter to his superiors dated August 25 that it was difficult to control the spread of disease "since it is all open country in which Spaniards and Indians live interspersed" (AGI, Chile 197). A second obstacle to the successful operation of quarantine was ongoing trade. The colonial authorities permitted, or tolerated, commercial exchanges between the Pehuenches, traditionally Spanish allies in the fight against the Indians of the Central Valley, and the garrisons at Santa Bárbara and San Carlos. Were this traffic to be prohibited, Spaniards would lose favor with the Pehuenches. In fact, it had been Spanish officials who first encouraged bartering between the Pehuenches and the garrisons, not only to cement the alliance but also to make the nomads dependent on Spanish products, especially on wine and metals (Métraux 1943). With this in mind, Francisco de la Mata recommended that the commanders of garrisons proceed "with the greatest prudence in granting passes allowing them [the Pehuenches] to deal with our people" (AGI, Chile 197). The chief administrator thus decided to grant freedom of movement to the Pehuenches, justifying his stance by observing, on July 29, that "as they show no signs of infection so far, I have, with the necessary degree of caution, allowed them to trade meat, apples, and so forth, but not suspicious-looking woolen items. They cannot live without us, and these measures give them more reason to believe this, so that they may carry on calmly in this knowledge" (AGI, Chile 197).

THE "EYES AND EARS" OF THE CROWN

The next step taken by the colonial administrators consisted of sending *capitanes de amigos*, the "eyes and ears"
of the Crown, to travel beyond the Bío-Bío and visit *rehues* that had been infected by the disease. These scouts
were to find out exactly what state of affairs prevailed
and the extent to which smallpox had developed. The
expeditions that set out from the frontier garrisons to
explore the infected lands did not have an easy task.
With its harsh winters and heavy rains, its swollen rivers and rugged terrain, natural conditions south of the
Bío-Bío had always guaranteed that relations between
Spaniards and Indians were in large part determined by
the rhythm of the seasons. The onset of winter, therefore, made it all the more difficult to accomplish reconnaissance operations. On the other hand, it was necessary to act quickly before summer arrived, for better
weather and travelling conditions during this season
would mean an increase in trade and contact, which
might exacerbate the situation considerably.

The reports that the *capitanes de amigos* delivered to
their superiors are revealing as well as informative.
They enable us to ascertain not only the course the disease took as it passed from one *rehue* to another but also
afford insights into relations between two mutually hostile societies, which, for the moment, lived side by side
under terms of uneasy peace.

ASSISTANCE AND MEDICATION OFFERED TO THE INDIANS

The *capitanes de amigos* sent on scouting expeditions
were also entrusted with the task of offering the Indians
the use of doctors, medicines, "curative methods," and
"healthy foods" and giving them useful advice on how
to prevent or put an end to the sickness that killed or
debilitated them.

We must remember that, in the eyes of imperial Spain,

the Indians were the royal subjects of His Catholic Majesty in spite of their also being "rebellious infidels." Indians, therefore, were deserving of the concern shown by the Crown's representatives. Governor O'Higgins, in a letter addressed to Chief Administrator de la Mata on July 21, insisted on this point:

> I advise you, Sir, that you see that these orders be made understood, through communication between the commanders and the Indian emissaries, to the *caciques* and principal *ayllus*, in order that those who need help may come and ask for it, but also so that they know that if they comply with the King's kind wishes I can offer them the help they need, treat them as a part of the state in their capacity as subjects of His Majesty. They will also retain his friendship and keep the other promises of loyalty they have made to this government.

That same day, however, in a letter addressed to Fray Francisco Pérez, the father superior of the Seminary of Franciscan Missionaries at Chillán, O'Higgins made perfectly clear the political objectives that lay behind his humanitarian actions:

> I have decided that, under the present circumstances in which smallpox has spread so quickly amongst the *butalmapus* and has caused the ravages of which Your Reverend Father is surely aware, I must offer them every kind of help possible. They should be ready and willing to accept this help in accordance with the inducements of humanity and the political goals recommended by our Sovereign Rulers, which is to possess as assets the souls of these natives through charitable acts.

The "political goals" O'Higgins alluded to include the neutralization of indigenous society through commerce, evangelization, the education of *cacique* offspring, and the convening of *parlamentos*, assemblies held to celebrate the successful negotiation of a peace treaty. Spaniards could then proceed to occupy Indian lands, or rather, to repossess towns and territory south of the Bío-Bío that had been lost since the great uprising of 1598 (Jara 1971). The recovery of these lands and settlements would permit the Crown to govern the Reino de Chile as a single unified territory, stretching from the Atacama Desert to the Chiloé archipelago. In effect, smallpox would be manipulated by the Spaniards as a means of carrying out the reconquest long dreamed of by successive governors.

O'Higgins, who possessed a thorough knowledge both of the frontier and his men, gave Chief Administrator de la Mata orders to the effect that only those "friendly captains and lieutenants" who were "most honorable and rational" should be sent to make contact with the *rehues* that had been affected by the disease. This was O'Higgins's way of saying he was well aware that the abuses, acts of force, and transactions that "the King's eyes and ears" inflicted upon the *rehues* had, on occasion, provoked rebellion.

Officers sent into the field were to inform Indians "of the curative method practiced by Spaniards" according to the instructions issued by the chief Crown physician during the epidemic that hit the city of Concepción in 1790 (Encina and Castedo 1980, 1:445). Unfortunately, we have no knowledge of what these instructions might have been. Officers were also to give the Indians "healthy foods" and medicines, of which we also have no record, with directions to "take the remedies according to their taste and their experience of its effects" (AGI, Chile 197). Indians, of course, were to be promised that doctors would be sent to assist them, along with a healer who had proven himself "useful" while engaged in fighting the epidemic at Concepción. O'Higgins also arranged for inoculation to be carried out should the virus reach the Isla de la Laja and endanger lives there. Naturally, these arrangements applied only to Spanish residents, for experience had long shown the Indians to be suspicious of any cure administered by the enemy.[2]

---

[2]Inoculation was carried out in Chile as early as 1765, in large part due to the hard work and expertise of Pedro Manuel de Chaparro, a missionary

The above stipulations were accompanied by certain suggestions that *capitanes de amigos* were supposed to make to the Indians, with the explicit aim of placing restrictions or bans on certain activities. One suggestion concerned what and what not to drink. Captain Villagrán advised Curincaguel, *lonco* of the *rehue* of Angol, "that while they were afflicted by the disease they should drink infusions made with *palqui* and other fresh herbs, and that they refrain from drinking *chicha*, wine and liquor, as they had been warned before." Another recommendation concerned burial habits. On August 31 Villagrán warned Tronolab and Rucalab, the *loncos* of the *rehues* of Quechereguas, "that the burials of those who died from the disease should only be attended and executed by members of their household." Other Indians, he went on, "should avoid contact with infected people until forty days have passed, because if things fail to be done in this way, then the contagion will not be eliminated." Villagrán also maintained that "compassion should be shown towards the children and wives" of the deceased "because they would all die of the fever when the hot season arrives" (AGI, Chile 197).

THE FINANCIAL BURDEN OF ASSISTANCE

Assistance to the Indians was financed by the royal treasury under the terms of the *agasajo*, a policy of "kindness" or "good treatment" designed to help preserve a strategic relationship between Spaniards and the people they had come to conquer. Awarding "kindnesses" usually involved offering gifts to the Indians to ensure their friendship or neutrality. The policy also entailed organizing feasts and ceremonies to accompany *parlamentos* (Casanueva 1987). Dr. Pérez de Uriondo, fiscal of the *audiencia*, described the policy well in a letter to Gover-

---

with experience in medical care. During the smallpox epidemic that swept through Chile in 1765, Fray Pedro inoculated some 5,000 people, thereby halting the spread of disease. See Encina and Castedo (1980:300–301).

nor O'Higgins on September 27: "The liberality with which funds for the costs of medicines and other vital expenses are being charged, without firm justification, to the *agasajos* and other treasury accounts is considered absolutely essential so that we can ingratiate ourselves to the Indians and thus entice them to our side by means of gentleness and persuasion."

As might be expected, certain limits were imposed on this economic "liberality," for the authorities always insisted on providing the Indians with the "cheapest and easiest remedies to administer." For example, Fray Francisco Pérez, who had been ordered by O'Higgins and de la Mata to help Indians in the infected area, informed his secular superiors that in the garrison of Los Angeles, missionaries would be provided with all they needed "to enter and subsist in that land." Fray Francisco made it clear, however, when writing to de la Mata on August 12, that missionaries "should never exceed levels of expenditure judged to be prudent and necessary." Pérez also believed that his brothers "will readily comply because they are rightly convinced that their being sent is not an excuse to indulge themselves and lead a pleasurable life, but to suffer in the name of Jesus Christ in an exercise most fitting to apostolic ministry." The father superior was acting not only with the humility required of a man of his position but also with full knowledge of the keen vigilance with which the royal treasury watched over the king's finances.

The mutual, deep-rooted suspicion with which Spaniards and Indians regarded each other in the frontier zone surfaces in official correspondence, even as the threat of war throughout the region diminished. Spaniards spoke of their "liberality" and "charitable measures." They congratulated themselves for acting with "the wisdom and firmness the situation requires." To them, however, Indians were still "ignorant and superstitious barbarians" who were "not moved by reason, but by their whims"—lesser beings whose rhetoric "like everything they say, has no structure" and who clung, always, to "heathen beliefs." From the Indian point of view, the greed of the Spaniards was perceived as insatiable. Unfortunately, we can see things only indirectly through Indian eyes, for they left behind few first-person testimonies. Their perspective comes through in the telling words used by Fray Francisco Pérez to convince Melignir and other *cacique* allies in the garrison of Nacimiento to enter the lands of infected "infidels": "Let it be known that those whom you call *cari patirus*, the fathers in brown habits, have no desire for your lands, your estates, or your women. What we desire is your greater happiness and advancement, best fulfilled in accordance with the most righteous intentions and Christian wishes of our Catholic Majesty."[3]

Spanish Political Concerns at the Time of the Epidemic

The presence of *capitanes de amigos* among the Indians, then, did not serve merely to give the impression that smallpox was being treated in a humane fashion and that it was being prevented from spreading north of the Bío-Bío. The role of these officers was considerably more expedient.

During the second half of the eighteenth century, hostile relations between Spaniards and Indians were modified as a result of two phenomena. First, due to the forging of peacekeeping pacts, the creation of stable trading relationships, and the patient labor of Jesuit and Franciscan missionaries, the Araucanian war lost the intensity with which it had been waged in earlier centuries, even if the Crown still thought it prudent to maintain a chain of fortifications along the frontier. Second, native peoples south of the Bío-Bío began at this time

[3] The Franciscans were called "fathers in brown habits" by the Indians to distinguish them from Jesuits, who wore black habits. Father Pérez wrote to Governor O'Higgins on September 24, 1791.

to migrate eastward across the Andes to settle lands in the southern part of the viceroyalty of Buenos Aires, lands that already were occupied by groups such as the Ranquelches, the Aucas, and the Tehuelches. This migration sparked an increase in intertribal feuding and caused an intensification in the level of aggression shown by Indians towards Spanish settlements on both sides of the mountains. Tension was released in the form of *malocas*, or attacks, on Spanish garrisons and farms. These attacks were carried out with the aim of robbing cattle or kidnapping Spanish settlers, both men and women. Afterwards, ransom would invariably consist of demands for horses, cattle, or firearms. Thus, somewhat paradoxically, as a state of all-out war was reduced, local raids and skirmishes increased.

The Crown's policy in Chile involved creating alliances with some tribes, especially the Pehuenches, to fight against others, but the Spaniards themselves were not a direct cause of intertribal warfare. The Pehuenches became their closest allies, at once indispensable and dependent, while to a certain extent the Spaniards became arbitrators between all native groups, a role that the Crown was anxious to preserve at all cost.

To implement this policy, the colonial authorities had recourse to a system of middlemen: *comisarios de naciones* (superintendents of Indian nations), *capitanes de amigos, tenientes de amigos* (friendly lieutenants), and *lenguas* (interpreters). The *comisarios* were the links between the *capitanes de amigos,* who played an important role as Indian advisors, and the principal military and civil authorities.

The appearance of smallpox threatened to upset the delicate balance that the Spaniards had established after much time and effort. Whenever *loncos* died came the risk that alliances forged by them would disintegrate. The authority of the *lonco,* even more so that of the *apogulmen,* was neither absolute nor undisputed. Divisions and rivalries within native society were common, and the Spaniards were well aware that certain *rehues*, led by adult males with aspirations of becoming *loncos* or *apo-gulmens* themselves, had to be watched carefully. *Loncos* had to maintain a constant vigil over these *aucas* (rebels) or *mocetones* (strong young men) since their actions could easily undermine authority and diminish personal prestige. This was an aspect of Mapuche society that many Spanish observers commented on. Accustomed to European mores, which promoted recognition of (and respect for) social hierarchy, Spaniards could not grasp that a young warrior might argue with or even strike his leader (Quiroga 1979:25).

The *capitanes de amigos* were thus charged, among other things, with reinforcing the authority of *loncos* loyal to the Crown. When, for example, Captain Villagrán suggested to the *lonco* of Nininco, Don Miguel Millagueque, "that he advise his people to behave quietly and peacefully" during a visit by the governor, Don Miguel replied that he would "do everything His Lordship suggested, and that he would see that his *mocetones* were under control so that there would be no cause for reproach" (AGI, Chile 197).

In some *butalmapus*, *capitanes de amigos* would artfully influence the most respected *loncos* to cajole weaker ones into following government directives. Captain Villagrán, for example, having been instructed by the commander of the garrison at Nacimiento, manipulated certain *caciques* from Angol to persuade other *loncos* of the *ayllarehue* to accept the presence of Franciscan missionaries in their *rehues*. Villagrán wrote: "In the knowledge that the *caciques* of Angol exert influence in other native settlements, I made every possible effort to convince them of the benefits which Your Lordship's kindness would afford them. We succeeded, in fact, in getting the *cacique* Melignir to go to the plaza at Nacimiento so that he could speak with, and make himself known to, the missionaries."

Another cause for concern at the time of the epidemic

was the frequency with which *malocas* were being carried out. In view of such instability and flux, it was crucial that Spaniards maintain their role as arbitrators. An awareness of this state of affairs was best expressed by the commander of the garrison at Nacimiento, Tadeo Rivera, who wrote to the chief administrator:

The poor living conditions that prevail in these settlements are a result of robberies and *malocas* in which Indians kill one another and destroy the *haciendas*. This leads me to think the worst of them and to consider all this a fatal beginning, for these acts are almost identical to those which marked the last uprising. Your Grace will recall that they did the same thing then, robbing, killing, and destroying property, before hunger and greed led them to do what happened, although things were not as safe then as they are today.

The fear that Rivera expresses here was a real one, for tribal wars triggered never-ending reprisals. These, in turn, disrupted normal agricultural routines and caused food shortages and hunger, which only exacerbated the crisis brought about by smallpox. The Spaniards well understood that social breakdown and disorder of this magnitude might degenerate into a general uprising, as had occurred in 1598, 1655, 1723, and 1766 (Encina and Castedo 1961, 1:135, 223–24).

The Epidemic and the "Spiritual Conquest"

Another measure taken by Spanish officials to combat the outbreak of smallpox was to send missionaries from the Franciscan Seminary at Chillán among the Indians. As they tended the sick, missionaries sought also to provide for the spiritual needs of the afflicted. A letter written by O'Higgins on July 21 to Father Superior Francisco Pérez sums up the government's position:

I have authorized the chief administrator and commander general of the frontier that he have distributed [to the Indians] those things I judge to be necessary, namely medicines, healthy foods, and cures, to be provided by the friendly captains and lieutenants in their settlements. I have also made it clear that Christian missionaries from Arauco, Santa Juana, and Santa Bárbara, and others from the Colegio de Conversores, would be good workers. Your Reverend Father knows best how to choose and deploy missionaries full of zeal, patience, and faith, all of which are necessary if, at the same time as showing compassion towards physical health, the opportunity is also taken to convert Indians to Our Faith, or help many of those wretches in their dying moments.

As far as O'Higgins was concerned, the epidemic served as an ideal pretext for renewing Spanish efforts at converting the Indians to Christianity, a process that had been seriously disrupted by the uprising of 1766 and the expulsion of missionaries by the Indians the following year.

Fray Francisco's reply is also instructive. In a letter to O'Higgins dated August 12, he writes:

Since this work comes naturally to those of us in apostolic ministry, there will be no shortage of necessary assistance from this community, whose members offer themselves to the challenge of making this sacrifice in the service of both Majesties. I hope that by this means we shall bring Faith through Holy Baptism to adults as well as to children, and even attain the cherished goal of establishing missions. To this end, and in view of the great number who might be led to the grace of religion and the state, I have no hesitation in pledging our careful cooperation and will ensure that the missionaries I have chosen for this expedition work without pause or rest.

Fray Francisco selected the four best missionaries from those available at the Chillán Seminary: Antonio de la Vega, Miguel López, Francisco Javier de Alday, and Matías Martínez, described as "well-educated in the language of these natives, known for their zeal, and proven in their ability to work and to organize." Pérez set out with his disciples for the garrison of Los Angeles on August 15, only twelve days after the commander of the garrison, Pedro Nolasco del Río, had warned that great precautions must be taken. Nolasco advised that the missionaries "should not prepare themselves for this expedition" until the results of Captain Villagrán's expedition were known. He also suggested delaying the expedition until it had been established that the Indians were willing to allow the Franciscans to enter their territory and undertake "the proposed task" (AGI, Chile 197). Nolasco's wariness was well founded. The report that Villagrán presented, based on a week's reconnaissance of "the lands of the interior," was not encouraging. Indians from Angol, Nininco, Quechereguas, Chacaico, Renaico, and Tub-Tub declared that they "had found herbs with which to cure themselves." Two *loncos*, Don Miguel Millagueque of Nininco and Curilab of Tub-Tub, accepted offers of medical assistance, but there was unanimous rejection of the plan to send in missionaries. Villagrán stated bluntly: "As for the missionaries, and the idea that they offer comfort during the present crisis, the Indians all refuse, saying that they do not need them" (AGI, Chile 197).

Fray Francisco responded to Villagrán's report by writing to O'Higgins on September 24, upon his return to Chillán. The manner in which he expresses himself affords valuable insight into the relationship between the church and the state, and the ultimate goals of both institutions:

The distress that the Indians' refusal caused us was as great as had been our hopes that access would be granted us, since we know that this would be a most advantageous step to take in achieving the spiritual conquest of these *butalmapus*. And although I urged that the enterprise be undertaken with a missionary accompanying each officer so that the proposal might be made with the utmost passion and effectiveness, this could not be done because, with great wisdom, the commander foresaw some of the fatal consequences that might ensue.

The "consequences" to which Pérez refers were well-recognized by the various branches of the colonial regime: suspension of peacekeeping arrangements, the breaking-off of alliances, and mass rebellion among all four *butalmapus*, which might trigger renewed attacks on garrisons and missions along the frontier and thus constitute a threat to colonial order throughout the entire Reino de Chile. It is also important to observe how Fray Francisco, writing at the end of the eighteenth century, speaks of the "spiritual conquest" of the Indians, employing a term more commonly associated with the first century of Spanish rule in America (Ricard 1966).

The words with which Pérez addressed the *lonco* Melignir in the garrison at Nacimiento are illustrative of Franciscan "political" rhetoric, very different in tone from that of the Jesuits. Fray Francisco tried throughout, as did other members of his order, to convince the Indians that it was necessary for them to take advantage of the governor's kind disposition and accept the missionaries he was sending:

I put it to them that Your Lordship, in expressing his great love for them, had shown them and the other natives a mark of concern that is without parallel, that he was providing them with timely assistance so that the disease would not put an end to them, and so that if any of them should die, they would not die like animals; that he had employed us so that we might help them in this great conflict, in matters worldly as well as spiritual, because he knew that no other would regard them with so much love and compassion, would look after them so carefully nor work on their behalf with such selflessness; that Your Lordship could feel nothing less than resentment against all those who were contemptuous of, or did not acknowledge, this most exceptional favor, having done it with no thought or intention other than that of looking after the common good of all. But I told them I expected that the people of Angol, who are exceptionally distinguished in their displays of affection, would not follow the bad example of the rest, because then his anger would have been greater, and his bitterness more justified.

Death on the Frontier: Indigenous Response

Native peoples affected by smallpox confronted it using the now traditional methods that experience had taught them after two and a half centuries of contact with innumerable sicknesses brought by Europeans and Africans to the New World. These methods, which Commander Tadeo Rivera of Nacimiento described as "strange and barbarous," involved the following remedies.

Consumption of medicinal herbs and plants. Native peoples chose medicinal herbs and plants from the vast array to be found among the flora of the Araucania (Rosales 1877–78, 1:231; J. I. Molina 1978:33–44). One plant used frequently, drunk with darnel, was *palqui*. According to the Jesuit missionary Diego de Rosales, one of the foremost authorities on Chilean flora, *palqui* was used by the Indians to treat "high fevers, was squeezed on wounds to remove a cancer or prevent it from spreading, and to clean wounds and leave them properly disinfected" (Rosales 1877–78, 1:236). *Chilco*, a tree similar to the pomegranate, was considered by Rosales (1877–78, 1:230) to be "the best medicine for the treatment of pain while urinating." Rosales (1877–78, 1:224) also believed that a species of the *canelo* tree was used "by medicine men and witchdoctors [*machis*] for medical cures and to summon up the devil." Another plant used in times of sickness was *concho de aniltun*, of which there is no mention in Padre Diego's classic work. The Indians must also have used other plants from "the natural pharmacy of herbs," as the Jesuit called it, to combat the high temperatures, shivering, vomiting, and head and back aches associated with the onset of smallpox.

Frequent baths. Scattered throughout official correspondence are references to the fact that Indians "bathe very often." The Mapuche and other native groups in Chile paid attention to personal hygiene at all times, something that struck Spaniards as unusual, for they

themselves were not disposed towards regular bathing
(Nuñez Pineda y Bascunan 1863, 3:58).

Staying in bed. One item of correspondence states that
"the number of days in bed varies according to the extent of the smallpox sores." This is surely a reference to
the different stages in the advance of the infection, from
the appearance of first symptoms through the period in
which pocks broke out (in blemishes, pimples, blisters,
and pustules) to the moment of suppuration.

Isolation of infected groups. The commander of the garrison at Los Angeles stated that certain precautions were
taken by the Indians "so as not to have contact with
infected groups. This has been done in Colguë, Bureo,
Mulchén, and Rucalgue, all of which lie on the Bío-Bío
frontier, and so far none of these places has been affected by the contagion." Indians would prevent any
stranger from entering their *rehue*. At Angol, Captain
Villagrán was informed that "up to the present the disease had not penetrated" and that the Indians "hoped
it never would," primarily because of the "great care
they take not to allow any outsider to enter."

Rituals and Interpretations

In Mapuche territory, the above cures and preventions
were accompanied by propitiatory ceremonies called
machitunes, referred to by the Spaniards as *curaciones su-
persticiosas* (superstitious treatments). A consequence of
the *admapu,* the spirit of veneration and commitment
that the Mapuches felt towards the customs of their
forefathers, this was a devotional tradition and a constant means of referring back to the world of their
mythic ancestors.

Mapuche custom held that if death did not come in
battle (considered by warriors the most honorable way
to die), it was brought about, as were all misfortunes,
by an evil spirit known as the *huecube,* which had been
sent by a *calcu,* or witch, consulted and paid to cause

harm by some enemy, either an individual or an entire family. The mourners of the victim would then consult a *machi*, usually a female shaman, or a *dungube*, a soothsayer, who would determine during a *machitun* ceremony the source of the evil spirit and identify the perpetrator. With this knowledge, the aggrieved family would call together its relations and organize a punitive expedition, which, in turn, would provoke the response of those whom they had attacked. Thus a vicious circle was created, providing such warlike societies a reason to be permanently at war.

Logically, then, many Indians attributed the epidemic of 1791 to the black arts of their enemies, be they Spaniards or rival *rehues*. Captain Villagrán, for example, attributed the collective response of the *rehue* of Quechereguas to suggestions made by him that they stop attending burial ceremonies and that the dead "be interred by those of their own household." The Indians declared to Villagrán that they "were not dying from the pestilence, but as a result of the harm that witches were inflicting on those who were infected." Similarly, the *cacique* known as Curilab informed Ignacio Cotar that at Painecura "most have been buried, although they are not dying because of disease, but because of witchcraft." Another person, Lieutenant Lizama, also told Commander del Río of the belief, held by the Indians of Repocura, that the epidemic was a form of revenge planned by Spaniards for the attack and robbery that *rehues* from the Cordillera de la Costa had carried out on the party led by the bishop of Concepción, José Marán, in 1787. One of the smallpox victims in Repocura was a *cacique* named Cayullanca, the chief instigator of the *maloca*. Lieutenant Lizama "heard it said that those Indians were complaining a great deal, attributing the epidemic, in their barbarous ignorance, to curses cast in order to avenge that occurrence" (AGI, Chile 197).

The *machi* was responsible not only for discovering the identities of those who sent the evil spirit, but also for trying to heal the victim, usually administering the traditional cures and medicines. The *machitun*, however, was always a source of potential infection, for it was attended by relatives and friends who were not given any of the treatments extended to the patient and who were thus, if not previously exposed to smallpox, considerably at risk.

Burials also required the presence of numerous relatives and friends of the deceased and thus facilitated infection. The infection could be transmitted either directly, from one person to another, or indirectly, thanks to the strength of the virus, which was able to survive periods of extreme heat and dryness as people handled contaminated objects.

Unanimous rejection of the Franciscan missionaries can therefore be attributed not only to inherent native suspicion of the strange, unarmed *cari-patirus* who wished to convert them, but also to their understandable fear that "the fathers in brown habits" might bring infection with them. *Rehues* from the *butalmapu* of the Central Valley gave a clear response to the *capitanes de amigos* who offered to send them missionaries. They told one of the captains, Tadeo Rivera, that they would "continue to refuse to admit the fathers, saying that they will kill them in boiling water, as has happened to other Spaniards." Under these circumstances, Indians often regarded missionaries as the precursors or emissaries of death, since it was the dying whom they would try to baptize or have confess. Miguel de Olivares (1874: 289–90), himself an experienced Jesuit missionary and an important colonial chronicler, observed:

Rebel Indians live according to their customs, which they favor very much, and very few of them have ever made a good confession in their life. Among the bad or worst things are the witchdoctors who live amidst the Indians, who speak with the devil, and who sow discord among them. They tell them that confession and baptism are Spanish inventions designed to deprive them of life. And so it is very rare for an Indian who is dying to ask or send for a priest to be called in order that he might baptize him or hear his confession.

The Final Outcome

For whatever reason, most likely a combination of the health measures implemented by both frontier societies, the most serious effects of the epidemic had been felt by the end of 1791. On October 14, Commander Rivera wrote to inform the chief administrator at Concepción that smallpox was by then "much diminished in settlements and homes affected by it." He further suggested that "the distance one group lives from another" helped the sickness abate, as did "the strange and barbarous manner in which they treat themselves." It is also clear that smallpox did not affect all four *butalmapus* to the same extent. Referring to the Cordillera de la Costa, Manuel de Santa María, commander of the Spanish garrison at Arauco, reported on September 2 that "until now we have had no reason to be cautious, since the smallpox suffered has been exceptionally benign and no one in these mountains, as far as I have been informed, has died from it" (AGI, Chile 197).

The situation in the *butalmapu* of the Central Valley was quite similar. In a letter sent on July 30, Commander Rivera of Nacimiento informed Chief Administrator de la Mata, in Quechereguas, that the disease "has spread over most of the area, but still with the same mildness as before, which the Indians are able to withstand." On September 6, writing to Governor O'Higgins, de la Mata offered the following summary:

Given the situation in which the *butalmapus* find themselves, and in view of the repugnance they show towards the physical and spiritual assistance offered them, because it has been stated that they are unanimous in their determination not to accept missionaries, I will again issue orders to the captains to explain to [the Indians] that by no means should we endeavour to establish permanent missions among [them], but that the fathers should only help them for as long as the situation demands, or for as long as it pleases them.

It is evident, then, that not even the epidemic gave Spaniards a clear opportunity to send missionaries among the "barbarous rebels." The authorities, however, were singularly patient in their pursuit of imperial objectives, and they pressed on always in the hope that whatever failed today might succeed tomorrow. The logic behind state policy was outlined by the Crown attorney, Dr. Pérez de Uriondo, in a letter written on September 27 to Governor O'Higgins:

If, in order to help those wretches who form a part of the state by virtue of their being subjects of the King and who are therefore obliged to maintain the friendship and promises of loyalty they have made to this government, the gestures of humanity which Your Lordship has righteously promoted do not produce the favorable results we ought to expect, given that the Indians have refused to accept the physical and spiritual assistance offered them, we should not be disappointed at the progress of this interesting matter, which is very normal with acts of Christian charity. In the case of our neighbors, a continuation of [our policy] is required for [the success of our] political goal of making those who were once our enemies see how important our friendship is to them, [especially when] we help them with medicines, doctors, and other means [in times of] such urgent necessity.

The policy of prudence and perseverance favored by O'Higgins, de la Mata, and Pérez de Uriondo would in fact bear fruit two years later, following the *parlamento* of Negrete.

Not everything, therefore, constituted a failure for the colonial regime. In the first instance, the strategic Isla de la Laja was apparently spared from infection, for there is no reference made to smallpox among Spaniards there. Second, the arrangements put in place during the epidemic laid the foundations for the *parlamento* held at Negrete in 1793, undoubtedly the most impor-

tant peace talks between the Spaniards and the Mapuche during the eighteenth century.

As early as July 1791, Governor O'Higgins had written to the chief administrator at Concepción about
the possibility "of holding a *parlamento* next summer,"
one which the Indians "had been offered" and which
O'Higgins said he would "not like to delay, nor make
my journey to the frontier a waste of time." The reply
from de la Mata, who was well informed about the
course of the epidemic, cautioned against this proposal.
He wrote to O'Higgins in August stating that, in his
reckoning, "it does not seem possible to convene a *parlamento* during the summer without exposing the Isla de
la Laja to the clear risk of infection for, in spite of the
present circumstances, smallpox will still be prevalent
as soon as warmer weather arrives." At the height of the
epidemic, the *rehues* of Quechereguas, Renaico, Tub-
Tub, and Maquegua also suggested to officers Villagrán
and Cotar that a *parlamento general* with O'Higgins be
organized.

For the Indians, the peace talks were always a good
opportunity not only to receive gifts (*agasajos*) and at-
tend banquets offered by the highest colonial authorities, but also to use the influence of meeting Crown
representatives in their dealings with enemy tribes. For
the Spaniards, the peace talks were, above all, a show
of strength against people they regarded as "barbar-
ian." Peace talks, moreover, were a means of obtaining
concessions from the Indians, although the Spaniards
knew, by experience, that these concessions were never
permanent.

When the much-talked about *parlamento* finally did
take place in 1793, it was, in the words of O'Higgins
himself, "the best attended of those that have been cele-
brated up to now" (AGI, Chile 199). The event, which
attracted to Negrete 187 *caciques*, 77 warrior chiefs,
2,380 Indian warriors from all four *butalmapus*, and a
large, highly visible contingent of Spanish troops, re-

sulted in the negotiation of several concessions long desired by the colonial power. It was at Negrete that O'Higgins obtained the consent of the Huilliches to reconstruct the town of Osorno, destroyed by Indian attacks in 1600, the ruins of which were not even seen by Spaniards until 1792. The resettlement of Osorno had been one of the Crown's most enduring ambitions. O'Higgins also reached an agreement about reestablishing a garrison at Río Bueno, about halfway between Valdivia and Osorno, and rebuilding the Franciscan mission in Valdivia, which the Indians had razed in 1787. Furthermore, an agreement was reached that enabled the Spaniards to improve communications between Concepción, Valdivia, Osorno, and Chiloé, and to embark once again on founding missions. Franciscans ventured as far south as Quilacahuín, Pilmaiquén, and Coyunco in 1794 and then established the last mission of the colonial period at San Juan de la Costa in 1806. These considerable achievements earned Governor O'Higgins the title of Marqués de Osorno and the post of viceroy of Peru.

The success of the Negrete *parlamento*, as always, hinged on skillful manipulation by imperial Spain of Indian tribal divisions. But the epidemic of smallpox that weakened native society in 1791 was also a key factor in enabling colonial rule to be extended south of the Bío-Bío River. In a wild frontier on the fringe of an empire destined to last only twenty years more, disease paved the way for the conquest that military strength, political ambition, and religious zeal had for centuries failed to impose.

UNRAVELING THE WEB OF DISEASE

*Noble David Cook
and W. George Lovell*

The Snuffles (*Florentine Codex*)

There was then no sickness; they had then no aching bones; they had then no high fever; they had then no smallpox; they had then no burning chest; they had then no abdominal pains; they had then no consumption; they had then no headache. At that time the course of humanity was orderly. The foreigners made it otherwise when they arrived here. They brought shameful things when they came.

11 Ahau was when the mighty men arrived from the East. They were the ones who first brought disease here to our land, the land of we who are Maya, in the year 1513.

Like a servant of God who bends his back over virgin soil, they recorded the charge of misery in the presence of our Lord God: the introduction of Christianity occurs; blood-vomit, pestilence, drought, a year of locusts, smallpox are the charge of misery, also the importunity of the devil.

The Book of Chilam Balam of Chumayel

The essays collected in this volume focus on the impact of epidemic disease on native peoples throughout colonial Spanish America. Our spatial range, from central Mexico to southern Chile, is vast, and the time span

covered by our inquiries stretches from the era of conquest to the eve of independence. Whether our attention is drawn to the beginning of the sixteenth century
or the end of the eighteenth, from Aztec core to Mapuche periphery it is incontestable that Old World infections markedly shaped New World destinies. Epidemics
struck early and lingered late. In some instances disease
outbreaks even preceded direct physical contact between natives and newcomers. The effects of disease
transfer, furthermore, continued throughout the nineteenth and well into the twentieth century. There
evolved in colonial Spanish America what might best be
considered a web of disease. This web, and its underlying dynamics, are what we attempt to unravel in this
concluding essay.

We tend, in the present century, to view pronounced
population growth as commonplace, an almost natural
state of affairs. In rapidly industrializing western societies, demographic expansion began in the late eighteenth century and generally continued until control of
births slowed the process. Growth continues at a dra-
matic rate in the nations of the so-called Third World,
where modern public health measures have sharply
lowered the death rate without providing for a corre-
sponding reduction in the number of births. For several
generations we have experienced almost continuous
population expansion, leading many to assume that the
demographic characteristics of the world today represent the normal pattern (Hollingsworth 1969; Wrigley
1969; Sánchez-Albornoz 1974).

In preindustrial times, population growth tended to
be slow and relatively continuous, until the approximate carrying capacity of the social and economic environment was reached, or until an alien element was introduced. At this point, conditions were propitious for
a sudden catastrophe, or "die-off," of a sizeable portion
of people. There were often sudden "spurts" of growth
when changed circumstances prevailed, as occurred

when plants and animals were domesticated (Sauer 1952) or when a new and valuable food resource was exploited (Crosby 1972). As populations neared a peak, however, the natural checks of war, famine, and pestilence, or some combination of all three, acted to limit further expansion. Social variables such as age at marriage, nursing patterns, spacing of children, the practice of infanticide or (in extreme cases) human sacrifice and cannibalism could depress demographic growth. These societal factors tended, in the short term, to be less significant as checks than the Malthusian trinity of conflict, hunger, and disease (Boserup 1988; Zubrow 1975; Hollingsworth 1969).

There are abundant examples of the process, especially from Europe, where the record of history is more complete. A plague beset the people of Athens during the Peloponnesian Wars. It led to the city's downfall and the ultimate victory of the Spartans and their allies. A series of epidemics, coming from the East, penetrated the Roman Empire beginning about A.D. 180, and another series struck in the middle of the third century. Mortality was highest in the urban complexes (Grmek 1989; McNeill 1976; Hopkins 1983). Towards the end of the fifth century the population of many cities was only a fraction of what it had been before the onset of sickness. Founded on the principles of orderly town life, Roman civilization failed to survive in its original form. The Black Death, also coming from the East, struck Europe in the mid-fourteenth century. City populations were again cut by half or more by outbreaks of the plague. The economic and demographic upswing of the previous century was reversed. European confidence was shattered as thousands of people, rich and poor alike, faced the specter of sudden death. In many parts of Europe, it took a century and a half for the population to recover from the devastation. These epidemics, and their social and economic consequences, have attracted close scholarly attention (Gottfried 1983; Ziegler 1976).

It is in the New World, however, and not in the Old, that disease outbreaks probably caused the greatest loss of life known to history. In all likelihood, the severest and most protracted human mortality ever to occur did so in the years following overseas expansion by Europeans in the late fifteenth century. Technological improvements in shipbuilding, advances in navigation and mapmaking, and increasing sophistication of the machinery of war, as well as fundamental changes in the way economic, political, and social life were organized, made possible long-range sea voyages and facilitated the conquest and colonization of lands new to Europeans. Non-European peoples who before had dwelled in virtual isolation became part of a wide and widening world. As Crosby (1986) has shown, European expansion brought about, across the globe, an unprecedented exchange of people, plants, animals, weeds, pests, and pathogens. From the standpoint of the native peoples of the Americas, who had been shielded from Old World diseases for a long period of time, contact with Europeans was catastrophic (Borah 1976). Within a century, perhaps 90 percent of the Indians of the New World had succumbed because of the ravages of disease, famine and warfare (Borah 1964; MacLeod 1973: 1–20).

The Agents of Death

The diseases that appear to have been most destructive of Native American lives are smallpox and measles. We will review the salient pathogenic features of these illnesses as they relate to recorded outbreaks in colonial Spanish America. Afterwards we will treat, in similar summary fashion, influenza, plague, typhus, yellow fever, malaria, leishmaniasis, syphilis, and tuberculosis. By so doing, various strands of the web of disease will be isolated and illuminated. We point out in advance, however, that the web is a complex gestalt, one in which the whole was decidedly more ruinous than the sum of its lethal parts.

SMALLPOX

As several contributors have observed, accurate diagnosis of disease symptoms reported by nonspecialists for nonmedical purposes is fraught with difficulty. Only during the past one hundred years has the germ theory of infection supplanted the medical belief systems of the ancient and medieval worlds (Cumston 1987). Compounding the problem of accurate diagnosis from scant, sketchy, or contradictory evidence is the fact that when a new disease agent infects a virgin population, abnormal symptoms often occur (Crosby 1976a). Explicit identification of smallpox provides a clear example of the difficulties we encounter when working with early colonial testimony.

Smallpox occurs in two principal forms: *variola major*, usually with mortality rates of 30 to 50 percent, and *variola minor*, with much lower mortality levels. Complicating the business of identification is the existence of five different types of *variola major*, all with varying levels of mortality: episodes of benign semiconfluent smallpox result in 10 percent mortality, benign confluent in 20 percent, malignant semiconfluent in 25 percent, malignant confluent in 70 percent, and fulminating smallpox in almost 100 mortality (Dixon 1962). Even with the advantages of twentieth-century health care, before the elimination of smallpox in the 1970s, people who contracted malignant or fulminating strains could not be significantly assisted. Mortality of pregnant women was especially high, some 50 percent and more.

The clinical symptoms of smallpox as we know it are well described in standard references: fever, malaise, and then a generalized eruption usually on the third day, which progresses from papules to vesicles and, finally, to pustules (Dixon 1962). In the past, those who

survived an attack were often marked by pitted skin
(Hopkins 1983:1–21; Anderson and Arnstein 1956:301–
11). The problem is that other diseases could have been
confused with smallpox as it passed through progres-
sive stages.

Smallpox is transmitted among human beings by individuals who are ill with the infection or convalescing
from it. The virus is passed through secretions in the
throat and the nose, and from the lesions themselves. It
is communicable until lesions are completely healed
and the scabs covering them have fallen off. Direct contact with the material containing the virus was necessary for the spread of smallpox. The virus enters the
human body through the respiratory tract and has an
incubation period of eight to ten days (Dixon 1962:68,
88; Joralemon 1982:120; Anderson and Arnstein 1956:
301–4).

Given the high communicability of smallpox, we might
well ask why the disease did not, as far as is known,
reach the Americas before 1518. One answer is probably the high percentage of immune Europeans who
crossed the Atlantic during the first voyages. Smallpox
in sixteenth- and seventeenth-century Europe primarily
affected children, so most adults who undertook the
journey had developed an immunity by being exposed
to the disease during childhood. The virus could remain
active for several weeks in the scab, but intense heat
and solar radiation, common conditions during the Atlantic crossing, usually destroyed it. The early crossings
were generally slow and subject to delay, the trips taking several weeks. Finally, however, the smallpox virus
made the fateful passage. It may have done so via scabs
hidden away in bundles of clothing or textiles, which
would provide the virus with ample protection. Alternately, a ship may have sailed across with enough infected and nonimmune passengers to keep the virus
alive through human transmission. The latter situation
certainly prevailed during the peak of the slave trade,

when large cargoes of young, susceptible blacks taken on board ships on the African coast provided ideal carrying conditions for the transfer of smallpox to port cities in the New World. The disease struck Santo Domingo in December 1518 or January of the following year, the time and place most contemporary scholars (Crosby 1972:35–40, 40–47; Dobyns 1983:11–16; McNeill 1976:183) assign to the origins of smallpox in the New World. Smallpox, however, may have made an earlier American landfall, for around the time of the expedition led by Francisco Hernández de Córdoba to the Yucatán, in 1517, a cruel and unfamiliar sickness had already devastated the peninsula. Writing in the 1560s, the Franciscan missionary Diego de Landa (1941:42) recorded the testimony of Maya survivors in his *Relación de las cosas de Yucatán*, which speaks of "great pustules, which rotted bodies with a great stench, so that the limbs fell in pieces in four or five days." Although no mention is made of pock marks, Inga Clendinnen (1987: 19) thinks the sickness "was almost certainly smallpox." She reaches this conclusion in sound scholarly company, for Ralph Roys (1967:138) in his translation of the *Book of Chilam Balam of Chumayel* observes that "an epidemic of smallpox swept through Yucatán in Katun 2 Ahau, and it may have been brought by the party of Spaniards who were shipwrecked and cast on the east coast in 1511."

What we do know, as Prem and others have observed, is that smallpox was said to have been introduced into Mexico by a black servant of Panfilo de Narváez who had been stricken by the disease. From the Gulf Coast, sickness then spread west and south. Many scholars, Lovell among them, note that a well-known passage in the *Annals of the Cakchiquels* tells of terrible sickness in Guatemala between 1519 and 1521. Diagnosis is problematical, but designation as smallpox has its supporters, including medical doctors. Newson, as have several researchers before her, establishes the presence of smallpox in the Andes in the 1520s, where it took a heavy native toll. According to Borah, the first outbreaks of smallpox in the Andean highlands, one of which killed the Inca ruler Huayna Capac, may have originated not as diffusions from Mexico and Central America but as overland transfers from the Río de la Plata region, far to the south. The first fully documented epidemic of smallpox to reach New Granada was recorded in 1558. It came from Hispaniola, and mortality associated with it was high. Smallpox flared up again in New Granada in 1588. This may have been the origin of part of the devastating sickness that swept Peru at this time. Evans, in Chapter 5, examines the impact of smallpox on the community of Aymaya, in present-day Bolivia, in 1590. Of 194 deaths that critical year, 147 were caused by smallpox. About a quarter of these deaths were among children under the age of five. This presents us with an unusual piece of evidence, for smallpox mortality in Europe in the sixteenth century would have evinced a far different pattern, with a much larger percentage of deaths among children than occurred in the Andes. Smallpox reappeared in Aymaya between 1609 and 1610. Thereafter, even in distant parts of the empire, smallpox occurred at fairly regular intervals throughout the colonial period, as Casanueva demonstrates in Chapter 7. By the early nineteenth century, however, scientific initiatives such as the royal expedition led by Francisco Xavier de Balmis had positive and beneficial effects (S. F. Cook 1941; M. M. Smith 1974; Lovell 1988), although smallpox enjoyed a post-Jenner existence in some areas that reflects poorly on republican-era governments.

MEASLES

Measles is an acute, short-term viral infection. Its classic symptoms include the onset of fever, the appearance of a spotted rash, and the development of a cough. The disease is highly communicable but has a relatively low level of mortality for people who have been exposed to it for generations. Measles is most serious for children under three years of age, fetuses, and secondarily for adults. Complications involve infections of the middle ear, pneumonia, and sometimes encephalitis. The last two can cause death. Measles is transmitted by direct contact with infected droplets via the respiratory passage. Incubation varies from eight to twenty-one days, the characteristic rash appearing around the third day of illness. Temporary immunity lasting about six months is passed from a mother who has previously contracted measles to her infant. The greater the population density, the more rapid the spread of disease. In large urban clusters, epidemics usually take place at intervals of two or three years. In rural districts, measles epidemics occur infrequently, only after infection from the outside (Anderson and Arnstein 1956:287–94).

A study of disease outbreaks during the late seventeenth and eighteenth centuries in Santa Ana de Triana, a parish of Seville, indicates that measles was virtually endemic in the port city, from which most official trade with the Indies was conducted (N. D. Cook et al. 1988). Almost all those who contracted the disease, as in the case of smallpox, were children. Given its relatively short incubation period and its brief span of being acutely infectious, it would be necessary to have a group of children on board a fleet to transfer measles across the Atlantic. This situation might not have prevailed early on, but by the 1530s surely did. In Chapter 1, Prem suggests that measles hit sixteenth-century Mexico in cycles of approximately thirty years, with a presumed first appearance in 1531. Lovell, in Chapter 2, discusses a measles pandemic in Central America between 1532 and 1534, one that occurred throughout Guatemala as well as in Honduras and Nicaragua. Both contributors, however, caution about the problems of accurate diagnosis. In Chapter 3, Newson argues that the measles present in Nicaragua in 1533 also reached Panama. From there, the human traffic ferried to Peru as part of the Nicaraguan slave trade (Radell 1976) could afterwards have transmitted measles to the Andes, certainly by the mid or late 1530s. A combination of measles and smallpox, according to Newson, reached Peru in 1558. By far the most devastating outbreaks of sickness, however, swept the Andes from 1585 to 1591, when several diseases, measles among them, were present. The Villamaríns, in Chapter 4, indicate that measles took a heavy toll in the Sabana de Bogotá in 1617–18. In Chapter 6, Alchon reports great devastation in Ecuador in 1785. Measles also hit the Sabana de Bogotá in 1788 and is recorded in Peru a year later. These eighteenth-century outbreaks appear to have struck Indian peoples with the same severity as earlier episodes.

Measles, then, proved a deadly sickness for Native Americans who came in contact with it. It is difficult for us to imagine what destruction this common childhood disease of the Old World produced in the "virgin soil" context of the Americas. Mortality must have been very high indeed. Dobyns (1983:270, 284–85) estimates 50-percent mortality during a hypothesized epidemic of 1531–33 in Florida, a 25-percent rate in 1596, and a 16-percent figure for 1727 or 1728. Measles, he contends, may have caused the death of more Native Americans than any other disease except smallpox.

INFLUENZA

Another communicable airborne disease is influenza, a condition characterized by fever, a general feeling of malaise, and prostration. We now know the agent is a virus, divided into two major strains, type A and type B, both of which are comprised of several substrains. Susceptibility is high. The virus is transmitted via droplets or secretions from the infected host. Influenza becomes deadly usually as a result of complications, the most common of which is the invasion of pneumonococci and streptococci organisms in the weakened respiratory tracts. Incubation appears to be two or three days for most strains. Although children are most susceptible, adults, especially the ill or elderly, suffer from a higher death rate (McGrew 1985:150).

Influenza occurs in waves, normally during the winter months. There are sharp variations in severity from one epidemic wave to the next. In fact, the influenza virus is extremely unstable and mutates with great frequency. Temporary immunity following one attack does not provide immunity against exposure to other strains. Accurate diagnosis of cases on the basis of colonial documentation is almost impossible because it is easy to confuse outbreaks of influenza with those of other viral infections (Crosby 1976b; Dobyns 1983:19). Guerra (1985, 1986) contends that the first major epidemic to reach America was influenza, or swine flu, which swept Hispaniola in 1493. Prem (Chapter 1) and Lovell (Chapter 2) mention that literature for Mexico and Guatemala correlates some early epidemics with influenza (McBryde 1940). Fevers, nosebleeds, severe coughs, and stiffness of the neck are some of the vaguely described symptoms. The last major pandemic occurred in 1918, when global mortality exceeded that of the recently ended Great War. During this outbreak young adult males were hit with exceptional virulence (Crosby 1976b).

INFECTIONS SPREAD BY ARTHROPODS

Several diseases affecting Native Americans were spread by arthropods, especially lice and fleas, and also by dipterans. These diseases warrant close examination as a group because of their complex etiology. Bubonic plague, typhus, yellow fever, malaria, and leishmaniasis are examples. The pool of infection is often in other mammals, and the epidemics usually appear in *Homo sapiens* as the result of an accidental explosion of the disease (epizootic) in the normal host population.

Environmental factors play a major part in the dissemination of these infections. International migrations of humans and rodents on ships contributed to the diffusion of these diseases during European expansion. If a suitable vector were not available in new territory, then diffusion was cut short, as was the case with leishmaniasis. Climatic variations obviously play a role in the passage of arthropod-borne disease. Yellow fever, which periodically entered the northern part of the United States, retreated with the onslaught of winter. On the other hand, in Europe during the Middle Ages epidemics of typhus most often took place in winter months because people tended to concentrate in buildings, where the body louse found an ideal setting. Infrequent bathing and the rare washing of woolen garments provided near perfect conditions for the propagation of lice and, in turn, the rapid transmission of typhus (Zinnser 1935; Anderson and Arnstein 1956:433–35).

Plague. Plague (*Pasteurella pestis*) was one of the major killers in medieval Europe. Various pandemics swept the continent, including the most famous of all, the Black Death, which caused heavy mortality in the mid-fourteenth century. Plague is spread from host rodent populations through the bite of the rat flea (*Xenopsylla cheopis*), or directly from person to person. There are two forms of the plague, bubonic and pneumonic, or pulmonary. The bubonic form, spread after infection by the flea, is characterized by swollen lymph nodes, often with fatal septicemia. Pneumonic or pulmonary plague is the more deadly, and mortality levels before the advent of antibiotics reached 100 percent. This highly communicable form is spread from person to person via sputum infected with *Pasteurella pestis*. Incubation requires from two to three days. Body temperature falls, there is a severe cough, then a bloody discharge. Coma and death follow.

Reexamining the Black Death in Europe, Gottfried (1983) reports sharp variations in mortality levels from one region to another. Total mortality from the plague that began in 1348, in an epidemic series that lasted in some locales up to eighteen months, was high. The range for Florence is from 45 to 75 percent, for Genoa 30 to 40 percent, for Milan only about 15 percent, but for Venice as high as 60 percent. Gottfried (1983:8, 42–76) calculates a mortality of from 33 to 50 percent for the whole of Italy, and for the entire Mediterranean basin some 35 to 40 percent. He estimates 35 to 50 percent for London, but only 20 to 25 percent for eastern Europe. Dobyns (1983:18–20, 30–31) argues that bubonic plague reached the New World in the 1540s, in a pandemic that included all of Mesoamerica, the Andean region of South America, and possibly Florida. Drawing on the evidence of Cieza de León, Newson suggests (Chapter 3) that pneumonic or pulmonary plague probably reached Ecuador in 1546 and spread from there throughout the Andes. This may have been an extension of the sickness noted by Prem and Lovell for, respectively, Mexico and Guatemala. Other plague epidemics broke out in 1576–80, 1612–19, and 1707. Mortality during these episodes, especially the one of 1545 to 1548, was high. Further research on the impact of plague in the New World is needed, however, before definitive conclusions can be reached (Dobyns 1983: 18–20, 30–31).

Typhus. Typhus is an acute infection manifest, like measles, by the onset of fever and the appearance of a rash. Three main forms are known: (1) epidemic or classical typhus, transmitted by the body louse (*Pediculus humanus*) and resulting in heavy mortality; (2) endemic or murine typhus, spread by the flea and producing lower rates of mortality; and (3) tsutsugamushi disease, carried by a mite and common in parts of Asia. The epidemic form is the most dangerous, usually occurring when people are densely concentrated without adequate sanitation. Periods of war and famine have provided ideal conditions for the spread of typhus. Incidence of typhus tends to be highest during the colder months of the year. The typhus agent is *Rickettsia prowazekii*, a microorganism living in cells lining the gut of the body louse. The agent is expelled in the feces, and the louse survives the infestation for about twelve to eighteen days. The microorganism can live for several days in the dried feces. *Rickettsia* usually enters human beings through cuts or abrasions in the skin, such as scratched insect bites. Incubation in human beings lasts anywhere from ten to fourteen days. The early symptoms include headache, loss of appetite, fever, and general malaise. Body temperature peaks at the end of the first week, remains elevated until about the twelfth day, then drops to normal among survivors between the fourteenth and sixteenth days. A rash appears on the fourth to sixth day and shows up as red or dark-red spots some two to five millimeters in diameter. Some spots rise slightly above the skin. In severe cases the rash might cover most of the body. Fatal episodes produce marked prostration followed by delirium and end in coma and cardiac arrest. Those who survive face a long and slow convalescence. Mortality can vary from approximately 5 to 25 percent. The level is much higher for the elderly, about 50 percent. Children, on the other hand, face mortality levels of less than 5 percent (Anderson and Arnstein 1956:449–51).

Typhus is a disease the Spaniards apparently knew well. One of the clearest European accounts of the illness comes from the period of conflict in which the kingdom of Granada was enmeshed in 1489–90. Spaniards called the disease *tabardillo*, in reference to its characteristic symptoms: spots covering the body like a tabard, or sleeveless cloak. It struck the Iberian peninsula repeatedly during the sixteenth century and could have accompanied the troops led by Hernán Cortés during the conquest of Mexico (Dobyns 1983:21, 31; McNeill

1976:194–95). Prem considers typhus a possible explanation of the dreadful epidemic that hit Mexico in 1545 and may have carried off more than 60 percent of those taken ill. Lovell connects this sickness with one that swept Guatemala that same year. Typhus seems to have reappeared in Mexico and Guatemala between 1576 and 1581, in combination with other serious ailments. Certainly the demographic consequences of sickness lasted well into the 1580s. Another wave of typhus beset Guatemala in 1607–8 and again in 1631–32. The 1630s outbreak may have been pan-American in scale, for the Villamarins report it from 1630 to 1633 in the Sabana de Bogotá, where possibly one-fifth or more of the population succumbed.

Yellow fever. Spread by the *Aedes aegypti* mosquito in normal epidemic form, yellow fever is a fatal viral infection mostly found in the tropics but which, during the months of high summer, can move into temperate zones. In the nineteenth century, for instance, a bout of yellow fever extended into the United States as far north as Boston and the upper Mississippi basin. The etiology of the disease is complex. An infected human being passes the virus to the mosquito. After ten to fourteen days' incubation in the mosquito, the virus can be passed until the death of the insect. In tropical areas of Africa and South America, it appears that yellow fever is endemic in certain primate populations and may be transmitted by other mosquito vectors. Symptoms include a sudden illness, fever, a slowed pulse, and finally jaundice—hence the name "yellow fever." Vomiting of blood of a dark, almost black hue also occurs. Tolerance among blacks suggests that yellow fever was endemic along the African coast for some time (Anderson and Arnstein 1956:468–74).

It is difficult to date precisely when yellow fever first entered the New World. One serious outbreak, acknowledged by Dobyns (1983:279–80) as the first, began in Barbados in 1647, reached the Yucatán in 1648, and is recorded for Guadeloupe, Cuba, and Saint Kitts in 1648 49. Another severe outbreak swept the northeast coast of Brazil from 1686 to 1694. Yellow fever reached Boston in 1693, having been brought there by the British fleet returning from Barbados. It hit Charleston and Philadelphia in 1699, with high mortality (Marks and Beatty 1976:149–50). Yellow fever epidemics were common in the eighteenth century. An epidemic lashed New York City in 1702, when 570 people died in a population of fewer than 8,000. Other epidemics hit the city in 1743, 1745, and 1748. Newson notes yellow fever as occurring, probably for the first time, in 1740 in Guayaquil, where it reappeared three years later.

Charleston was ravaged by yellow fever in 1706, perhaps also in 1711, then again in 1728 and 1732. There was a serious outbreak in 1745, a mild outbreak in 1758, then a major series in 1790, 1791, 1792, 1795, 1798, and 1799. Philadelphia was hit in 1741 and 1747. In 1762 the disease entered the city again, having been carried from Veracruz to Cuba in 1761, there infecting British troops who, after attacking Havana, sailed to Philadelphia. Another severe epidemic hit Philadelphia in 1793. Between 1794 and 1805, yellow fever contaminated the port cities of Charleston, Norfolk, Baltimore, New York, and Boston. Smaller cities were also affected. New Orleans suffered in 1796 and throughout much of the nineteenth century (Duffy 1968:100–112). Baltimore, Philadelphia, and Boston were struck by a devastating series in 1819. Mortality was often high. Of a population of about 50,000 in the 1790s, New York City lost 732 in the 1795 outbreak and more than 2,000 in 1798. Epidemics of yellow fever abound in the nineteenth century. A classic example of the effect of yellow fever is seen in Haiti. There Napoleonic troops attempted, in 1802, to suppress an independence movement led by Pierre Toussaint L'Ouverture. Over 40,000 Europeans died from the disease, thus destroying Napoleon's plans for political aggrandizement in the New World (Marks and Beatty 1976:150–60).

Malaria. The etiology of malaria is even more complex than that of yellow fever. Malaria is caused by three strains of plasmodium: (1) *Plasmodium vivax*, called "tertian malaria" because chills come every third day; (2) *Plasmodium malariae*, or quartan type, characterized by chills at four-day intervals; and (3) *Plasmodium falciparum*, which is the cause of most deaths from malaria and is associated with irregularly spaced, nearly daily occurrences of chills. Malaria is transmitted by several species of the anopheles mosquito. In *Homo sapiens*, the plasmodium invades red blood cells, becoming a mature trophozoite. At this point, it ruptures both itself and the membranes of the red blood cells, becoming a large number of merozoites. Chills are associated with the rupture of the cell membranes. The merozoites then enter new red blood cells, becoming trophozoites, having multiplied themselves asexually. Some of the trophozoites in the human body become sexually differentiated gametocytes. If the gametocytes enter the mosquito, they can reproduce sexually. The gametocytes, drawn into the mosquito's stomach, finally penetrate the insect's body cavity, forming an oocyst. After ten to fourteen days, these break into sporozoites, invade the mosquito's salivary glands, and then may be injected into another person. The mosquito is infectious for its entire life. Infection may be carried in hibernating mosquitos from one season to the next. Malaria persists in afflicted individuals for an indefinite period, during which time there may be spells of chills and anemia. Populations in regions where malaria is endemic can be greatly weakened and debilitated (Anderson and Arnstein 1956:468–74).

Leishmaniasis. Also called *uta, espundia,* or *jukuya,* leishmaniasis is brought on by the action of the protozoan *Leishmania braziliensis,* found in the foothills of the Andes. The infection is passed to *Homo sapiens* or a mammal that can act as host (dogs and rodents) by the bite of an infected sand fly of the *Lutzomyia* genus. According to Gade (1979: 271), leishmaniasis "was one of the few ecopathogenic diseases found in South America before the arrival of the Europeans." It is endemic to the American tropics and subtropics from 22 degrees north to 30 degrees south. The impact of leishmaniasis, in contrast to diseases that sicken and cause distress almost immediately, is long term. In that sense it resembles tuberculosis. Gade (1979:269) describes succinctly the normal course of the disease:

The syndrome begins with a primary skin lesion where the bite occurs, usually on the arm or leg, which later heals. One to six months later, pathological organisms may appear in the nasal mucosa, but more typically, a long period—sometimes many years—of dormancy passes before the characteristic facial lesions develop. The nose, palate and upper lip may become ulcerated; the underlying cartilage may also be destroyed. If the larynx becomes infected, the vocal chords may fail, the necrosis of the trachea can limit food intake. Ultimately the disease may result in death through gangrene, bronchopneumonia or starvation.

Fortunately, the sand-fly vector responsible for leishmaniasis has a restricted altitudinal range on the slopes of the Andes. Dense populations lived above that range, well in excess of 2,500 meters, and were consequently less endangered.

Syphilis and Tuberculosis. Like leishmaniasis, syphilis and tuberculosis are not ordinarily acute, communicable diseases, but they can shorten life and debilitate their victims. It is possible, however, for a person to carry any one of these three diseases for a long period of time and still survive. In his introduction, Borah touched briefly on the possible New World origins of syphilis, transmitted by *Treponema pallidum* during sexual intercourse. Syphilis appears to be communicable for up to five years from spirochetes present in open lesions often not visually detectable. A primary lesion may appear within three to four weeks, but sometimes as short as eight days or as long as eight weeks after exposure. The secondary stage may consist of malaise, fever, a generalized rash, and a sore throat. This stage can go undetected easily, and a period of latency follows. This latent condition might last as long as the life of the host. The final stage consists of a concentrated attack usually on one of the major systems of the victim: the central nervous, skeletal, or cardiovascular system. At this point the disease becomes fatal. Congenital infections are often fatal before the birth of an infant (Anderson and Arnstein 1956:376–80; Dobyns 1983:34–35).

Especially acute during the nineteenth century, tuberculosis is another disease that erodes physical welfare slowly. Caused by the tubercle bacillus *Mycobacterium tuberculosis*, the illness seems to be particularly influenced by population density, general economic and nutritional levels, prevalence of milk-borne infection, and ethnic background. Mortality rates vary significantly. Death from tuberculosis in the United States fell from 153.8 per 100,000 in 1910 to 26.3 in 1949. The disease can attack most parts of the human body. The response is to replace areas of tissue destroyed by the disease with fibrous tissue, or calcification. Anderson and Arnstein (1956:354) state that "the outcome of any case depends on the tissue involved and whether or not the fibrous repair processes develop more rapidly than the necrotic action." Tuberculosis is manifest in three different strains: human, bovine, and avian. The bovine strain tends to concentrate in the bones and joints, whereas the human strain is primarily pulmonary. Bacillus is expelled in lung infections in the sputum, where it can exist for up to several weeks, protected by mucin covering. Human beings with active progression of the disease are potential carriers. The bacilli are sensitive to heat, hence the success of pasteurization of milk with regard to eliminating the bovine strain as a major threat (Anderson and Arnstein 1956:354–71). S. F. Cook (1946: 324) and Dobyns (1983:34–36) suggest that in pre-Columbian times Native Americans enjoyed an existence relatively free of infectious diseases, suffering mostly from respiratory disorders such as tuberculosis and a number of gastrointestinal disturbances.

The Key Variables

Epidemiologists have long been interested in the study of the causal chain of disease, as best it can be discerned from past outbreaks of sickness. For them, a major purpose of such research is to establish the basis for predicting the course of future epidemics. For scholars interested in past epidemics and their impact on human societies, the reverse is true: a better understanding of history is attained by present knowledge of disease characteristics.

Mass outbreaks of sickness are predicted by analyzing various factors, including the nature of the causative agent, the exposure of the individual to that organism, the disposition of the host (immunity, resistance, susceptibility), and the environment that influences the process (Sinnecker 1976:23). Susceptibility of the human host is a key epidemiological factor. Individual susceptibility determines the spread of a disease, but it is the susceptibility of the population as a whole that differentiates a series of ill people from a mass outbreak. Population density and communication patterns are also important variables. Resistance to a disease may be genetic or acquired. A mother passes to her infant temporary immunity or resistance to certain diseases if she has herself experienced them. It is also possible that slightly longer protection is afforded by the breast-feeding of infants.

Invasion of an infant's system by an infectious agent provokes a response to contain and ultimately destroy the foreign organism. This response varies in different individuals and depends again on a number of factors, especially nutrition. In some illnesses, if the dose of the infectious agent is small, the infant will be able to suppress the agent. Increasing doses leads to stronger internal defenses against the infection. This may go on until the mass infection is too great for the body response to handle, or if the internal defenses are weak, as might occur when a person is suffering from exhaustion or is malnourished. At that point, the disease temporarily wins the battle, and clinical manifestations become evident. In the case of most viral diseases, the size of the dosage or inoculum does not appear to be a significant factor, and the disease tends to run its course with no subclinical infections (Anderson and Arnstein 1956:13–41).

Genetic factors also play a role in the individual's response to infection. Precise measurement of the role of genetic variation, however, is difficult to obtain. Blood factors influence the ability of some African groups to survive in malarial areas, but that same blood factor has had one detrimental side-effect: the tendency to acquire sickle-cell anemia (Sinneker 1976:63–64). The response of Native Americans to what are often considered European childhood diseases is a subject the contributors of this volume have addressed. Perhaps the sharpest mortality differences between Europeans and Amerindians lie in the experience of measles and smallpox, where the exposure of Europeans, subjected to the ravages of both diseases over many generations and centuries, led to a mortality level that allowed the continuation of both the virus and its host.

Epidemiologists have studied the relationship between host and parasite with regard to the introduction of an alien species into a new environment (Sinnecker 1976:55–58). The individual's response to the onslaught of an infection also depends on the virulence of that particular outbreak, for the severity of a disease organism for a host population can and does vary over time.

Here the mechanism is probably natural selection, for a disease that destroys an entire host population ultimately destroys itself. There is thus a premium for the selection of less fatal forms of the disease agent, as Zinsser (1935) recognized. The classic example of this process was the introduction of the myxomatosis virus into Australia in an attempt to control the explosive growth of the wild rabbit population. In the first epizootic, rabbit mortality reached 97 to 99 percent. In the second epizootic, it registered 85 to 95 percent. By the third epizootic, mortality had fallen to 40 to 60 percent. Natural selection might favor rabbits resistant to the myxomatosis virus, but given the duration of rabbit generations, this advantage must have been minimal. It is more likely that natural selection of less virulent forms of the virus played a role in the lower levels of mortality in the later epizootics.

Human generations, of course, are chronologically much longer than rabbit generations. The factor influencing an advantage for less virulent infections has probably always been at play in human epidemics. Problems arise if there is a human population that can acquire and transmit a disease with a low mortality experience, living side by side with a population that lacks this resistance. In such cases, there may be virtually no premium for natural selection of weaker forms of the infection, and so the new or "virgin" population may be completely destroyed (N. D. Cook 1981:72–73, 268; Sinnecker 1976:59–61).

Other biological factors enter into the disease equation. Mortality levels are related to both age and sex in certain illnesses. Old people and infants commonly suffer highest mortality during certain epidemic outbreaks. Heightened mortality during influenza epidemics, for example, is evident among elderly folk, who often succumb to ensuing pneumonia infections. On the other hand, direct deaths from influenza in the 1918 pandemic were, in the isolated Maori, highest among young, adult, working males, a mortality pattern that holds also for the same pandemic in the United States (Crosby 1976b). For women, mortality levels due to infectious diseases tend to be highest during pregnancy. Some infections, including smallpox, measles, and syphilis, affect the fetus as well as the mother (N. D. Cook 1981: 66–67; Sinnecker 1976:135–47).

The latent and infectious periods are clear-cut factors regulating the speed of progression of an epidemic. Once the disease agent has entered the human body, there is a period of development until the body's defenses are overwhelmed and clinical symptoms appear. As we noted in our survey of disease agents, the incubation period varies from one illness to another, and there are fluctuations also in the latency period within the disease itself. The longer the chronological time involved in the latency period, the greater the possibility that the disease can be spread without detection from one locale to another. The extent of transmission is dependent on the speed of communications. Also related is the period of infectiousness. Once again, the longer the period of infectiousness, the more likely it is that disease will spread over vast regions because infected persons carry it to a point where sickness can be transmitted to another individual. With arthropod-spread epidemics, the feeding cycle of the vector is also a factor (Sinnecker 1976:180–82).

The latency and infectious periods, essential biological factors involved in epidemic propagation, relate directly to social factors, particularly communication networks and population densities. The latter is in fact both a biological and cultural variable. It can be controlled by societal decisions: concepts of ideal family size, spacing of infants, age at marriage, a decision of allowable population concentration, colonization efforts to limit high densities, celibacy, and even cannibalism, infanticide, and human sacrifice. How quickly disease is transmitted is directly related to population density:

the greater the number of inhabitants in a confined, crowded space then the greater the degree of contact between individuals, resulting in the rapid spread of infection from one person to another. Some epidemiologists maintain that major epidemics as we know them would not have existed in hunting, fishing, and gathering societies that had little outside contact and low population densities (McNeill 1976; Boserup 1988).

When dealing with communication networks, technological developments are crucial. With modern air travel, virtually all major world regions are less than twelve hours flying distance one from another. This condition allows an acute communicable epidemic in one region almost immediately to reach each other one. The rapid spread of influenza epidemics to almost all sections of the globe is a consequence of this transportation revolution. Although the speed of ships in the era of Columbus was slow, velocity was fast enough to have significant demographic consequences. Indeed, as Parry (1963) so vividly demonstrates, technological innovations in shipbuilding, navigation, and armaments made possible the creation of a global network dominated by Europeans in the Age of Reconnaissance. From the late fifteenth to the end of the nineteenth century, passage across land and water accelerated rapidly as a result of further improvements in transportation (Crosby 1972: 35–63; McNeill 1976:176–207). Native Americans, as we have seen, paid a high price during this period of European domination.

Hygiene and sanitation are other factors that influence the spread of infections, especially the transmission of water-borne epidemics such as cholera and typhoid. Contaminated sewage leads to the rapid dissemination of the infectious agent and the outbreak of an epidemic. Recognition of the relationship between polluted water supplies and disease led public officials in many nations during the late nineteenth century to provide purified drinking water. The consequence was a rapid fall in the incidence of water-related epidemics. During the colonial period, however, such was not the case, and so water-borne infections, although not much discussed, must have taken a toll in human lives.

Sanitation goes beyond merely providing purified water. Diseases spread by contact with droplets suspended in the air are also amenable to control by hygienic measures. Societal customs with regard to sneezing and disposal of nasal secretions can have a marked effect on the spread of epidemic infections. Attempts to deflect a sneeze into a handkerchief, for example, can reduce drastically the number of disease agents that can enter the air and thus be transmitted to other individuals. Likewise, careful washing with a disinfectant can help to reduce the number of disease agents that are transferred by direct contact.

Towards the end of the nineteenth century, before scientific recognition of the process by which infectious diseases are transferred, most sanitary measures were a result of social custom and existed in large part by chance. Attempts by sixteenth-century Europeans to restrict bathing in tropical and subtropical regions reduced the cleanliness of aboriginal residents and directly contributed to spreading disease and death (Anderson and Arnstein 1956:43–58). In some cases, however, native healing practices were detrimental to the sick during times of illness. Indians in Mesoamerica, for example, as well as in North America, used sweat treatments followed by quick cold baths or swims in frigid waters to cure fevers. Such treatments only served to increase the mortality associated with measles and smallpox, for the weakened cardiovascular system was just not able to stand the shock (Dobyns 1983:16).

Societal practices for the care of the ill can also influence the recovery rate. Sickness in the New World before the arrival of Europeans was in general not life threatening for aboriginal inhabitants, a circumstance that Old World diseases changed markedly. Age-old cures prescribed by knowledgeable shamans were simply no longer effective, breeding wariness and fear and provoking new forms of reaction. In some instances, after the lethal nature of Old World infections was recognized, Indians abandoned sick persons to die or to fend for themselves, as friends and relatives fled their homes to avoid contagion. We even have evidence from late in the colonial period of full-scale abandonment of settlements, where the living did not bury the dead, but instead left them behind to rot (Lovell 1988). In such a situation, all semblance of normality disappeared. Crops were neither sown nor harvested, animals roamed untended, chores and routines were forgotten. Communal life disintegrated. When, months later, hungry survivors returned to their villages, Bosch-like scenes of horror awaited them.

Seasonal factors are yet another consideration, for fluctuations in temperature and humidity affect both the conditions diseases operate in and how human beings decide to live. Measles, for example, occurs usually in the late autumn and winter, appearing perhaps because of increased indoor crowding and a higher incidence then of respiratory infections brought on by the cold and damp. Smallpox in Europe tended to peak during the drier summer months, when people and goods moved around more. Cholera seems also to occur most often in the summertime. In disease transmitted by arthropods, seasonal variation is clearly marked. Yellow fever and malaria are restricted in temperate zones to the warmer months, when mosquitoes are most active. Plague in Eurasia had two peaks, one in January and another in summer. The summer epidemics are related to the greater activity of the flea and rodent vectors as well as people working outdoors. The January peak represents the maximum concentration of humans and rodent pests indoors. The common cold is most prevalent in winter. Even minor cooling of the body can alter resistance to infection. Lowest resistance also seems to be associated with changes in human physiological activities, which in Europe occur in the months of August and February (Sinnecker 1976:203–15).

Warfare and pilgrimages have a major impact on the spread of disease. Armies mobilize comparatively large numbers of men. Living at close quarters, often malnourished, ill-clad, and seldom if ever clean, warriors have frequently suffered higher disease mortality preparing to fight than in actual combat. Soldiers conducting sieges have been especially subject to crowd diseases, foremost of all typhus and plague, which can then infect civilians. Similarly, famous pilgrimages, such as the ones to Mecca, Jerusalem, and Santiago de Compostela, have been associated with sickness and contagion (Omar 1957; Sinnecker 1976:203).

The role of the environment is also crucial. A number of variables clearly influence the spread of disease, among them altitude, temperature, and the presence or absence of water. Seasonal variations in the distribution of malaria are based on the activity of the mosquito vector. Malaria would not be expected, even in areas near the equator, where the elevation is high enough for water to freeze during certain times of year. Humidity, too, is an important consideration. Floods, of course, influence how people and commodities circulate. Some diseases slow down during months of heavy rainfall, when transportation lines are disrupted. At the same time, other diseases flourish in times of flood because of water contamination. The complexity of relationships between the environment and the passage of sickness makes it difficult to ascertain accurately how all of these variables interact (Sinnecker 1976:206–210).

Caught in the Web of Disease

A communicable disease is simply what the term suggests. Diseases are "communicated," or transferred, from one person to another along established routes of transportation. Even diseases carried by arthropod vectors must run parallel to lines of communication. A network, a web of disease is soon established, but it depends at all times on human traffic. The spread of the first smallpox pandemic helps us visualize the process. If we leave aside the possibility of smallpox in the Yucatán prior to 1518, a pattern of pandemic spread is reasonably well documented, even allowing for chronological imprecision or spatial gaps: from Caribbean islands (Hispaniola and Cuba) late in 1518 or early in 1519, Mexico in 1520, throughout Guatemala that same year and the next, then showing up some five years later in Peru. A mainland course south from Mexico as far as Central America is evident. Far less so, but likely, is diffusion north from Mexico, perhaps even across large areas of North America, as Dobyns (1983:11–16; 1989) has asserted. Such claims, whether smallpox reached Florida overland from movement along the Gulf Coast or from native canoes or Spanish ships approaching the peninsula from Cuba, demand a meticulous appraisal of the information at hand, as Henige (1985-86; 1986; 1989) pointedly cautions and as Borah, in this volume, more charitably reiterates.

That the first diseases introduced from the Old World to the New found ideal conditions for the rapid transmission of sickness across vast distances is indisputable. Sizeable populations existed that were immunologically defenseless against the quick work of unknown pathogens. Diseases passed back and forth as long as the chain of vulnerability was unbroken. After a century or so, during which time depopulation in many regions of the order of 90 percent or more had occurred, pandemic activity abated, probably because both the size and density of Indian populations had been reduced to a level at which the possiblity of the spread of new diseases was curtailed. Epidemics that originated as "visiting people" (Greek *epidemos*) became endemic, ones that stayed among or "in people" (Greek *endemos*). The dynamics of the web of disease adapted to a new reality, one in which patterns of sickness changed both in impact and manifestation, with more and more small-scale incidents and fewer and fewer large-scale outbreaks. Certainly by the eighteenth century, as Lovell (1988) indicates in the context of Guatemala, it was possible for disease to break out in some communities without necessarily spreading to neighboring ones only a short distance away. Serious epidemics, however, did still occur during late colonial times, as the chapters by Alchon and Casanueva clearly attest.

In retrospect, an aura of inevitability surrounds the demographic collapse suffered centuries ago by Native American populations, decidedly the most tragic feature of the colonial experience in Spanish America. Given the limited state of knowledge, then, about what epidemic disease was, how it was transmitted, and what possible measures could restrict its spread, once Europeans reached the New World the fate of native peoples was effectively sealed. Several eyewitnesses drew a direct correlation between outbreaks of sickness and Indian depopulation, but most Spaniards did not understand the reasons behind aboriginal demise, even if they soon became aware of what it would mean for their chances of material enrichment or their desires for religious converts (Phelan 1970:92–96). Non-Spaniards who witnessed or were informed about goings on, the English in particular, attributed the loss to demoniacal acts of cruelty on the part of Spanish conquerors and colonists, a view that was enhanced by the disturbing accounts of Fray Bartolomé de Las Casas. The controversial Dominican, however, conveniently overlooked the role disease played in shaping the colonial experience, even among the native groups he knew and grew to love best. Regardless of how we choose to rank the key elements of survival, the fact remains that when Spaniards (even those moved by the most enlightened of intentions) set out to conquer Indians, unforeseen things happened. The year 1492, for all Native Americans, came to represent disaster. A Maya plaint tolls a collective epitaph: "There was then no sickness. The foreigners made it otherwise when they arrived here. They brought shameful things when they came."

GLOSSARY

Achaque. Ailment, complaint, illness.

Adelantado. Leader of an expedition of conquest who has been granted special military and political authority.

Agasajo. Policy of gifts to ensure friendly relations.

Alcalde mayor. A Spanish official in charge of a district known as an *alcaldía mayor.*

Anexo. Small settlement subordinate to a nearby larger one.

Audiencia. Either the governing body of a region or, by extension, the region itself.

Arroba. A unit of measure of approximately eleven kilograms.

Ayllu. Andean kin unit.

Botica. Pharmacy.

Butalmapu. In Chile, a group of forty-five *rehues.*

Cabildo. Municipal town (or city) council.

Cacique. Native chief or ruler.

Cahuin. In Chile, a Mapuche bonding ritual.

Calenturas. Fevers.

Calenturas cuartanas. A form of malaria in which chills occur every four days.

Calenturas tercianas. A form of malaria in which chills occur every three days.

Capitanes de amigos. Friendly captains.

Carga. A variable measure of volume, a bundle.

Castas. Mixed groups.

Catarro. Comon cold, influenza.

Chaac. In Cakchiquel Maya, any eruptive disease.

Chicha. In the Andes, corn beer.

Chorillos. Small textile mills.

Cocoliztli. In Nahuatl, sickness, pestilence, plague.

Comisarios de naciones. Superintendents of Indian nations.

Corregidor. A Spanish official in charge of a district known as a *corregimiento.*

Corregimiento. Province, Indian district.

Curandero. Healer.

Disentería de sangre. Bloody dysentery.

Dolor de costado. Chest or side pain.

Encomendero. Holder of an *encomienda.*

Encomienda. Grant of Indian tributaries from whom goods and services could officially be extracted.

Enfermedad de robles. Onchocerciasis.

Entrada. A military expedition, early reconnaissance.

Esquilencia. Scarlet fever.

Forasteros. Immigrants, outsiders.

Fuertes fluxiones. Diarrhea.

Garrotillo. Diphtheria.

Gucumatz. An undetermined pestilence that may have been pneumonic or pulmonary plague.

Hueycocoliztli. In Nahuatl, great sickness (or pestilence).

Hueyzahuatl. In Nahuatl, big rash, smallpox.

Legua. League, a distance of about 4.2 kilometers.

Loncos. In Chile, native chiefs or rulers.

Machi. Mapuche shaman, usually female.

Machitun. Mapuche propitiatory ceremony.

Mal de pujos. Dysentery.

Matlaltotonqui. In Nahuatl, green fever, perhaps typhus.

Matlazahuatl or matlalzahuatl. In Nahuatl, a disease that may have been typhus.

Mestizo. Person of mixed Indian and European descent.

Mita. In the Andes, a draft of forced native labor.

Mulato. Person of mixed black and European descent.

Noveno. Ecclesiastical tax on agricultural production.

Obraje. Textile mill.

Oidor. Judge of royal court or *audiencia.*
Originario. A person who resides in his or her place of birth.
Palqui. In Chile, medicinal plant.
Paperas. Mumps.
Páramo. High plateau, wide barren plain.
Parcialidad. A small social division associated with certain sections of a town or village.
Parlamento. Peace convention.
Peso. A monetary unit worth two *tostones* or eight *reales.*
Peste. An unspecified epidemic.
Pian. Disease similar to *verruga peruana.*
Pinto. Spirochete-caused disease.
Protomédico. Medical examiner.
Puna. An upland zone in the Andes.
Quechpozahualiztli. In Nahuatl, mumps, swelling in the neck.
Real. A Spanish coin, eight of which make one *peso.*
Regidor. Member of a municipal council.
Rehues. Independent tribes of Southern Chile.
Relación geográfica. A geographical report.
Repartimiento. A draft of native labor in Mesoamerica; in Andes, same as *encomienda.*
Romadizo. Respiratory infection.
Sarampión. Measles.
Scarlatina. Scarlet fever.
Tabardillo. A fever usually considered to be typhus.
Tenientes de amigos. Friendly lieutenants.
Tomín. Small unit of currency.
Tomín. Small unit of currency.
Toqui. In Chile, chief of a *butalmapu.*
Tos. Cough.
Tostón. Half a *peso,* or four *reales.*
Totomanaliztli. Nahuatl term for a disease that may have been smallpox.
Tributario. An Indian tribute payer.
Vecino. A resident of a town or city, with legal status.
Viruelas. Smallpox.
Visita. A tour of inspection.
Verruga peruana. Form of Carrion's disease.
Xaltic zahuatl. In Nahuatl, sandy, pock-forming rash that may have been measles.

Bibliography

Aberle, S.D., J. H. Watkins, and E. H. Pitney
  1940 "The Vital History of San Juan Pueblo." *Human Biology* 12(2):141–87.
Ackerknecht, Erwin H.
  1963 *Geschichte und Geographie der wichtigsten Krankheiten.* Stuttgart: Enke.
Actas del Cabildo de la Ciudad de México, Guía de las
  1970 México: Fondo de Cultura Económica.
Aguado, Fray Pedro
  1956–57 *Recopilación historial.* 4 vols. Bogotá: Academia Colombiana de Historia.
Albornoz, V.M.
  1948 *Cuenca: Monografía histórica.* Cuenca: Editorial Austral.
Alchon, Suzanne Austin
  1984 *See* Browne 1984.
Alden, Dauril and Joseph C. Miller
  1987 "Out of Africa: The Slave Trade and the Transmission of Smallpox to Brazil, 1560–1831." *Journal of Interdisciplinary History* 18:195–224.
Allison, M.J., and E. Gerszten
  1982 *Palaeopathology in South American Mummies: Application of Modern Techniques.* Richmond, Va.: Virginia Commonwealth University.

Anales antiguos de México y sus contornos
1948 Prepared by José Fernando Ramírez and edited by Luis Vargas Rea. 4 vols. México: Vargas Rea.

Anales de Cuauhtitlán
1938 "Geschichte der Königreiche von Colhuacán 1938 und Mexico." In *Quellenwerke zur alten Geschichte Amerikas* vol. 1, ed ited by Walter Lehmann. Stuttgart: Kohlhammer.

Anales de San Gregorio Acapulco, 1520–1606
1949–57 *Tlalocán* 3: 103–41.

Anales de Tecamachalco
1897–1903 "Crónica local y colonial en idioma náhuatl, 1398 y 1590." In *Colección de documentos para la historia mexicana*, edited by Antonio Peñafiel. 6 vols. México: Secretaría de Fomento.

Anales de Tlatelolco y códice de Tlatelolco
1948 Versión preparada y anotada por Heinrich Berlin, con un resumen de los anales y una interpretación del códice por Robert H. Barlow. México.

Anales mexicanos Azcapotzalco
1900 "México-Azcapotzalco, 1426–1589." *Anales del Museo Nacional de México* 7:49–74.

Anda Aguirre, A.
1980 *El adelantado don Juan Salinas Loyola y su gobernación de Yaguarsongo y Pacamoros.* Quito: Casa de la Cultura Ecuatoriana.

Anderson, Gaylord West, and Margaret G. Arnstein
1956 *Communicable Disease Control.* New York: Macmillan.

Antúñez de Mayolo R., Santiago Erik
1981 *La nutrición en el antiguo Perú.* Lima: Banco Central de Reserva del Perú, Oficina Numismática.

Archibald, Robert
1976 "The Economy of the Alta California Mission, 1803–1821." *Southern California Quarterly* 58(2): 227–40.

Archila, Ricardo
1961 *Historia de la medicina en Venezuela. Epoca colonial.* Caracas: Tipografía Vargas.

Arcos, Gualberto
1979 *Evolución de la medicina en el Ecuador.* 3rd ed. (1st. ed., 1933). Quito: Casa de la Cultura Ecuatoriana.

Aschmann, Homer
1959 *The Central Desert of Baja California: Demography and Ecology.* Ibero-Americana 42. Berkeley: University of California Press.

Ashburn, Percy M.
1947 *The Ranks of Death: A Medical History of the Conquest of America.* New York: Coward-McCann.

Asturias, Francisco
1958 *Historia de la medicina en Guatemala.* Guatemala: Editorial Universitaria.

Baker, Brenda J. and George J. Armelagos
1988 "The Origin and Antiquity of Syphilis: Paleopathological Diagnosis and Interpretation." *Current Anthropology* 29(5): 703–37.

Balcázar, Juan Manuel
1956 *Historia de la medicina en Bolivia.* La Paz: Ediciones Juventud.

Ball, A.P.
1977 "Measles." In *A World Geography of Human Diseases,* edited by G. Melvyn Howe, pp. 237–54. New York: Academic Press.

Barbier, Jacques A.
1980 *Reform and Politics in Bourbon Chile, 1755–1796.* Ottawa: Ottawa University Press.

Barros Arana, Diego
1884–1902 *Historia general de Chile.* 16 vols. Santiago: R. Jover.

Barrow, Mark V., Jerry D. Niswander, and Robert Fortune
1972 *Health and Disease of American Indians North of Mexico: A Bibliography, 1810–1969.* Gainesville: University of Florida Press.

Batres Jaureguí, Antonio
1920 *La América Central ante la historia.* Guatemala: Tipografía Sánchez y De Guise. 3 vols.

Benzoni, Girolani
1967 *La historia del Mundo Nuevo.* Caracas: Academia Nacional de Historia.

Berthe, J.P.
1983 "Les épidemies au Mexique au XVIè siècle." *Asclepio* 35: 357–63.

Bett, Walter R.
1954 *The History and Conquest of Common Diseases.* Norman: University of Oklahoma Press.

Black, Francis L.
1975 "Infectious Diseases in Primitive Societies." *Science* 187: 515–18.

Black, Francis L., Francisco de P. Pinheiro, Walter J. Hier and Richard V. Lee
1976 "Epidemiology of Infectious Disease. The Example of Measles." In *Health and Disease in Tribal Societies,* pp. 115–35. Ciba Foundation Symposium 49. Amsterdam: Elzevir.

Borah, Woodrow W.
1964 "America as Model: The Demographic Impact of European Expansion upon the Non-European World." Paper presented in 1962 and published in *Actas y memorias del XXXV Congreso Internacional de Americanistas* 3:379–87, México, D.F.
1976 "Renaissance Europe and the Population of America." *Revista de Historia* 105: 17–61.

Boserup, Ester
1988 "Environment, Population, and Technology in Primitive

Societies." In *The Ends of the Earth: Perspectives on Modern Environmental History*, edited by Donald Worster, pp. 23–38. New York: Cambridge University Press.

Brinton, Daniel G.
1885   *The Annals of the Cakchiquels*. Library of Aboriginal American Literature, no. 6. Philadelphia.

Browne, Suzanne A.
1984   "The Effects of Epidemic Disease in Colonial Ecuador." Ph.D dissertation. Durham, N.C., Department of History, Duke University.

Bullen, Adelaide K.
1972   "Paleoepidemiology and Distribution of Prehistoric Treponemiasis (Syphilis) in Florida." *Florida Anthropologist* 25(4):133–74.

Burnet, MacFarlane
1953   *Natural History of Infectious Disease*. Cambridge: Cambridge University Press.

Bustamante, Miguel E.
1958   *La fiebre amarilla en México y su origen en América*. México, D.F.

Busvine, J.R.
1976   *Insects, Hygiene and History*. London: Athlone Press.

Caballero, J. M.
1902   "En la Independencia." In *La patria boba*, edited by Eduardo Posada and P. M. Ibáñez, pp. 75–274. Bogotá: Biblioteca de Historia Nacional, Imprenta Nacional.

Cabello de Balboa, Miguel
1945   *Obras*. 2 vols. Quito: Editorial Ecuatoriana.
1951   *Miscelánea antártica*. Lima: Instituto de Etnología, Universidad de San Marcos.

Cabildo de Quito
1978   "Descripción de Quito en 1577." In *Museo Histórico* 56:45–70.

Campos, F.
1894   *Compendio histórico de Guayaquil desde su fundación hasta el año 1820*. Guayaquil: Filantrópica.

Carmack, Robert M.
1973   *Quichean Civilization: The Ethnohistoric, Ethnographic, and Archaeological Sources*. Berkeley: University of California Press.

Carmagnani, Marcello
1967–68   "Colonial Latin American Demography: Growth of Chilean Population, 1700–1830." *Journal of Social History* 1(2): 179–91.
1973   *Les mécanismes de la vie économique dans une société coloniale: le Chili 1680–1830*. Paris: S.E.V.P.E.N.

Carmona García, Juan I.
1979   *El sistema de la hospitalidad pública en la Sevilla del Antiguo Régimen*. Sevilla: Diputación Provincial.

Carreras Panchón, Antonio
1976   *La peste y los médicos en la España del renacimiento*. Ediciones

del Instituto de Historia de la Medicina Española. Salamanca: Universidad de Salamanca.

Cartas de Indias
1877 Madrid: Manuel G. Hernández.

Carter, Henry R.
1931 *Yellow Fever: An Epidemiological and Historical Study of Its Place of Origin*. Baltimore: Williams and Wilkins.

Carter, Hodding, ed.
1968 *The Past as Prelude: New Orleans, 1718–1968*. New Orleans: Tulane University Press.

Carvajal, Gaspar de
1958 *Descubrimiento del río de Orellana*. Vol. 28. Quito: Libros de Cabildo de Quito, Imprenta Municipal.

Casanueva, Fernando
1981 "La société coloniale chilienne et l'Eglise au XVIIIè. siècle: les Tentatives d'évangelisation des indiens rebelles." Ph.D. dissertation, Ecole des Hautes Etudes en Sciences Sociales, Paris.
1987 "Politiques, évangelisation et révoltes indiennes à la fin du XVIIIè. siècle." In *L'Amérique espagnole à l'époque des lumières*, pp. 203–19. Paris: Ed. du CNRS.

Castellanos, J. de
1955 *Elgías de varones ilustres de Indias*. 4 vols. Bogotá: Editorial A.B.C.

Cavo, Andrés
1949 *Historia de México*. México, D.F.: Editorial Patria, S.A.

CDI
1864–84 *Colección de documentos inéditos relativos al descubrimiento, conquista y organización de las antiguas posesiones españoles de América y Oceanía*. Edited by L. Torres de Medoza. 42 vols. Madrid.

CDIE
1842–95 Colección de documentos inéditos para la historia de España. 112 vols. Madrid.

Chamberlain, Robert S.
1953 *The Conquest and Colonization of Honduras, 1502–1550*. Washington: Carnegie Institution.

Chandler, David L.
1981 *Health and Slavery in Colonial Colombia*. New York: Arno Press.

Chimalpahin, Domingo Francisco de San Antón Muñón
1965 "Die Relationen Chimalpahins zur Geschichte Mexicos." Teil 2: *Das Jahrhundert nach der Conquista*. Hamburg: Cram, de Gruyter.

Christie, A. B.
1977 "Smallpox." In *A World Geography of Human Diseases*, edited by G. Melvyn Howe, pp.255–70. New York: Academic Press.

Cieza de León, Pedro de
1984–85 *Obras completas*. Madrid: Consejo Superior de Investigaciones Científicas, Instituto Gonzalo Fernández de Oviedo. 3 vols.

Clastres, Pierre
1974   *La société contre l'Etat: recherches d'anthropologie politique.* Paris: Editions de Minuit.
Clendinnen, Inga
1987   *Ambivalent Conquests: Maya and Spaniard in Yucatan, 1517–1570.* New York: Cambridge University Press.
Cobo, Bernabé
1956   *Historia del nuevo mundo.* 2 vols. Madrid: Real Academia de Historia..
Cockburn, Aidan
1976   "Where Did Our Infectious Diseases Come From? The Evolution of Infectious Diseases." In *Health and Disease in Tribal Societies.* Ciba Foundation Symposium, 49. Amsterdam: Elzevir.
Codex Aubin
1981   "Geschichte der Azteken. Der Codex Aubin und verwandte Dokumente." In *Quellenwerke zur alten Geschichte Amerikas 13,* edited by Walter Lehmann and Gerdt Kutscher. Berlin: Mann Verlag.
Codex Mexicanus
1952   *Journal de la Société des Américanistes,* 2:41. Bibliothèque Nationale de Paris.
Códice en Cruz
1981   Edited by Charles E. Dibble. 2 vols. Salt Lake City: University of Utah Press.
Códice Telleriano-Remensis
1963   *Pictografía mexicana del siglo XVI,* edited by Carmen Cook de Leonard. México: Echaniz.
Cole, Jeffrey A.
1981   "The Potosí Mita under Habsburg Administration: The Seventeenth Century." Ph.D dissertation. Amherst, Mass.: Department of History, University of Massahcusetts.
1985   *The Potosí Mita 1573–1700.* Stanford: Stanford University Press.
Colmenares, Germán
1970   *La provincia de Tunja en el Nuevo Reino de Granada.* Bogotá: Universidad de los Andes.
1975   *Historia económica y social de Colombia, 1537–1719.* 2nd ed. Medellín: Editorial La Carreta.
Cook, Noble David
1975   ed. *Tasa de la visita general de Francisco Toledo.* Lima: San Marcos.
1981   *Demographic Collapse: Indian Peru, 1520–1620.* Cambridge: Cambridge University Press.
1982   *People of the Colca Valley: A Population Study.* Boulder, Colo.: Westview Press.
Cook, Noble David, José Hernández Palomo, María Luz Peña Fernández, and Alexandra Parma Cook
1988   "Epidemics in the Parish of Santa Ana de Triana, 1665–

1850." Paper presented at the 46th International Congress of Americanists, Amsterdam.

Cook, Sherburne F.
1935 "Diseases of the Indians of Lower California in the Eighteenth Century." *California and Western Medicine* 43: 432–34.
1937 *The Extent and Significance of Disease among the Indians of Baja California, 1697–1773.* Ibero-Americana: 12. Berkeley: University of California Press.
1939a "Smallpox in Spanish and Mexican California, 1770–1843." *Bulletin of the History of Medicine* 7:153–91.
1939b "The Smallpox Epidemic of 1797 in Mexico." *Bulletin of the History of Medicine* 7:937–69.
1941 "Francisco Xavier de Balmis and the Introduction of Vaccination to Latin America." *Bulletin of the History of Medicine* 11: 543–60, 12: 70–101.
1943 *The Conflict between the California Indian and White Civilization.* Ibero-Americana: 21–24. 4 vols. Berkeley: University of California Press.
1946 "The Incidence and Significance of Disease among the Aztecs and Related Tribes." *Hispanic American Historical Review* 26:320–35.
1973 "Significance of Disease in the Extinction of the New England Indian." *Human Biology* 45:485–508.

Cook, Sherburne F. and Woodrow Borah
1971–79 *Essays in Population History.* 3 vols. Berkeley: University of California Press.

Cooper, Donald B.
1965 Epidemic Disease in Mexico City, 1761–1813: An Administrative, Social and Medical Study. Austin: University of Texas Press.

Costa-Casaretto, C.
1980 "Las enfermedades venéreas en Chile desde el Descubrimiento hasta la Colonia." *Revista Médica Chilena* 108(10): 969–76.

Crosby, Alfred W., Jr.
1967 "Conquistador y Pestilencia: The First New World Pandemic and the Fall of the Great Indian Empires." *Hispanic American Historical Review* 47: 321–37.
1972 *The Columbian Exchange: Biological and Cultural Consequences of 1492.* Westport, Conn.: Greenwood Press.
1976a "Virgin Soil Epidemics as a Factor in the Aboriginal Depopulation in America." *William and Mary Quarterly*, 3rd ser., 33(2):289–99.
1976b *Epidemic and Peace, 1918.* Westport, Conn.: Greenwood Press.
1978 "God . . . Would Destroy Them, and Give their Country to Another People." *American Heritage* 29(6): 38–43.
1986 *Ecological Imperialism: The Biological Expansion of Europe, 900–1900.* Cambridge: Cambridge University Press.

Cumston, Charles Green
   1987   *An Introduction to the History of Medicine from the Time of the Pharaohs to the End of the XVIIIth Century.* New York: Dorset Press.
Davidson, William V., and James J. Parsons
   1980   *Historical Geography in Latin America: Papers in Honor of Robert C. West.* Baton Rouge: Louisiana State University Press.
Denevan, William M.
   1966   *The Aboriginal Cultural Geography of the Llanos de Mojos of Bolivia.* Ibero-Americana: 48. Berkeley: University of California Press.
Denevan, William M., ed.
   1976   *The Native Population of the Americas in 1492.* Madison: University of Wisconsin Press.
Descripción de San Bartolomé, del Partido de Atitlán, 1585
   1965   *Anales de la Sociedad de Geografía e Historia de Guatemala* 38: 262–76.
Díaz del Castillo, Bernal
   1960   *Historia verdadera de la conquista de la Nueva España.* México: Editorial Porrúa.
Diccionario de Autoridades
   1726–39   *Diccionario de la lengua castellana [etc.].* Madrid: Hierro.
Dixon, C.W.
   1962   *Smallpox.* London: J. and A. Churchill.
Dobyns, Henry F.
   1963   "An Outline of Andean Epidemic History to 1720." *Bulletin of the History of Medicine* 37:493–515.
   1966   "Estimating Aboriginal American Population: An Appraisal of Techniques with a New Hemispheric Estimate." *Current Anthropology* 7: 395–449.
   1976a   "Brief Perspective on a Scholarly Transformation: Widowing the 'Virgin' Land." *Ethnohistory* 23:95–104.
   1976b   *Native American Historical Demography. A Critical Bibliography.* The Newberry Library Center for the History of the American Indian, Bibliographical Series. Bloomington: Indiana University Press.
   1983   *Their Number Become Thinned. Native American Population Dynamics in Eastern North America.* Knoxville: University of Tennessee Press.
   1989a   "More Methodological Perspectives on Historical Demography." *Ethnohistory* 36: 285–99.
   1989b   "On Issues in Treponemal Epidemiology." *Current Anthropology* 30(3) 342–43.
Duffy, John
   1953   *Epidemics in Colonial America.* Baton Rouge: Louisiana State University Press.
   1968   "Pestilence in New Orleans." In *The Past as Prelude: New Orleans, 1718–1968,* edited by Hodding Carter, pp. 88–115. New Orleans: Tulane University Press.

1972   *Epidemics in Colonial America*. Port Washington, New York: Kennikat Press.

Dunn, Frederick L.
1965   "On the Antiquity of Malaria in the Western Hemisphere." *Human Biology* 37:385–93.

Dutertre, Jean Baptiste
1667–71   *Histoire générale des Antilles habitées par les français*. 4 vols. Paris: T. Iolly.

Encina, Francisco A., and Leopoldo Castedo
1980   *Resumen de la historia de Chile*. 2 vols. Santiago: Editorial Zig-Zag.

Estete, Miguel de
1918   "El descubrimiento y la conquista del Perú." *Boletín de la Sociedad Ecuatoriana de Estudios Históricos Americanos* 1(3): 300–350.

Eugenio Martínez, María A.
1977   *Tributo y trabajo del indio en Nueva Granada*. Sevilla: Escuela de Estudios Hispano-Americanos.

Evans, Brian M.
1981   "Census Enumeration in Late Seventeenth-Century Alto Peru: The *Numeración General* of 1683–1984." In *Studies in Spanish American Population Studies*, edited by David J. Robinson, pp. 25–44. Boulder, Colorado: Westview Press.
1983   "Migration in Alto Peru in the Late Seventeenth Centuy: The Evidence of the *Numeración General*." Paper presented at the Symposium on Unity and Diversity in Latin America, Tulane University, New Orleans.
1985   "The Structure and Distribution of the Indian Population of Alto Peru in the Late Seventeenth Century." In *Yearbook of the Conference of Latin Americanist Geographers*, pp. 31–37.

Fenner, F., D.A. Henderson, I. Arita, Z. Jezek, and I.D. Ladnyi
1988   *Smallpox and its Eradication*. Geneva: World Health Organization.

Fieldsteel, A. Howard
1983   "Genetics of Treponema." In *Pathogenesis and Immunology of Treponemal Infection*, edited by Ronald F. Schell and Daniel M. Musher, pp. 39–55. New York: Marcel Dekker.

Figueroa, F. de
1904   *Relación de las misiones de la Compañía de Jesús en el país de los Maynas*. Madrid: Lib. General de V. Suárez.

Figueroa Marroquín, Horacio
1983   *Enfermedades de los conquistadores*. Guatemala: Editorial Universitaria.

Florescano, Enrique, and Elsa Malvido, eds.
1980   *Ensayos sobre la historia de las epidemias en México*. 2 vols. México: Instituto Mexicano del Seguro Social.

Flórez de Ocáriz, Juan
1943, 1946, 1955   *Genealogías del Nuevo Reino de Granada*. 3 vols. Bogotá: Prensas de la Biblioteca Nacional y Editorial Kelly.

Fortune, Robert
1971   "The Health of the Eskimos as Portrayed in the Earliest Written Accounts." *Bulletin of the History of Medicine* 45(2): 97-114.
Fragoso Uribe, R.
1979   "Algunas observaciones que apoyan el origen precolom bino de la 'enfermedad de Robles' en América." *Salud Pública de México* 21(6):697-706.
Friede, Juan, ed.
1955-60   *Documentos inéditos para la historia de Colombia.* 10 vols. Bogotá: Academia Colombiana de Historia.
Fuentes y Guzmán, Francisco Antonio de
1932-33   *Recordación Florida.* 3 vols. Guatemala: Sociedad de Geografía e Historia.
Gade, Daniel W.
1979   "Inca and Colonial Settlements, Coca Cultivation and Endemic Disease in the Tropical Forest." *Journal of Historical Geography* 5(3): 263-79.
Gage, Thomas
1928   *The English American: A New Survey of the West Indies.* London: George Routledge and Sons.
García Bernal, M. Cristina
1978   *Yucatán: Población y encomienda bajo los Austrias.* Sevilla: Escuela de Estudios Hispano-Americanos.
García Icazbalceta, Joaquín, ed.
1858-66   *Colección de documentos para la historia de México.* 2 vols. México: J.M. Andrade.
Garcilaso de la Vega
1960   *Comentarios reales de los incas.* 3 vols. Madrid: Biblioteca de Autores Españoles.
Gerhard, Peter
1972   *A Guide to the Historical Geography of New Spain.* Cambridge: Cambridge University Press.
1977   "Congregaciones de Indios en la Nueva España antes de 1570." *Historia Mexicana,* 26:347-95.
Gibson, Charles
1964   *The Aztecs under Spanish Rule. A History of the Indians of the Valley of Mexico. 1519-1810.* Stanford: Stanford University Press.
Goodyear, J.C.
1985   "Medicine in New Spain." *Bulletin of the History of Medicine* 59:117-20.
Gottfried, Robert S.
1983   *The Black Death: National and Human Disaster in Medieval Europe.* New York: Free Press.
Graham-Cumming, George
1967   "Health of the Original Canadians, 1867-1967." *Medical Services Journal of Canada* 23(2):115-66.

Grmek, Mirko D.
1989   *Diseases in the Ancient Greek World.* Baltimore: Johns Hopkins University Press.
Groot, José M.
1889–93   *Historia eclesiástica y civil de Nueva Granada.* 5 vols. Bogotá: Casa Editorial de M. Rivas.
Grumbach, A., and W. Kikuth, eds.
1971   *Die Infektionskrankheiten des Menschen und ihre Erreger.* Stuttgart: Thieme.
Gsell, O., and W. Mohr
1965   *Infektionskrankheiten.* Berlin: Springer.
Guerra, Francisco
1975   "The Problem of Syphilis." In *First Images of America: The Impact of the New World on the Old,* edited by Fredi Chiapelli, pp. 845–51. 2 vols. Berkeley: University of California Press.
1978   "The Dispute over Syphilis: Europe versus America." *Clio Medica* (Netherlands) 13(1):39–62.
1985   "La epidemia americana de influenza en 1493." *Revista de Indias* 45: 325–47.
1986   "El efecto demográfico de las epidemias tras el descubrimiento de América." *Revista de Indias* 46:41–58.
1987   "The Cause of Death of the American Indians." *Nature* 326:449–50.
1988   "The Earliest American Epidemic: The Influenza of 1493." *Social Science History* 12(3): 305–25.
Halberstein, Robert A., Michael H. Crawford, and Hugo Nutini
1973   "Historical-Demographic Analysis of Indian Population in Tlaxcala, Mexico." *Social Biology* 20:40–50.
Harvey, R.R.
1967   "Population of the Cahuilla Indians: Decline and Its Causes." *Eugenics Quarterly* 14(1):185–98.
Heinbecker, Peter, and Edith I.M. Irvine-Jones
1928   "Susceptibility of Eskimos to the Common Cold and a Study of Their Natural Immunity to Diphtheria, Scarlet Fever and Bacterial Filtrates." *Journal of Immunology* 15(5): 395–406.
Henige, David
1985–86   "If Pigs Could Fly: Timucuan Population and Native American Historical Demography." *Journal of Interdisciplinary History* 16:701–20.
1986   "Primary Source by Primary Source? On the Role of Epidemics in New World Depopulation." *Ethnohistory* 33(3): 293–312.
1989   "On the Current Devaluation of the Notion of Evidence: A Rejoinder to Dobyns." *Ethnohistory* 36: 304–7.
Hermida Piedra, César
1951   "Apuntes para la historia de la medicina en el Azuay." *Anales de la Universidad de Cuenca* 7(2–3):5–155.

Hermosilla Molina, Antonio
 1970   *Cien años de medicina sevillana.* Sevilla: Consejo Superior de
        Investigaciones Científicas.
Hernández, Francisco
 1959–60 *Obras completas.* 3 vols. México· Universidad Nacional
        Autónoma de México.
Herrera, Pablo, and Alcides Enríquez
 1916   *Apuntes cronológicos de las obras y trabajos del cabildo y munici-
        palidad de Quito.* 2 vols. Quito: Imprenta Municipal.
Herrera y Tordesillas, Antonio de
 1934   *Historia general de los hechos de los castellanos en las islas y tierra
        firme del Mar Océano.* 17 vols. Madrid: Real Academia de la
        Historia.
Hoeppli, R.
 1969   *Parasitic Disease in Africa and the Western Hemisphere. Early
        Documentation and Transmission by the Slave Trade.* Acta Tro-
        pica, Supplementum 10. Basel.
Hoffman, B.H., and A.J. Haskell
 1984   "The Papago Indians: Historical, Social, and Medical Per-
        spectives." *Mount Sinai Journal of Medicine* 51(6):707–13.
Hollingsworth, Thomas H.
 1969   *Historical Demography.* Ithaca: Cornell University Press.
Hopkins, Donald R.
 1983   *Princes and Peasants. Smallpox in History.* Chicago: University
        of Chicago Press.
Hovind-Hougen, Kari
 1983   "Morphology." In *Pathogenesis and Immunology of Treponemal
        Infection,* edited by Ronald F. Schell and Daniel M. Musher,
        pp. 3–28. New York: Marcel Dekker.
Howe, G. Melvyn, ed.
 1977   *A World Geography of Human Diseases.* New York: Academic
        Press.
Hrdlicka, Ales
 1908   *Physiological and Medical Observations among the Indians of
        Southwestern United States and Northern Mexico.* U.S. Bureau
        of American Ethnology. Bulletin 34. Washington.
 1932   "Disease, Medicine, and Surgery among the American
        Aborigines." *Journal of the American Medical Association* 99:
        1661–66.
Hudson, Ellis Herndon
 1965   "Treponematosis and Man's Social Evolution." *American
        Anthropologist* 65: 885–901.
Humboldt, Alexander Freiherr von
 1811   *Essai politique sur le royaume de la Nouvelle-Espagne.* 5 vols.
        Paris: Chez F. Schoell.
 1966   *Ensayo político sobre el reino de la Nueva España.* México: Edi-
        torial Porrúa.
Ibáñez, Pedro
 1913–23 *Crónicas de Bogotá.* 4 vols. Bogotá: Imprenta Nacional.

1935 *Isagoge Histórica apologética de las Indias Occidentales y especial de la provincia de San Vicente de Chiapa y Guatemala de la orden de Predicadores.* Guatemala: Sociedad de Geografía e Historia.

Iscán, M. Yasar, and P. Miller-Shaivitz
1985 "Prehistoric Syphilis in Florida." *Journal of the Florida Medical Association* 72(2):109–13.

Jackson, Robert H.
1981 "Epidemic Disease and Population Decline in the Baja California Missions, 1697–1834." *Southern California Quarterly* 63(4): 308–46.
1984 "Demographic Patterns in the Missions of Central Baja California." *Journal of California and Great Basin Anthropology* 6(1):91–112.

Jacobs, Wilbur R.
1974 "The Tip of the Iceberg: Pre-Columbian Indian Demography and Some Implications for Revision." *William and Mary Quarterly*, 3rd series, 31(1): 123–32.

Jara, Alvaro
1971 *Guerra y sociedad en Chile.* Santiago.

Jaramillo Uribe, J.
1964 "La población indígena de Colombia en el momento de la conquista y sus transformaciones posteriores." *Anuario Colombiano de Historia Social y de la Cultura* 1(2):239–93.

Jarco, Saul
1964 "Some Observations on Disease in Prehistoric North America." *Bulletin of the History of Medicine* 38(1):1–19.

Jiménez de la Espada, Marcos, ed.
1965 *Relaciones geográficas de Indias. Perú.* 3 vols. Madrid: Biblioteca de Autores Españoles.

Johansson, S. Ryan
1982 "The Demographic History of the Native Peoples of North America: A Selective Bibliography." *Yearbook of Physical Anthropology* 25:133–52.

Joralemon, Donald
1982 "New World Depopulation and the Case of Disease." *Journal of Anthropological Research* 38(1):108–27.

Jouanen, José
1941–43 *Historia de la Compañía de Jesús en la antigua provincia de Quito, 1570–1774.* 2 vols. Quito: Editorial Ecuatoriana.

Juan, Jorge, and Antonio de Ulloa
1758 *A Voyage to South America.* 2 vols. London: L. Davies and C. Reymers.

Keehn, Pauline A.
1978 *The Effect of Epidemic Disease on the Natives of North America: An Annotated Bibliography.* London: Survival International.

Kempper, Rosemary
1973 "Prevention of Smallpox in Alta California during the Fran-

ciscan Mission Period, 1769–1833." *California Medicine* 119: 73–77.

Kiple, Kenneth F., and Virginia H. Kiple
1980 "Deficiency Disease in the Caribbean." *Journal of Interdisciplinary History* 11(2):197–215.

Landa, Diego de
1941 *Landa's Relación de las cosas de Yucatán*. Translated and edited by Alfred M. Tozzer. Cambridge: Peabody Museum, Harvard University.

Lanning, John T.
1985 *The Royal Protomedicato: The Regulation of the Medical Profession in the Spanish Empire*. Durham: Duke University Press.

Larraín Barros, H.
1980 *Demografía y asentamientos indígenas en la sierra norte del Ecuador en el siglo XVI. Estudio etnohistórico de las fuentes tempranas (1525–1600)*. 2 vols. Otavalo: Instituto Otavaleño de Antropología.

Lastres, Juan B.
1951 *Historia de la medicina peruana.* 3 vols. Lima: San Marcos.

León, L.A.
1951 *Relación cronológica del tifus exantemático en el Ecuador.* Quito: Imprenta de la Universidad.

León, Nicolás
1919 *¿Qué era el Matlazahuatl y qué el Cocoliztli en los tiempos precolombinos y en la época hispánica?* México, D.F.: Imprenta Franco Mexicana.

LeRoy Ladurie, Emmanuel
1973 "Un concept: l'unification microbienne du monde (XIVè-XVIIè siècles)." *Schweizerische Zeitschrift für Geschichte* 23(4): 627–94.

Lizárraga, Reginaldo de
1968 *Descripción breve de toda la tierra del Perú, Tucumán, Río de La Plata y Chile*. Madrid: Ediciones Atlas.

Long, Esmond R.
1935 "The Rise and Fall of Tuberculosis in Certain American Peoples." *Journal of Public Health and Tropical Medicine* (Puerto Rico), 10:270–87.

López de Gomara, F. de
1918 "Hispania victrix: Historia general de las Indias." In *Historiadores primitivos de Indias.* 1:155–455. Madrid: Biblioteca de Autores Españoles.

1966 *Historia general de las Indias.* Barcelona: Iberia.

Lovell, W. George
1982 "Historia demográfica de la sierra de los Cuchumatanes, Guatemala, 1520–1821." *Mesoamérica* 4:279–301.

1985 *Conquest and Survival in Colonial Guatemala: A Historical Geography of the Cuchumatán Highlands, 1500–1821*. Kingston and Montreal: McGill-Queen's University Press.

1988 "Enfermedades del Viejo Mundo y mortandad amerindia:

La viruela y el tabardillo en la sierra de los Cuchumatanes de Guatemala (1780–1810)." *Mesoamérica* 16: 239–85.

1990 *Conquista y cambio cultural: la sierra de los Cuchumatanes de Guatemala, 1500–1821.* Antigua, Guatemala: Centro de Investigaciones Regionales de Mesoamérica and South Woodstock, Vermont: Plumsock Mesoamerican Studies.

Lovell, W. George, Christopher H. Lutz, and William R. Swezey

1984 "The Indian Population of Southern Guatemala, 1549–1551: An Analysis of López de Cerrato's Tasaciones de Tributos." *The Americas* 40(4):459–77.

Lucena, Manuel

1965 *Nuevo Reino de Granada. Real Audiencia y presidentes: Presidentes de capa y espada (1605–1628).* Bogotá: Academia Colombiana de Historia.

Lutz, Christopher H.

1982 *Historia sociodemográfica de Santiago de Guatemala, 1541–1773.* Antigua, Guatemala: Centro de Investigaciones Regionales de Mesoamérica.

MacLeod, Murdo J.

1973 *Spanish Central America: A Socioeconomic History, 1520–1720.* Berkeley: University of California Press.

1983 "Modern Research on the Demography of Colonial Central America: A Bibliographical Essay." *Latin American Population History Newsletter* 3(3/4):23–39.

1986 "The *Matlazáhuatl* of 1737–1738 in Some Villages of the Guadalajara Region." *Studies in the Social Sciences.* West Georgia College. 25:7–15.

MacLeod, Murdo J., and Robert Wasserstrom

1983 *Spaniards and Indians in Southeastern Mesoamerica: Essays on the History of Ethnic Relations.* Lincoln: University of Nebraska Press.

Madero, M.

1955 *Historia de la medicina en la provincia del Guayas.* Guayaquil: Casa de la Cultura Ecuatoriana.

Major, Ralph Hermon

1945 *Classic Descriptions of Diseases.* Springfield.

Malvido, Elsa

1975 "Efectos de las epidemias y hambrunas en la población colonial de México (1591–1810): El caso de Cholula, Puebla." *Salud Pública de México* 17(6):793–802.

Malvido, Elsa, and Carlos Viesca

1985 "La epidemia de cocoliztli de 1576." *Historias* (México, D.F.), 11:27–33.

Malvido, Elsa, Josefina Mansilla, and José A. Pompa

1986 "Un cementerio indígena del siglo XVI en Huexotla, Estado de México." *Travaux et Recherches dans les Amériques du Centre* 10:39–51. México, D. F.: CEMCA.

Manson-Bahr, P.H.

1941 *Manson's Tropical Diseases.* London: Cassel and Co.

Marks, G., and W.K. Beatty
    1976   *Epidemics.* New York: Charles Scribner's and Sons.
Márquez, Morgin L.
    1984   *Sociedad colonial y enfermedad.* México, D.F.: Instituto Na-
           cional de Antropología e Historia.
Martínez Durán, Carlos
    1941   *Las ciencias médicas en Guatemala: Origen y evolución.* Guate-
           mala: Tipografía Sánchez y De Guise.
McAfee, Byron, and Robert H. Barlow, eds.
    1948   "Únos anales coloniales de Tlatelolco, 1519–1633." *Tlate-
           lolco a través de los tiempos* 10. México.
McBryde, Felix Webster
    1940   "Influenza in America during the Sixteenth Century (Gua-
           temala: 1523, 1559–1562, 1576)." *Bulletin of the History of
           Medicine* 8(2):296–302.
McGrew, Roderick E.
    1985   *Encyclopedia of Medical History.* London: Macmillan Press.
McFalls, J.A., and McFalls, M.H.
    1984   *Disease and Fertility.* New York: Academic Press.
McNeill, William H.
    1976   *Plagues and Peoples.* Garden City, New York: Anchor Press/
           Doubleday.
    1978   "Disease in History." *Social Science and Medicine* 12:79–81.
Mendieta, Fray Jerónimo de
    1945   *Historia eclesiástica indiana.* 2d ed., 4 vols. México, D.F.: Edi-
           torial Salvador Chávez Hayhoe.
Metraux, Alfred
    1943   "Le caractère de la conquête jésuitique." *Acta Americana,*
           México. 1.
Micheli, A. de
    1979   "La viruela en la Nueva España." *Prensa Médica Mexicana*
           44(9–10): 201–7.
Milner, G.R.
    1980   "Epidemic Disease in the Postcontact Southeast: A Reap-
           praisal." *Midcontinental Journal of Archaeology* 5(1):39–56.
Minchom, Martin
    1986   "Demographic Change in Ecuador During the Eighteenth
           Century." Unpublished manuscript, Quito.
Mitchem, Jeffrey M., and Dale L. Hutchinson
    1987   *Interim Report on Archaeological Research at the Tatham Mound,
           Citrus County, Florida: Season III.* Florida State Museum, De-
           partment of Anthropology, Miscellaneous Project Report
           Series, 30. Gainesville.
Molina, Alonso de
    1970   *Vocabulario en lengua castellana y mexicana y mexicana y castel-
           lana.* México: Editorial Porrúa. [Originally appeared 1555
           (Part 1) and 1571 (Part 2).]
Molina, Antonio de
    1943   *Antigua Guatemala.* Guatemala: Unión Tipográfica.

Molina, Juan Ignacio
1978 *Historia natural y civil de Chile*. Santiago: Editorial Universitaria.
Monroy, J.L.
1938 *El Convento de la Merced de Quito, 1534–1617*. Quito: Editorial Labor.
Montesinos, D.F.
1906 *Los anales del Perú*. 2 vols. Madrid.
Morúa, Martín de
1962–64 *Historia general del Perú, origen y descendencia de los Incas* (1590–1611). Madrid: Instituto Gonzalo Fernández de Oviedo.
Motolinía o Benavente, Toribio de
1971 *Memoriales o libro de las cosas de la Nueva España y de los naturales dello*. México: UNAM.
Muñoz Camargo, Diego
1892 *Historia de Tlaxcala*. México: Secretaría de Fomento.
Murra, John
1975 *Formaciones económicas y políticas del mundo andino*. Lima: Instituto de Estudios Peruanos.
Neel, James V.
1976 "Health and Disease in Unacculturated Amerindian Populations." In *Health and Disease in Tribal Societies*. pp. 155–68. Ciba Foundation Symposium. 49. Amsterdam: Elzevir.
Newson, Linda A.
1976 *Aboriginal and Spanish Colonial Trinidad. A Study in Culture Contact*. London and New York: Academic Press.
1982 "The Depopulation of Nicaragua in the Sixteenth Century." *Journal of Latin American Studies* 14(2):253–86.
1985 "Indian Population Patterns in Colonial Spanish America." *Latin American Research Review* 20(3):41–74.
1986 *The Cost of Conquest: Indian Decline in Honduras under Spanish Rule*. Boulder, Colo.: Westview Press.
1987 *Indian Survival in Colonial Nicaragua*. Norman: University of Oklahoma Press.
Numbers, Ronald L., ed.
1987 *Medicine in the New World. New Spain, New France, and New England*. Knoxville: University of Tennessee Press.
Núñez de Pineda y Bascuñán, Francisco
1863 *Cautiverio feliz . . . y razón individual de las guerras dilitadas del reino de Chile*. Santiago: Imprenta del Ferrocarril.
Oberem, Udo
1978 "El acceso a recursos naturales de diferentes ecologías en la sierra ecuatoriana (siglo XVI)." *42nd International Congress of Americanists, Paris*. 4:51–64.
Olivares, Miguel de
1874 *Historia de la Compañía de Jesús en Chile (1592–1736)*. Santiago: Imprenta A. Bello.

Omar, W.
1957 "The Mecca Pilgrimage." *World Health Organization Chronicles*, 11: 337–42.

Orellana, Sandra L.
1987 *Indian Medicine in Highland Guatemala.* Albuquerque: University of New Mexico Press.

Pacheco, Juan M.
1959 *Los jesuitas en Colombia.* 2 vols. Bogotá: Editorial Eudes.

Paredes Borja, V.
1963 *Historia de la medicina en el Ecuador.* 2 vols. Quito: Casa de la Cultura Ecuatoriana.

Parry, John H.
1963 *The Age of Reconnaissance.* London.

Paso y Troncoso, Francisco del, ed.
1905 *Papeles de Nueva España.* 9 vols. Madrid.
1939–42 *Epistolario de la Nueva España, 1505–1818.* México: Robredo. 16 vols.

Phelan, John Leddy
1967 *The Kingdom of Quito in the Seventeenth Century.* Madison: University of Wisconsin Press.
1970 *The Millennial Kingdom of the Franciscans in the New World.* Berkeley: University of California Press.

Pike, Ruth
1972 *Aristocrats and Traders. Sevillian Society in the Sixteenth Century.* Ithaca: Cornell University Press.

Pollitzer, R.
1954 *Plague.* World Health Organization Monograph Series (Geneva) 22.

Polo, José Toribio
1913 "Apuntes sobre las epidemias del Perú." *Revista Histórica* 5:50–109.

Poma de Ayala, Felipe Guaman
1980 *El primer nueva corónica y buen gobierno*, edited by J.V. Murra and R. Adorno. 3 vols. México: Siglo Ventiuno.

Posada, Eduardo, and P. M. Ibáñez, eds.
1910 *Relaciones de mando.* Bogotá: Biblioteca de Historia Nacional, Imprenta Nacional.

Quiroga, Jerónimo de
1979 *Memoria de los sucesos de la guerra de Chile.* Santiago.

Radell, David R.
1976 "The Indian Slave Trade and Population of Nicaragua during the Sixteenth Century." In *The Native Population of the Americas in 1492*, edited by William M. Denevan, pp. 67–76. Madison: University of Wisconsin Press.

Ramenofsky, Ann R.
1987 *Vectors of Death: The Archaeology of European Contact.* Albuquerque: University of New Mexico Press.

Raynaud, Georges, Miguel Angel Asturias and J.M. González de Mendoza
1946 *Los Xahil.* México: UNAM.
Real Academia Española
1956 *Diccionario de la lengua española.* Madrid: Espasa Calpe.
Recinos, Adrián
1950 *Memorial de Sololá.* México: Fondo de Cultura Económica.
Recinos, Adrián, and Delia Goetz, eds.
1953 *The Annals of the Cakchiquels.* Norman: University of Oklahoma Press.
Relación de Michoacán, 1541. See Tudela de la Orden, José
Relación de Santiago Atitlán, 1585
1964 *Anales de la Sociedad de Geografía e Historia de Guatemala* 37: 87–106.
RGI
1965 *Relaciones geográficas de Indias: Perú.* 3 vols. Edited by Marcos Jiménez de la Espada. Madrid: Biblioteca de Autores Españoles.
Ricard, Robert
1966 *The Spiritual Conquest of Mexico: An Essay on the Apostolate and Evangelizing Methods of the Mendicant Orders in New Spain, 1523–1572.* Berkeley: University of California Press.
Risse, Guenter
1987 "Medicine in New Spain." In *Medicine in the New World: New Spain, New France, and New England,* edited by Ronald L. Numbers, pp. 12–63. Knoxville: University of Tennessee Press.
Robinson, David J., ed.
1979 *Social Fabric and Spatial Structure in Colonial Latin America.* Ann Arbor, Mich.: University Microfilms.
1981 *Studies in Spanish American Population History.* Boulder, Colo.: Westview Press.
Robles, Antonio
1972 *Diario de sucesos notables.* México: Editorial Porrúa.
Romoli de Avery, K.
1962 "El suroeste del Cauca y sus indios al tiempo de la conquista española." *Revista Colombiana de Antropología* 11: 239–300.
Rosales, Diego de
1877–78 *Historia general de el reyno de Chile, Flandes indiano.* 3 vols. Valparaíso: Mercurio.
Rothschild, H. ed.
1981 *Biocultural Aspects of Disease.* New York: Academic Press.
Roys, Ralph L., ed.
1967 *The Book of Chilam Balam of Chumayel.* Norman: University of Oklahoma Press.

Ruiz Rivera, Julián
 1975   *Encomienda y mita en Nueva Granada en el siglo XVII.* Sevilla:
        Escuela de Estudios Hispano-Americanos.
Rumazo González, J.
 1948–49 *Colección de documentos para la historia de la Audiencia de
          Quito.* 8 vols. Madrid.
Sahagún, Bernardino de
 1950–69 *Florentine Codex: General History of the Things of New
          Spain,* Translated from the Aztec into English, with notes
          and illustrations by Arthur J.O. Anderson and Charles E.
          Dibble. Santa Fe: The School of American Research and the
          University of Utah.
St. Hoyme, L.E.
 1969   "On the Origins of New World Paleopathology." *American
        Journal of Physical Anthropology* 31(3):295–302.
Salinas Cantú, Hernán
 1975   *Sombras sobre la ciudad: Historia de las grandes epidemias de vi-
        ruela, cólera morbus, fiebre amarilla e influenza española que ha
        sufrido Monterrey.* Monterrey, N.L.: Editorial Alfonso Reyes.
Salomon, Frank L.
 1978   "Ethnic Lords of Quito in the Age of thc Incas: The Political
        Economy of North-Andean Chiefdoms." Ph.D. disserta-
        tion, Cornell University.
Sánchez-Albornoz, Nicolás
 1974   *The Population of Latin America. A History.* Berkeley: Univer-
        sity of California Press.
 1983   "Mita, migraciones y pueblos: variaciones en el espacio y
        en el tiempo." *Revista Boliviana* 3: 31–59.
Sanders, William T., and Carson Murdy
 1982   "Population and Agricultural Adaptation in Highland Gua-
        temala." In *The Historical Demography of Highland Guatemala,*
        edited by Robert M. Carmack, Christopher H. Lutz, and
        John D. Early, pp. 23–34. Albany: Institute of Mesoameri-
        can Studies.
Santa Cruz Pachacuti Yamqui, Juan de
 1968   *Relación de antigüedades deste reyno del Pirú.* Madrid: Edi-
        ciones Atlas.
Sarmiento de Gamboa, Pedro de
 1960   *Historia índica.* Madrid: Biblioteca de Autores Españoles.
Sauer, Carl O.
 1952   *Agricultural Origins and Dispersals.* New York: American
        Geographical Society.
 1966   *The Early Spanish Main.* Berkeley: University of California
        Press.
 1971   *Sixteenth-Century North America.* Berkeley: University of Cal-
        ifornia Press.
Schell, Ronald F. and Daniel M. Musher, eds.
 1983   *Pathogenesis and Immunology of Treponemal Infection.* New
        York: Marcel Dekker.

Scholes, France V., and Eleanor B. Adams, eds.
1961 "Cartas del licenciado Jerónimo de Valderrama y otros documentos sobre su visita al gobierno de Nueva España,
1563–1565." *Documentos para la historia del México colonial*
(México) 7.
Shattuck, George Cheever
1938 *Medical Survey of the Republic of Guatemala.* Washington: Carnegie Institution.
Shea, Daniel S.
1976 "A Defense of Small Population Estimates for the Central
Andes." In *The Native Population of the Americas in 1492*, edited by William M. Denevan, pp. 157–80. Madison: University of Wisconsin Press.
Sherman, William L.
1979 *Forced Native Labor in Sixteenth-Century Central America.* Lin-
coln: University of Nebraska Press.
1983 "Some Aspects of Change in Guatemalan Society, 1470–
1620." In *Spaniards and Indians in Southeastern Mesoamerica:
Essays on the History of Ethnic Relations*, edited by Murdo J.
MacLeod and Robert Wasserstrom, pp. 169–88. Lincoln:
University of Nebraska Press.
Simmons, J.W.
1932 "Influence of Epidemic Disease on Early History of the
Western Hemisphere." *Military Surgeon* 71:133–43.
Simmons, Marc
1966 "New Mexico's Smallpox Epidemic of 1780–1781." *New
Mexico Historical Review* 41(4):319–26.
Simón, Fray Pedro
1882–92 *Noticias historiales de las conquistas de tierra firme en las
Indias Occidentales.* 5 vols. Bogotá: Imprenta de Medardo
Rivas.
Simpson, Lesley Byrd
1950 *The Encomienda in New Spain: The Beginnings of Spanish Mex-
ico.* Berkeley: University of California Press.
Sinnecker, Herbert A.
1976 *General Epidemiology.* New York: Wiley.
Smith, Michael M.
1974 "The *Real Expedición Marítima de la Vacuna* in New Spain and
Guatemala." *Transactions of the American Philosophical Society*, New Series, no. 64, Part 1.
Smith, Michael T.
1987 *Archaeology of Aboriginal Culture Change in the Interior South-
east: Depopulation During the Early Historic Period.* Florida
State Museum, Ripley B. Bullen Monographs in Anthropology and History, 6. Gainesville: University Presses of
Florida.
Snow, Dean, and Kim M. Lanphear
1988 "European Contact and Indian Depopulation in the North-

east: The Timing of the First Epidemics." *Ethnohistory* 35(1):
15–33.

1989   "More Methodological Perspectives: A Rejoinder to Dobyns." *Ethnohistory* 36(3): 299–304.

"Sobre los tributos de los indios de Yaguachi (1579)"
1972   *Revista del Archivo Histórico del Guayas* 1:70–97.

Solano, Francisco de
1974   *Los mayas del siglo XVIII.* Madrid: Ediciones Cultura
Hispánica.

Soriano, Andrés
1966   *La medicina en el Nuevo Reino de Granada durante la conquista
y la colonia.* Bogotá: Universidad Nacional de Colombia, Imprenta Nacional.

Speck, F.L., and R.G. Wheeland
1984   "Cutaneous Histopathology of Southwestern American Indian Mummies." *International Journal of Dermatology* 23(7):
487–92.

Spiegelman, Mortimer
1968   *Introduction to Demography.* Cambridge: Harvard University
Press.

Stage, H.H., and C.M. Gjulin
1935   "Anophelines and Malaria in the Pacific." *Northwest Science*
9(3):5–11.

Sticker, George
1923   Summary of paper on leprosy and syphilis in Hither Asia
before 1000 A.D., delivered at 16th meeting of Deutsche
Gesellschaft für Geschichte der Medizin und der Naturwis-
senschaften, Bad Stehen, 18–19 September, reported in *Ja-
nus, Archives Internationales pour l'Histoire de la Médicine et la
Géographie Médicale* 28 (1924): 394.

1924   "Krankheiten in Mittelamerika zur Zeit des Columbus." *Ja-
nus, Archives Internationales pour l'Histoire de la Médicine et la
Géographie Médicale* 28:232–304.

1931   "Epidemias que los conquistadores blancos llevaron al
Nuevo Mundo." *Boletín de la Revista de Higiene y Tuberculosis*
24:78–84.

1932–33 "Die Einschleppung europäischer Krankheiten in Ame-
rika wahrend der Entdeckungszeit; ihr Einfluss auf den
Ruckgang der Bevölkerung," *Ibero-Amerikanisches Archiv* 6:
62–83, 194–224.

Storey, R.
1985   "An Estimate of Mortality in a Pre-Columbian Urban Population." *American Anthropology* 87:519–35.

1986   "Perinatal Mortality at Pre-Columbian Teotihuacán." *American Journal of Physical Anthropology* 69:541–48.

Swann, Michael M.
1980   "The Demographic Impact of Disease and Famine in Late
Colonial Northern Mexico." In *Historical Geography in Latin
America: Papers in Honor of Robert C. West,* edited by Wil-

liam V. Davidson and James J. Parsons, pp. 97–109. Baton
Rouge: Louisiana State University Press.
Sweet, David Graham
1969 "The Population of the Upper Amazon in the 17th and 18th
Centuries." M.A. thesis, University of Wisconsin.
Tira de Tepechpán
1978 *Códice colonial procedente del valle de México*, edited by Xavier
Nóguez. México: Biblioteca del Estado.
Tolhausen, Luis
1892 *Neues spanisch-deutsches und deutsch-spanisches Wörterbuch.*
Leipzig: Tauchnitz.
Torquemada, Juan de
1723 *Monarquía indiana.* Madrid: Rodríguez Franco.
Torres de Mendoza, L. ed.
1864–84 *Colección de documentos inéditos relativos al descubrimiento,
conquista y organización de las antiguas posesiones españolas de
América y Oceanía.* 42 vols. Madrid.
Tudela de la Orden, José, ed.
1977 *Relación de las ceremonias y ritos y población y gobierno de los
indios de la provincia de Michoacán, 1541.* Morelia: Editorial
Balsal.
Tyrer, Robson B.
1976 "The Demographic and Economic History of the Audiencia
of Quito." Ph.D. dissertation, University of California.
Valle, R.K.
1973 "Prevention of Smallpox in Alta California during the Franciscan Mission Period." *California Medicine* 119:73–77.
Vargas Jurado, J.M.
1902 "Tiempos Coloniales." In *La patria boba*, edited by Eduardo
Posada and P.M. Ibáñez, pp. 1–71. Bogotá: Biblioteca de
Historia Nacional.
Vázquez, Francisco
1937–44 *Crónica de la provincia del santísimo nombre de Jesús de Guatemala.* 4 vols. Guatemala: Sociedad de Geografía e Historia.
Vázquez, Francisco de
1909 "Relación verdadera de todo lo que sucedió en la Jornada
de Omagua y Dorado." *Historiadores de Indias.* Madrid.
2:423–84.
Veblen, Thomas T.
1977 "Native Population Decline in Totonicapán, Guatemala."
Annals of the Association of American Geographers 67(4):
484–99.
Velasco, J. de
1977–79 *Historia del reino de Quito en la América meridional.* 3 vols.
Quito: Casa de la Cultura Ecuatoriana.
Vetancurt, Agustín de
1698 *Teatro mexicano; crónica de la provincia del Santo Evangelio de
México y menología cristiana.* México: Benavides.

Villacorta Calderón, J. Antonio
  1934   *Memorial de Tecpán Atitlán.* Guatemala: Tipografía Nacional.
Villacorta Cifuentes, Jorge Luis
  1976   *Historia de la medicina, cirugía y obstetricia prehispánicas.*
         Guatemala.
Villamarín, Juan
  1972   "Encomenderos and Indians in the Formation of Colo-
         nial Society in the Sabana de Bogotá, 1537–1740." Ph.D.
         dissertation, Brandeis University. Ann Arbor: University
         Microfilms.
Villamarín, Juan, and Judith Villamarín
  1979   "Chibcha Settlement Under Spanish Rule, 1537–1810." In
         Social Fabric and Spatial Structure in Colonial Latin America,
         edited by David J. Robinson, pp. 1–84. Ann Arbor, Mich.:
         University Microfilms.
  1981   "Colonial Censuses and Tributary Lists of the Sabana de
         Bogotá Chibcha: Sources and Issues." In *Studies in Spanish
         American Population History,* edited by David J. Robinson,
         pp. 45–92. Boulder, Colo.: Westview Press.
Vives Azancot, Pedro A.
  1982   "Entre el esplendor y la decadencia: la población de Mi-
         siones, 1750–1759." *Revista de Indias* 42(169–70):469–543.
Vogel, Virgil, Jr.
  1970   "Indian Health and Disease." *Ecologist* 5 (7): 254–58.
Washburne, Douglas
  1983   "The Bourbon Reforms: Creole Elites in the Audiencia of
         Quito." Ph.D. dissertation, University of California.
Way, A.B.
  1981   "Diseases of Latin America." in *Biocultural Aspects of Dis-
         ease,* edited by H. Rothschild, pp. 253–91. New York: Aca-
         demic Press.
Wood, C.S.
  1975   "New Evidence for a Late Introduction of Malaria into the
         New World." *Current Anthropology* 16:93–104.
Worster, Donald, ed.
  1988   *The Ends of the Earth: Perspectives on Modern Environmental
         History.* New York: Cambridge University Press.
Wrigley, E.A.
  1969   *Population and History.* New York: McGraw-Hill.
Zamora, Fray Alonso de
  1930   *Historia de la provincia de San Antonio del Nuevo Reino de Gra-
         nada.* Caracas: Editorial Sur América.
Zamora Acosta, Elías
  1985   *Los mayas de las tierras altas en el siglo XVI. Tradición y cambio
         en Guatemala.* Sevilla: Diputación Provincial.
Zárate, Agustín de
  1913   *Historia del descubrimiento y conquista del Perú.* Madrid: Bibli-
         oteca de Autores Españoles.

Ziegler, Philip
    1976   *The Black Death.* Hammondsworth: Pelican Books.
Zinsser, Hans
    1935   *Rats, Lice and History, Being a Study in Biography, Which, after
            Twelve Preliminary Chapters Indispensable for the Preparation of
            the Lay Reader, Deals with the Life History of Typhus Fever.* Bos-
            ton: Little, Brown.
    1949   *Ratten, Lause und die Weltgeschichte.* Stuttgart: Hatje.
    1960   *Rats, Lice, and History.* New York: Bantam Books.
Zubrow, Ezra B.W.
    1975   *Prehistoric Carrying Capacity: A Model.* Menlo Park, Calif.:
            Cummings.
Zulueta, J. de, and S.C. Ayala
    1978   "Malaria in Pre-Columbian America." *Paleopathology News-
            letter* 23:1?–15.

CONTRIBUTORS

Suzanne Austin Alchon is Assistant Professor of History at the University of Delaware in Newark. Her book *Native Society and Disease in Colonial Ecuador* was published in 1991 by Cambridge University Press.

Woodrow Borah is Abraham D. Shepard Professor of History, Emeritus, at the University of California, Berkeley. His collaborative work with Sherburne F. Cook, of which the three-volume *Essays in Population History* (California, 1971–79) is a culminating endeavour, occupies a classic niche in the field of Latin American historical demography.

Fernando Casanueva is a member of the Faculté des Sciences Economiques at the Université de Bordeaux in France. His research focuses primarily on the relationship between natives, church, and state in colonial Chile.

Noble David Cook is the William Bentsen Chair of History at the University of Bridgeport, Connecticut. He is the author of *Demographic Collapse: Indian Peru, 1520–1620* (Cambridge, 1981) and co-author, with Alexandra Parma Cook, of *Good Faith and Truthful Ignorance: A Case of Transatlantic Bigamy* (Duke, 1991).

Brian M. Evans is Professor of Geography at the University of Winnipeg in Manitoba, Canada. His wide-ranging interests include native colonial experiences in Alto Perú (Bolivia) and Welsh settlement of the New World.

W. George Lovell is a member of the Department of Geography at Queen's University in Kingston, Canada. His regional monograph on the Cuchumatán highlands, *Conquest and Survival in Colonial Guatemala* (McGill-Queen's 1985), appeared in a revised Spanish edition as *Conquista y cambio cultural* (Centro de Investigaciones Regionales de Mesoamérica and Plumsock Mesoamerican Studies, 1990).

Linda A. Newson is Reader in Geography at King's College, University of London. To her work on *Aborginal and Spanish Colonial Trinidad* (Academic, 1976) was recently added *The Cost of Conquest: Indian Decline in Honduras under Spanish Rule* (Westview, 1986) and *Indian Survival in Colonial Nicaragua* (Oklahoma, 1987).

Hanns J. Prem is a member of the Seminar für Völkerkunde at Universität Bonn in Germany. A longstanding commitment to the field of Mesoamerican ethnohistory has resulted in numerous publications, among them his definitive edition of the *Matricula de Huejotzingo* (Akademische Truck, 1974).

Juan A. Villamarín is Associate Professor and Chair of Anthropology at the University of Delaware in Newark. Judith E. Villamarín is a private scholar. Two Villamarín monographs on the Sabana de Bogotá during colonial times, one on *encomenderos*, the other on Indians, are forthcoming.

INDEX